William III

This is a political biography of William III (1650–1702): prince of Orange; stadhouder in the Netherlands from 1672; and (in a novel joint monarchy with his wife, Mary), king of England, Scotland, and Ireland after the revolution of 1688–9.

William III explains how William overcame huge disadvantages at his birth to regain his family's traditional dominance of Dutch politics; how he dedicated his life to the defeat of Louis XIV of France; how this brought him to the Stuart thrones in Britain and Ireland; and how he managed a war from 1689 which shifted the balance of Europe. William achieved these remarkable successes by being a new kind of 'hybrid' ruler. He befitted the traditional roles of aristocratic leadership and royalty: acting as a war leader, displaying personal and court magnificence, manipulating dynastic ties, and performing an authoritative masculinity. Yet he was also a master of an emerging public politics in which the opinions of others, and even wide populations, mattered. He persuaded his countries to fight Louis XIV of France with a brilliant mixture of mass print propaganda; skills of persuasion, compromise, and consent-building; a strong partnership with his popular wife; and a presentation of himself as his people's servant. For all this significance, and innovation, he deserves to be far better known than he has been among anyone interested in the origins of modern Europe.

This book will appeal to scholars and students alike studying the life and rule of William III, as well as more general audiences interested in the history of early modern England, Scotland, and Ireland within the political landscape of Western Europe.

Tony Claydon is Professor of Early Modern History at Bangor University in Wales. He is author of numerous books and articles on the political and religious culture of later Stuart England, concentrating on national and confessional identity, perceptions of time, and the ideology of the regime of William III after the 1689 revolution.

Routledge Historical Biographies
Series Editor: Glenn J. Richardson

Routledge Historical Biographies provide engaging, readable and academically credible biographies written from an explicitly historical perspective. These concise and accessible accounts will bring important historical figures to life for students and general readers alike.

In the same series:

Henry VII by Sean Cunningham
Henry VIII by Lucy Wooding (second edition 2015)
Hitler by Michael Lynch
Ho Chi Minh by Peter Neville
Isabella d'Este by Christine Shaw
John F. Kennedy by Peter J. Ling
John Maynard Keynes, by Vincent Barnett
Lenin by Christopher Read
Louis XIV by Richard Wilkinson (second edition 2017)
Martin Luther by Michael A. Mullet (second edition 2014)
Martin Luther King Jr. by Peter J. Ling (second edition 2015)
Mao by Michael Lynch (second edition 2017)
Marx by Vincent Barnett
Mary Queen of Scots by Retha M. Warnicke
Mary Tudor by Judith M. Richards
Mussolini by Peter Neville (second edition 2014)
Nehru by Benjamin Zachariah
Neville Chamberlain by Nick Smart
Oliver Cromwell by Martyn Bennett
Queen Victoria by Paula Bartley
Richard III by David Hipshon
Stalin by Christopher Read
Thatcher by Graham Goodlad
Thomas Cranmer by Susan Wabuda
Trotsky by Ian Thatcher
Wolsey by Glenn J. Richardson
William III by Tony Claydon

William III

Tony Claydon

LONDON AND NEW YORK

Designed cover image: Delftware charger with a portrait of William III, English, c.1689–1702.

First published 2025
by Routledge
4 Park Square, Milton Park, Abingdon, Oxon OX14 4RN

and by Routledge
605 Third Avenue, New York, NY 10158

Routledge is an imprint of the Taylor & Francis Group, an informa business

© 2025 Tony Claydon

The right of Tony Claydon to be identified as author of this work has been asserted in accordance with sections 77 and 78 of the Copyright, Designs and Patents Act 1988.

All rights reserved. No part of this book may be reprinted or reproduced or utilised in any form or by any electronic, mechanical, or other means, now known or hereafter invented, including photocopying and recording, or in any information storage or retrieval system, without permission in writing from the publishers.

Trademark notice: Product or corporate names may be trademarks or registered trademarks, and are used only for identification and explanation without intent to infringe.

British Library Cataloguing-in-Publication Data
A catalogue record for this book is available from the British Library

Library of Congress Cataloging-in-Publication Data
Names: Claydon, Tony, author.
Title: William III / Tony Claydon.
Description: New York : Routledge, 2024. | Series: Routledge historical biographies | Includes bibliographical references and index.
Identifiers: LCCN 2024018335 (print) | LCCN 2024018336 (ebook) | ISBN 9781032212777 (hardback) | ISBN 9781032212784 (paperback) | ISBN 9781003267621 (ebook)
Subjects: LCSH: William III, King of England, 1650-1702. | Netherlands--History--1648-1795. | Netherlands--Politics and government--1648-1795. | Netherlands--Kings and rulers--Biography.
Classification: LCC DJ187 .C57 2024 (print) | LCC DJ187 (ebook) | DDC 949.2/04092--dc23/eng/20240503
LC record available at https://lccn.loc.gov/2024018335
LC ebook record available at https://lccn.loc.gov/2024018336

ISBN: 978-1-032-21277-7 (hbk)
ISBN: 978-1-032-21278-4 (pbk)
ISBN: 978-1-003-26762-1 (ebk)

DOI: 10.4324/9781003267621

Typeset in Galliard
by SPi Technologies India Pvt Ltd (Straive)

Contents

	List of illustrations	*vii*
	Acknowledgements	*viii*
	Chronology and chronological note	*ix*
	Introduction: A painting on a wall: William III and his meanings	1
1	The death of a prince, 1650: the predicament of the infant William III	10
2	Slaughter in the streets, 1672: the Orangist revolution in the Netherlands	27
3	An invitation, 1688: Dutch politics and the path to the invasion of England	49
4	A coronation, 1689: William and the Glorious Revolution in England	73
5	A triumph in Ireland, 1690: the establishment of William's regime in the Stuart realms, and the start of the war with France	89
6	The end of a siege, 1695: success in European war	110
7	The loss of the army, 1698: challenges and defeats for William after the Glorious Revolution	136

| 8 | A new hope, 1701: William's recovery at the last years of his reign | 155 |

Conclusion: A stone in the floor: the legacies of William III — 172

Suggestions for further reading — *182*

Index — *186*

Illustrations

1 Former mural depicting William III, Shankill Parade, Belfast.
   HYYGCD © lowefoto / Alamy Stock Photo   2
2 Willem van Honthorst, *Mary Henrietta Stuart with
   William III of Orange-Nassau* (1662), oil on canvas. Collection
   Stedelijk Museum Breda; Ioan Gemeente Breda   12
3 The tomb of William the Silent, Nieuwe Kerk, Delft.
   Author's own picture   15
4 Attributed to Pieter Nason, *Four Generations of the Princes
   of Orange: William I, Maurice and Frederick Henry,
   William II, and William III* (c.1664), oil on canvas.
   SK-A-855. Rijksmuseum   17
5 Peter Lely, *William III, prince of Orange* (c.1677),
   oil on canvas. Royal Armouries Museum   56
6 Frontispiece to *The royal assembly of Europe, consulting
   about the affairs of Christendom* (London, 1691),
   ink on paper. Houghton Library, Harvard University   115
7 Godrey Kneller, *Equestrian portrait of William III*
   (1701), oil on canvas. Royal Collection Trust © His Majesty
   King Charles III   165
8 Leonard Knyff, *A view of Hampton Court Palace* (c.1703),
   oil on canvas. Royal Collection Trust © His Majesty
   King Charles III   167

Acknowledgements

The author would like to thank friends – both academic and personal – who read parts of the manuscript of this book to see it they thought they worked, or with whom he had conversations on broad approach or style. I am especially grateful to Andrew de Csilléry, Stephen Jones, Charles-Édouard Levillain, Esther Mijers, Johanna Murphy, David Onnekink, Hilary Rossington, Rosamund Rossington, and Lucy Wooding (whose excellent contribution to this series, her biography of Henry VIII, was held up as a model to emulate). I extend my thanks to Laura Pilsworth at Routledge, and to her team, including an anonymous reader of a late draft of the whole manuscript, who gave very useful feedback; and to the series editor, Glenn Richardson, for conceiving the volume, and for his wise advice along the way (again based on his own authorship of work in this series: his fine biography of Wolsey). The doubtless numerous mistakes and infelicities are my own. The book is dedicated to my husband, Jeremy Gregory.

Chronology and chronological note

Events in this chronology are dated according to years which are held to run from 1 January to 31 December – as is the modern convention. In the early modern world, however, some people used an older system, which conceived numbered years as running for twelve months from Lady Day onwards (so from 25 March to 24 March). This explains why events that we would think happened in the early weeks of 1689 were sometimes called the revolution of 1688 (some people were waiting for 25 March before they changed the year number in their dating system). In the chronology which follows, however, and throughout the text of this book, years are described as starting on 1 January. In an additional complication, Britain and Ireland employed a different way of calculating the day of the month from the calendar in use in much of continental Europe during William's lifetime (the Stuart realms had not kept up with more sophisticated calendrical calculations that had spread through Europe from the mid-sixteenth century). This meant that until 1700, the numbering of dates in the Britain and Ireland ran ten days behind the conventions which obtained in France, Spain, much of Germany, the Spanish Netherlands, and Holland (though not all of the Dutch provinces, or all of the German states). After 1700, Britain and Ireland fell an additional day behind (their calendar insisted they take a leap year, when most other people did not); but to complete the confusion, some Dutch provinces and German states swopped dating systems in that year, or in the early weeks of the next. In the text of the book, an attempt has been made to make clear which system is being used every time a specific date is given: the reader is asked to wish the author luck with this.

Main events of William's life

1650   Death of William II, prince of Orange, William III's father
       William III born
1651   Dutch constitutional revolution leads to exclusion of William from traditional family offices, and initiates the era of 'True Freedom' under Johan de Witt
       William moves from The Hague to Leiden, to receive a university-level education

x *Chronology and chronological note*

1660	Restoration of William's uncle, Charles II, in England
	Death of William's mother, Mary Stuart
1666	'Child of State' scheme sees de Witt take a role in William's education
1688	'Harmony' offers William a future role in the Netherlands, but excludes him from stadhouderships
	William become first noble of Zeeland, and achieves legal majority
1670	William takes a position on the Dutch Council of State
1672	Eastern provinces of Netherlands overrun by France and her allies, England and Münster, in the '*rampjaar*'
	Murder of de Witt brothers
	William become captain- and admiral-general of the Netherlands, and stadhouder of Zeeland and Holland
	William coordinates military defence of Netherlands from France
	William raids Bonn
1673	William concludes formal alliance with the Habsburg powers against France
	Ejection of French and allies from most of the Netherlands
1674	England and Münster make peace with the Netherlands
	William suffers heavy loss to the French at the battle of Seneffe
1675	William is offered the dukedom of Gelderland, but refuses it after opposition in other provinces
1677	William's marriage to Princess Mary of England
	William fails to retake Maastricht from the French
1678	Peace of Nijmegan with France
1679	Exclusion crisis begins in the in Stuart realms, and creates Whig and Tory parties
1684	Tension between William and Amsterdam over control of the Dutch army
1685	James II succeeds to English throne – William aids him against Monmouth's rebellion
1687	William builds contacts with English opposition to James II
1688	Birth of a male heir to James II
	Invitation to William to intervene in England by the 'Immortal Seven'
	Preparation and embarkation of an invasion fleet to convey William to England
	Publication of William's *Declaration of reasons*
	William lands at Torbay, advances on Salisbury
	James II retreats from Salisbury and escapes from England
	William occupies London
1689	Convention meets at Westminster to determine constitutional future of England
	William is offered crowns of England and Ireland, in a joint monarchy with his wife, who becomes Mary II

	Declaration of Rights defines royal power in England
	Coronation in Westminster
	William sponsors toleration act to grant freedom of worship to England's Protestant dissenters
	Scottish convention offers William the Scottish Crown in a joint monarchy with Mary
	'Claim of right' limits royal power in Scotland
	Jacobite rebellion in Scotland
	Irish rebellion, James II arrives in Ireland in an attempt to regain his crowns
	Siege of (London)Derry by James II, relieved by William's forces
	Construction of first Grand Alliance against Louis XIV
1690	William campaigns in Ireland, gains victory at battle of the Boyne
	William turns against Whigs in England
1691	William returns to the Netherlands for first time since 1688
	William chairs congress of the allies in The Hague
	William witnesses Louis XIV capture Mons
	Treaty of Limerick ends Irish war with concessions to William's Catholic opponents
1692	Glencoe massacre damages William's reputation
	Battle of Steenkerk sees William and French forces fight to a draw
1693	William rallies forces after loss at the battle of Landen
	William turns to the 'junto' Whigs to manage Parliament in England
1694	William's veto of place bill leads to tensions with Westminster Parliament
	William accepts triennial bill to soothe relations with Westminster Parliament
	Death of Mary II
1695	New policy of conciliation with Irish Parliament, initiation of management via 'undertakers'
	Company of Scotland formed to advance Scottish commercial interests, but is opposed by William, leading to growing unpopularity in Scotland in late 1690s
1696	Jacobite assassination plot against William rallies flagging support for the king in England
1697	Treaty of Ryswick brings peace with France
	Press and parliamentary campaign against standing army in England begins
	Campaign for regular meetings of church's convocation in England begins
	William's rupture with Hans Willem Bentinck: Arnold Joost van Keppel becomes new favourite
	Tension begins with Ireland over the woollens act
1698	Work to complete William's apartments at Hampton Court begins

	First Partition Treaty to avoid war with Louis XIV over future of Spanish empire
1700	Second Partition Treaty
1701	General election forces William to work with Tory-country alliance in England
	Louis XIV accepts Carlos II of Spain's will, breaking the partition treaties
	Conclusion of Second Grand alliance against Louis XIV
1702	Death of William

Introduction
A painting on a wall: William III and his meanings

On the end of one of the houses in Shankill Parade, Belfast, there was a mural (see Figure 1). It stood in a tradition of painting in Northern Ireland that went back to the early twentieth century, and it depicted a man in a magnificent seventeenth-century costume, riding a rearing white charger as he crosses a river. The man was William III. William was prince of Orange from his birth in 1650; he was captain-general of the United Provinces of the Netherlands from 1672; and he was the most influential person in Dutch politics for three decades from that date, in his capacity as 'stadhouder' (a sort of governor) of five of those provinces. He was also king of England, Scotland, and Ireland, from 1689 until his death in 1702. The river in the mural is the Boyne. This was the site of its subject's most famous military victory.

The wall painting was produced because William had become a symbol for Northern Ireland's Unionist, Protestant, and Loyalist communities. Their use of this figure remained the most famous and vibrant commemoration of him to survive into the twenty-first century: though William is still remembered as an important member of the reigning royal house in the Netherlands; as the founder of William and Mary College in Virginia; and in a number of statues and place names around the world. Elsewhere, however, the king's image has faded since his death. As we will explore at the end of this book, changing trends in historical writing, some embarrassments in the countries he affected about his role in their histories, and perhaps some difficulty putting him in a clear and comprehensible category of ruler have meant he has not stuck in people's minds. Even the mural on Shankill Parade has gone. Local information suggests it was painted over when the owner of the end-terrace house on which it appeared was trying to sell the property, and feared the decoration was reducing its value.[1] This biography will do what it can to rescue William from such obscurity and shame. It will argue that his impacts on Dutch, British, Irish, European, and indeed global history deserve to be far better acknowledged, and understood, than they have been.

To appreciate William's significance, the Belfast murals are a useful place to start. What exactly this king has meant to the communities that produced such art is debateable, and it has shifted constantly since his lifetime. Yet two broad

DOI: 10.4324/9781003267621-1

Figure 1 Former mural depicting William III, Shankill Parade, Belfast. HYYGCD © lowefoto / Alamy Stock Photo.

themes have remained fairly constant. First, William's victory at the Boyne has been presented as the salvation of the particular ways of being Irish, and of being – at the same time – British, that has marked the Protestant experience in Ulster. Second, the prince's career has been seen a preservation of the wider Protestant faith that the people who value him have espoused. Both of these understandings have roots in the realities of William's career, and can start to illustrate his importance. For the first: it is undeniably true that before the battle of the Boyne, Ireland's Protestant culture had genuinely faced an existential crisis. A Catholic rebellion against English rule had gained control of nearly all the country, leading many of its opponents to conclude they must flee the land. William's victory at the Boyne reasserted control from London, and so rescued a cause that had looked desperate. As for the second meaning of the mural, it is certain that without William, the prospects for European Protestantism would have been far darker. Through the seventeenth century, Roman Catholicism had been advancing in multiple countries, to the point that many Protestants had begun to fear that their faith was in mortal danger. In the hundred years before the Boyne, the Roman Church had increased its hold over the western European population: it had started with the adherence of about half the continent's people, but ended with something much closer to three-quarters of them. In multiple ways, however, William halted this trend, and perhaps ensured the survival of Protestantism in the continent. As we shall see, he not only defeated Catholic forces in Ireland to secure their religious rivals there; but he saved his native and Protestant Netherlands from being overrun by Catholic armies; he intervened in England and Scotland to remove the Catholicising regime of his uncle James II; and he built an international alliance which, among other objectives and achievements, defended the Protestant princes of Germany from encroachment by French forces bent on imposing the Roman Church.

Ulster's commemoration of William thus points us to some highlights of his life and significance. Yet, as will become clear, it distorts as much as it illuminates, and it ignores whole swathes of his legacy. We need to see William as far more than a protestant Crusader, charging across rivers for a Unionist, or divine, cause. He affected many more areas than those. He was a man whose actions crucially shifted the geopolitical balance of Europe and so shaped great power politics through the eighteenth century and beyond. He was a ruler whose approach to authority diverted the constitutional history of all the places he controlled, and who fostered new political cultures of open and popular discussion. He was a king of the Stuart realms whose priorities so tangled relationships between England, Scotland, Ireland, and a wider empire that they have still not been unknotted. And despite the image (and yes, the partial reality) of his zeal for Protestantism, he was someone with a personal commitment to religious toleration which permitted exploration of new ways of living with a diversity of faiths. Before diving into William's life itself therefore this biography must expand a little on these reasons we should care about this extraordinary figure.

We can start with the geopolitics. The seventeenth century was a time of profound shifts in the relative power of the states of Europe. In the sixteenth century, the emperor Charles V, and then his successors, the allied Habsburg crowns of Austria and Spain, had dominated the continent. In the next hundred years, by contrast, France emerged first as a rival to, and then as a potential displacer of, that dominance. That country first matched the Habsburgs in the Thirty Years War in Germany, and then engaged in long set of aggressions on her borders, which had the Austrian diplomat Franz Paul de Lisola warning all Europe that the balance of power was being destroyed.[2] The future had therefore looked French until William organised resistance. Assembling a stable international alliance to resist France's ambitions, the prince of Orange stopped them in their tracks. As a result, the eighteenth century was not marked by French hegemony, as had once seemed inevitable. France would still be a considerable power, but there remained room for the Habsburg states, and space had been created for the emergence of new claimants to control influence.

One of these new claimants would be Prussia. Since this eventually permitted the emergence of Germany on to the world stage, it had long-term consequences through to the twenty-first century. But more immediately, and more immediately traceable to William, England advanced to a powerful global position. Since the days of Henry VIII, English attempts to intervene in foreign wars had been limited, and often laughably unsuccessful. Elizabeth I (reigning from 1558–1603) had defended her realm from Spanish aggression, but this bare survival had been about all she could boast of; and then the rule of the first two Stuart kings (reigning from 1603–49) had been marked by embarrassingly poor showings abroad, even before the kingdom collapsed into internal conflict. There had been successes in later decades, particularly under Oliver Cromwell, the victor of the civil wars, but there had also been further humiliations, as when an enemy fleet sank much of the Royal Navy at anchor in 1667. As a result, in 1689, when William became king of England, Scotland, and Ireland, those realms had little reputation in Europe or beyond. Yet his brief eleven-year reign would change this. Incorporating the Stuart kingdoms into his anti-French alliance, and leading their military mobilisation, William would craft his realms into a major force and lay the foundations for their pre-eminence in the world over the next quarter of a millennium. Much of this was logistical. As we shall see, the king found ways of persuading subjects to build a modern state. In the 1690s, the English in particular would raise navies and armies, and find the provisions and funds for such forces, not only on an unprecedented scale, but with an unprecedented efficiency. Without William's transformation, England's – and soon Britain's – later global empire would probably be unimaginable. Similarly impossible would have been the nation's defeat of French expansion in the later eighteenth century under Napoleon; her nineteenth-century hegemony; and her defeat of German pretensions in the twentieth century.

England would therefore become a new kind of place, infrastructurally, as a result of William's rule. But this was only possible because of his political and constitutional impact. Before his arrival, the country had been in prolonged turmoil. It had found no way to reconcile its beliefs in monarchy, and in rulers' vigorous independent exercise of their authority, with a commitment to government by consultation and subjects' consent. This had partly explained its earlier ineffectiveness on the international stage. It was hard to be a continental power with Parliament constantly carping against the executive (the dominant political pattern of the 1620s, 1660s, and 1670s); and impossible to be so when disputes about the limits of court power had brought the nation to full political crisis or actual civil war (effectively the position in the 1640s and 1680s). One of William's greatest achievements was to resolve these tensions. As we will see, he did so by reconceiving monarchy. Taking lessons from the rather different political structures of his native Netherlands, he brought representatives of the people more fully into the exercise of power; he allowed greater scrutiny of his actions; he accepted clear restrictions on what he could do; and he presented himself as a service ruler – one whose highest objective was the welfare of his people, rather than promoting his personal reputation or glory. This did not necessarily reduce the power of the Crown (it could often do more with consent than without it), but it did end the sterile debates of the earlier seventeenth century; and it also ensured that the constitutional future of England and Britain would be marked by partnership between the Crown and the political nation. This was a framework that later allowed the gradual evolution of monarchy into a symbolic, and sometimes unifying, figurehead.

In a related development, William's style of rule promoted a vibrant 'public sphere'. This is the term historians have used to describe the open and vigorous debate in the press, pulpit, playhouse, and many other venues, which particularly characterised William's reign, and which would mark the history of Britain ever after. Used to such political rough and tumble in the Netherlands, the Dutch king of the Stuart realms was unphased by having his rule and policies openly discussed. He was therefore happy to tolerate quite free expression of disagreement: indeed, he joined in, and so encouraged, debate through his own polemic propaganda. William found that influencing the public sphere was more effective than trying to suppress it. This king thus turned a page in political culture. His realm, which had recently been a place where fears of monarchical arbitrary power drove constant instability, became somewhere that achieved an – albeit fluid – equilibrium by encouraging popular participation in, and argument about, the exercise of power.

Constitutionally, William also had a huge impact in his native Netherlands, though perhaps in the opposite direction to his effect on the Stuart realms. Before William came to power in the Dutch provinces, they had been engaged in a republican experiment. Following a doctrine of 'True Freedom', the country had rejected the quasi-monarchical role in government that had traditionally been played by William's family. William's countrymen had excluded him from the offices of the state which he would normally have expected to inherit as the head of his clan; and instead, they had dispersed power widely, particularly among the urban merchant elite. A crisis in 1672, as we shall see, ended this experiment. It swept William to leadership of the Netherlands, not only granting him the official posts that his predecessors had filled, but ensuring he had probably more informal influence than any of them had enjoyed. It is true that this reversal was not permanent. When William died in 1702, the Netherlands reverted to its largely republican model. However, the interlude under his rule had re-enforced the reputation of his family – and it had strengthened a Dutch tradition of looking to a single strongman to save the nation, a tendency which had long competed with a suspicion of monarchy as an actual form of government. As a result of this, William's dynasty continued to play a central role in the nation's affairs. It retained authority in some of the provinces through the eighteenth century; and when Napoleon's occupation of the Low Countries ended in 1814, it was appointed to rule as hereditary monarchs of the whole nation. A popular affection for the family continues to ensure that the Netherlands can claim to be one of the most monarchist countries in Europe, for all that the Dutch also value their republican heritage.

William also had an impact on relations between the various parts of his British and Irish realms, and one that is still very much playing out in the twenty-first century. This was rooted in the king's priority once he became the ruler of England, Scotland, and Ireland. As we have already hinted, this was the defeat of France. As noted above, William gained huge resource from England for this enterprise, but his other kingdoms and dependencies were not in a position to contribute in quite the same way. Scotland and Ireland were poorer and less populated than England; and as we shall see, the king's very right to rule them was more contested, so they simply cost more to secure for William's regime. England had overseas colonies, both of settlements in North America, and commercially across the globe, but the economic links which would later generate considerable wealth were only starting to develop. As a result, William did not see his territories outside England as game changers in providing war funds or manpower. His main aim was just to keep them peaceful, and his main strategy to ensure this was to try to work with local elites, and to hope they could be left to run their own affairs. For example, his predecessors' policy of centralising control over New England was abandoned; and William called frequent parliaments in Scotland and Ireland, in an attempt to recruit local representatives into his grand anti-French project.

This approach looked like a parallel for what he had done in England. However, we shall see that it met with far less success. William could not be present in Dublin, Edinburgh, and the colonies around the world, so he gained far less experience and sense of common purpose with their inhabitants than with the English elites. He also knew that it was most important to keep the English on board with the war effort because they controlled far more of the resources he was going to need. Conflict between the interests of England and other places therefore had to be resolved in favour of the former. The result of all this was a troublesome legacy in governing non-English places. Some, such as the American colonies, were so neglected that they drifted off into semi-separatist self-government. They would prove hard or impossible to recover for a more coordinated empire in the later eighteenth century. Others, particularly Ireland and Scotland, were pushed into understandable resentment at losing out to the demands of England, and found they had forums for their discontents in their local assemblies. As we will show, they had become almost ungovernable by the end of William's reign. Sometimes, too, the king's attempts to let Scottish and Irish elites run their own shows ended with dominant communities oppressing others: Ireland's Catholics suffered particularly, though those Scots who objected to a new Presbyterian national church also came off badly. All of this has cast very long shadows. Attempts to resolve Scottish problems through a union with England, which was being floated by the end of William's reign, and anger in all communities in Ireland against the style of rule from London, ultimately generated nationalist movements that have shaped and troubled politics for centuries.

Thus, Belfast's murals miss multiple dimensions of William's historical significance. And they misrepresent his impact even in the areas they celebrate, hiding one more contribution he made to European life. Yes, William rescued the Irish Protestant cause, and perhaps the religion more widely. As we shall see, his action was partly rooted in a deep personal commitment to a brand of Protestantism: that of the Dutch Reformed Church. But he was never a champion of any narrow version of Christianity, in the sense of wishing to impose this on others. The pages that follow will explore a subtle position on matters of faith that offered a way out of the confessional bitterness and warfare which had marked history across the continent since the early sixteenth century. Emphasising that following Christ could never mean coercing people on matters of belief, William was prepared to work with those who adhered to a wide variety of creeds, and he pressed himself for flexible and inclusive religious settlements wherever he had influence and when this was politically possible. Groups attempting to recruit him to any intolerant denominational campaign – and this included Irish Protestants – would be disappointed. His vision pointed to a future of religious pluralism, and though it was some way from later liberal insistence on freedom of conscience, it meant he was the opposite of the zealot for his faith that some strands in his Ulster commemoration might have wanted to portray him as.

William therefore had an enormous impact in multiple fields. Yet telling the story of these effects presents challenges for a biographer. To start, there is the standard objection to relating history through accounts of individual careers. Life narratives may sometimes be interesting studies in character, but they rarely have the greatest explanatory force in the practice of history – whatever claims we might want to make about William's importance. The processes and developments that account for change in societies, and for the overall shape of the past, tend not to run neatly through the careers of individuals. Rather, these forces cut across biographies. They mould what people do only at points in a life, before being replaced by other sets of influences; and individuals get to advance or modify them only at rare and particular moments. Biography may therefore tell us little about what was truly important in an era: it gets distracted by its need to refract everything through one human's experience. Compounding this is the fact that a person's impact on the world is never fully planned. Individuals may have convictions – in William's case his opposition to French hegemony, and his horror of religious persecution – but it is unusual for these to alter the world in any straightforward way. As we shall see, many of the changes that this king wrought were unintentional, or they were implemented because they seemed the best way to secure some other objective, or they were the result of political trial and error, or they stemmed from how other actors reacted to William rather than directly from the man himself. As with most figures therefore his significance sprang from complex narrative: it was not dictated by a preset script. And in the endeavour to make sense of William, the man himself will not help us much. Although it was often clear what he was trying to achieve, and the techniques he used can be reconstructed, he was rarely forthcoming about his core hopes or aims. He was not given to the recorded introspection that would allow us access to his inner thoughts and feelings, and frequently he concealed these deliberately. As we shall see, his childhood taught him the importance of hiding his emotions, and his political career showed him he could often succeed best by making no clear statements of what he wanted, but instead waiting for circumstances to bring him advantage. As we shall also see, he surrounded himself with tight-knit groups of friends and advisors, which were difficult for others to penetrate. Many contemporaries viewed him as a cold, odd man, and complained that it was impossible to get close to him. Historians have tended to feel the same. Here was someone who did a great deal, but who left few intimate records of why exactly he had done it, and only occasional glimpses of any interior personality.

These challenges have shaped the approach, structure, and nature of this biography. First, readers should recognise that the book was written from the conviction that an account of William's life has an unusual power to explain the course of his age. Because of the ways in which his skills, objectives, and personality interacted with the circumstances of his time, this work will argue that this ruler's career shaped the past to an extraordinary degree, even among other powerful leaders. The work will therefore use biography to try to clarify what was happening in late seventeenth century Europe; and it accepts that there will be some cost involved. The richness of a life will be edited down to show how its subject affected crucial processes in the development of the world. Second, the book will attempt to balance the large themes of William's contribution to the story of Europe, with acknowledgement that his impact came from a real life, with all its ambiguities, compromises, changes of direction, and reversals of fortune. It will therefore try to reflect complexity without descending into a meaningless parade of incidents; and will do so by adopting a mildly unconventional structure. Instead of the chapters advancing a strictly chronological story – which might become confusing – each will start with a turning point in William's career. Each will then go back in time to examine the often-intricate events, actions, and forces which led to its opening moment. Chapters will build towards the death of William's father in 1650; William's seizure of power in the Netherlands in 1672; the invitation to him to intervene in England in 1688; and his capture of the Scottish, Irish, and English crowns in 1689 (Chapters 1–4). Following that triumph, we shall look at his military victories at the Boyne in 1690; and at Namur in 1695; his political defeat over the standing army in 1698; and his final diplomatic success in reassembling an international alliance against France in 1701 (Chapters 5–8). In this way, the book hopes to acknowledge the eddying flows of actual history, and the paradoxes of power and human action within these, whilst maintaining a focus that will makes sense of the detail and reveal how William transformed his world.

As for its subject's intractability: there is no real way round William's privacy and reluctance to create evidence that would let us see behind his masks. We cannot get to the heart of this man. Yet this may be a smaller problem than it appears. The situation in which William operated was a fascinating one of rapid and innovative change – politically, socially, culturally – and it can provide much of the colour which our hero himself may lack. Tracing William's path through this world creates a fast-paced narrative, for all that it will, inevitably, be more of a political than a personal one. And one of the changes this period saw was the opening of space for public opinion and discussion. In this new sphere, the appearance and reputation of leaders were everything. So, although we may not be able to get close to a 'real' William, he was a master of the sort of public presentation which was vital to this new environment, and we can examine how he created images of himself which shaped entire political situations. Those masks may therefore be as important as the person. William may indeed have been cold and unknowable. His story, however, is anything but.

Notes

1 I am extremely grateful to Professor Ramona Wray, of Queens University Belfast, for going to the Shankill, and investigating the picture's fate.
2 [Franz Josef Lisola], *The bukler of state and justice* (London, 1667).

1 The death of a prince, 1650
The predicament of the infant William III

At first, it had seemed only a modest health scare. Certainly William II, prince of Orange, and captain-general of the United Provinces of the Netherlands, had fallen quite ill after a month's hard hunting from his lodge in rural Gelderland during a cold October in 1650. He had had to return by water to his main residence in The Hague, the Dutch capital, because this had allowed him to travel without getting out of bed, and he had run a high fever for the next couple of days. All this, however, could be put down to overexertion at the chase. Although the emergence of pustules soon suggested smallpox, recovery remained a strong possibility. Members of William's close family, including his mother, had survived the disease; and its mortality rate had been under fifty per cent, even before Edward Jenner developed the world's first vaccine to combat the illness at the end of the eighteenth century. A week after arriving back in the Hague, the pox broke out, but even this could be a hopeful sign. The prince seemed to be getting better soon after it happened, and his physicians left the sickroom, attempting to get some rest. Yet from this point, things rapidly worsened. William's fever returned with a vengeance; those experienced in the course of smallpox despaired; and prayers were said around the patient. At around nine o'clock in the evening of 6 November (in Holland; 27 October in England, Scotland, and Ireland, which still used an older and unreformed calendar), the prince of Orange died.[1] Thus perished the father of William III, who will be the hero of this book.

But our William had not yet even been born. He only entered the world ten days later, in a birthing chamber still draped in black, with attendants in full mourning clothes. His mother was Mary Stuart, a daughter of the English king, Charles I. She would supervise her son's upbringing through his earliest years, and, with her husband now out of the picture, she appears to have bestowed on him a strong sense of belonging to her own Stuart family. She was keenly aware of her clan's honour, claims, and rights as the ruling dynasty in Britain and Ireland; and William came to share many of these priorities. Later in his career, as we shall see, he married back into the Stuart family through an alliance with another Mary, one of Charles I's granddaughters. Two of his uncles would be the Stuart monarchs in London between 1660

DOI: 10.4324/9781003267621-2

and 1688; and William would frequently offer these rulers his advice, if not always his support. When he invaded England in 1688, it was to protect the interests of his Stuart wife, and to prevent a possible subversion of the Stuart succession (or so he claimed); and the result of that invasion was to put him on the Stuart thrones, as the fifth monarch of the line. The prenatal loss of his father, and the assertive personality of his mother, thus meant the new prince would have an identity well beyond the Netherlands. His British and Stuart heritage must always be weighed against his Dutch one if we are fully to understand this man.

Sadly, though, in the circumstances of 1650, William's membership of the Stuart house counted for far less than his mother would have liked. In a vivid demonstration of the family's congenital incompetence (it achieved the astonishing feat of losing seven British and Irish thrones in only four generations), it had been chased from power in all of its three kingdoms. From his accession in 1625, Charles I had advanced religious and constitutional policies that had led to rebellion in Scotland in 1637. He had reduced Ireland to chaos by 1641 and provoked many of his English subjects to revolt in 1642. Losing the resulting civil wars and plotting against the victors – though he had no talent for conspiracy – Charles was tried for treason and executed in January 1649. By 1650, a republican government had extended its authority over all three Stuart realms, so the family's prospects were dim. Certainly, when William III was born, Charles's eldest son, also a Charles, was in Scotland trying to raise support. But he was making little progress. His enemies occupied the rich lowland regions of the country, and he was proving incapable of mobilising his sympathisers in England or Ireland. The next autumn would see Charles hiding in an oak tree, and escaping the country in disguise, after a push south had ended in defeat at the battle of Worcester. From The Hague, William's mother did what she could to lobby for aid from other European monarchs, but her appeals were ineffective, and her efforts damaged relations with her son. Mary may have encouraged William to think of himself as a proud Stuart, but he was otherwise neglected as she intrigued for the interests of her British family. Indeed, Mary was to prioritise visiting branches of her clan, scatted in exile across Europe, over close attendance on William.[2] In later years the prince would rarely speak about his early years, and never did so with nostalgia or affection.

We can, perhaps, imagine that these emotions are depicted in the first portrait of the infant prince. Painted by Willem van Honthorst in 1652, this shows William in a garden and held aloft, somewhat precariously, by Mary (the artist seemed not to have grasped how gravity works) (see Figure 2). The ties between parent and child, however, seem loose. Mary stares out from the canvas, in a pose that suggests some hauteur, but pays absolutely no attention to her offspring. The prince, meanwhile, looks rather past his mother, and leans away from her. With a tiny finger he points to an orange tree in planter. This type of shrub was fashionable in seventeenth-century gardens, both as a source of exotic fruit and as a demonstration of the owner's wealth (the trees had to

12 The death of a prince, 1650

Figure 2 Willem van Honthorst, *Mary Henrietta Stuart with William III of Orange-Nassau* (1662), oil on canvas. Collection Stedelijk Museum Breda; Ioan Gemeente Breda.

be taken into greenhouses in their pots each winter to avoid northern European frosts, so only the very rich could afford to cultivate them). But obviously, the tree was also a symbol of his father's family: the Orange-Nassaus. The William in van Honthorst's picture seemed aware that, even after the misfortune of his father's death, it was from that paternal side of his heritage that he had to draw his most immediate advantages. The young prince was now the head and hope of a dynasty that had dominated the Dutch republic. Even before he could do much more than point at pot plants, that dynasty brought William prestige and political support, even if they also earned him the wary suspicion of some of his countrymen. For all the glamour of being a Stuart, it was his position as an Orange-Nassau that would enable and shape his early career.[3]

The Orange-Nassaus' position in the Netherlands was rooted in the circumstances of the nation's birth. In the mid-sixteenth century, the more northerly of Spain's Burgundian provinces had revolted against Madrid's rule (the Spaniards had controlled the lands of modern Belgium and the Netherlands since the early sixteenth century: the result of the sort of marriage alliances which produced some strange territorial conjunctions in the early modern period). The protest had started at erosions of local autonomy, but it had taken on a religious dimension as many the Dutch had adopted a rigorous Protestantism at odds with the Spanish monarchy's championing of the Catholic Church. The rebellion had then deepened into a patriotic movement (which had ultimately led to national independence) in reaction to Spain's brutal, and near successful, attempts at suppression. A reign of terror by the duke of Alba, Madrid's governor in the Low Countries from 1567 to 1573, had seared itself into the popular imagination as an image of tyranny which the people of the Netherlands must resist; whilst the miraculous recovery of their cause from almost total collapse in the face of Alba's repression had bred a pride in the resilience, heroism, and divine favour that seemed to characterise the Dutch in their defiance of Spanish might.

At the heart of all these events had been William I, prince of Orange. It had been this William, a member of the Nassau family which dominated the lands around the city of Breda, who had led the complaints of the Burgundian provinces against Spanish misrule. It had been this William, nicknamed 'the Silent', who had taken up arms against foreign governance; and this William who had refused to surrender even in the darkest days of the struggle. It had been he who had provided an ideological basis for the revolt with his published *Apology* (an instructive prefiguring of William III's own extensive use of the press); and it had been he who had encouraged a process in which the northern provinces would finally federate into a new nation, the Republic of the Seven United Netherlands. William the Silent had also become the country's first great martyr. When he was assassinated by a Spanish partisan in 1584, he provided a supreme moment of personal tragedy and political drama. Whether or not children really did cry in the streets on hearing of his death, as later folklore insisted, his position as father of the country was secured. His descendants – including our William, even as a baby – could bathe in the legacy of this extraordinary charisma.

The later leaders of the Orange-Nassau family carved out roles of their own in Dutch history and the Dutch imagination. The 1581 declaration of independence from Spain marked the birth of an autonomous polity in the eyes of Netherlanders, but, unsurprisingly, Spain did not accept this. For the next seven decades, off and on, Madrid tried to regain control of her old territories, often launching expeditions from the provinces that Spain still held around Brussels (provinces which were to become Belgium in the long run of a tortuous history). In this fight, members of the Orange-Nassau house were as prominent as William I had been. William's son Maurice inherited leadership of the military effort for independence, reorganising the Dutch army, and rounding out the frontiers of the new country by capturing Spanish outposts on its borders. In fact, the last decade of the sixteenth century became known as Maurice's 'Ten Glory Years'. When he died in 1625, Maurice was succeeded by his brother, Frederick Henry, who proved at least as capable a commander, and pushed the borders of the Netherlands southwards to provide more of a buffer against the enemy. Frederick Henry's son, William II (who was our William's father), took over in 1647, and finally achieved recognition of the new Dutch state by Spain. Madrid gave up its claims to rule the Northern Netherlands in the 1648 Westphalian settlement, the series of peace treaties which ended the much wider Thirty Years War in central Europe.[4]

This Orange-Nassau leadership had been formally recognised by the new state. The successive heads of the clan had been appointed captain-general and admiral-general by five of the provinces in revolt, and eventually by the whole Netherlands. These were posts created to command the collective land and naval forces of the new nation, and the Orange-Nassau family had enjoyed other powerful offices. Most importantly, the princes had been stadhouders of most of the individual provinces (a junior branch of the family tended to take this role in the most northerly regions of Friesland and Groningen). Stadhouderships had been offices under the Spanish king, but they had been repurposed in the new Dutch republic. Originally a sort of lieutenant for the distant ruler, they became both honorific heads of each province, and wielders of real power within them. Responsible for internal order and the administration of justice, including the issuing of pardons, stadhouders also held considerable rights of patronage. In places, they were even able to appoint the town magistrates. As we shall see, these urban elites were crucial to the political structures of the new nation as a whole.

By 1650, this tradition of Orange-Nassau pre-eminence meant the infant prince was expected to play a major role in Dutch affairs. Many assumed that he would take the roles and the offices of his forebears; though of course he would have to grow up before he could exercise them personally. The baby William could also bask in a popular affection and respect for a dynasty that had played such key roles in the birth of the republic. And, of huge further importance, he also inherited a substantial portfolio of symbolic power. The Orange-Nassau family had presented themselves as charismatic patriarchs of the nation. The clan had wormed their way to the very core of Dutch culture and had become personifications of Dutch patriotism. As William Temple, an English ambassador to the Netherlands, pointed out, the United Provinces were technically a republic, but ordinary people liked an individual on which to focus their loyalty. Folks in the street, Temple maintained, were pleased with the 'Pomp and Splendour' of a government headed by a prince, and saw this figure representing the 'Greatness, Honour, and Riches' of their country.[5]

The House of Orange-Nassau had exploited such sentiments by presenting its leaders as quasi-monarchical figures. The princes of Orange had assembled a splendid court around themselves, and generations of the dynasty had spent magnificently on the accoutrements of early modern rule. They had laid out vast sums on servants, guards, horses, wardrobes, jewels, liveries, ceremonies, art collections, and so on.[6] They had also built a string of country residences and hunting lodges; and they had occupied a suite of rooms in the Binnenhof – a palatial building in The Hague, originally built for the counts of Holland, which included the Ridderzaal, the state's chief ceremonial space. Finally, they had had themselves buried together beneath the magnificent tomb which had been erected in the Nieuwe Kerk (New Church) in Delft to celebrate the heroics of William I. This was an extraordinary affair, in black-and-white Italian marble and bronze, which had cost over thirty thousand guilders, and had taken six years to build. This monument became both a place of popular pilgrimage and an icon in Dutch art, reproduced in numerous paintings and engravings; and it featured allegorical statues of liberty, religion, valour, and justice, who surrounded a recumbent figure of William (and his dog), whilst an inscription praised the prince as the 'father of the fatherland' (see Figure 3).[7] All this meant, as Temple remarked, that the Orange-Nassaus could claim to represent the 'dignity' of the state.[8] The sovereignty of the United Provinces technically rested elsewhere, but it was this family who gave the country its glitter and glamour.

William's ancestors had been able to afford all this magnificent display because they were by far the richest family in the country. Not only had their

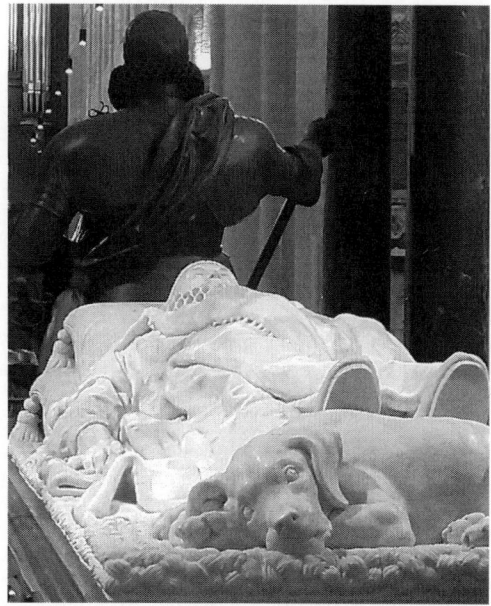

Figure 3 The tomb of William the Silent, Nieuwe Kerk, Delft. Author's own picture.

public offices brought considerable profit, but they remained substantial landowners. They held extensive estates in the Netherlands, and owned further lands across Flanders, Germany, and France. For example, they still held territories around Nassau in the mountains of the middle Rhineland, the region from which the family had originated in the Middle Ages, and which explained that element of their surname. Another of their foreign patrimonies was the city of Orange. Orange was an independent microstate, on the banks of the Rhone in southern France, which William's family had inherited in 1544. They had not just gained the land, however, but had become – as their title as 'princes of Orange' suggested – its sovereigns and rulers. This gave the dynasty still further prestige. They may not have been royalty in the Netherlands themselves, but they were the ruling royal house of somewhere, even if they never bothered to visit that realm, and even if it covered only a very limited tract of the earth's surface. When William invaded England in 1688, his manifesto for the expedition was issued in his capacity as prince of Orange, not by the Dutch state, or from any office he held in the Netherlands. It was therefore William's hereditary sovereignty of an independent political entity that he claimed gave him the right to make such a dramatic intervention in international affairs.

A final bequest to the infant prince from his forebears was an effective propaganda machine. The enthusiasm of a vigorous print industry had been part of this. William the Silent had used the press to garner support for his rebellion – as we have seen, his *Apology* became a quasi-official justification for the revolt – and his successors had benefitted from waves of pro-Orange publication in a Dutch book market which was one of the most sophisticated in Europe. Print culture in the Netherlands was somewhat rough and tumble. Censorship was never effectively imposed, and an urban, and remarkably literate, populace had an appetite for a wide variety of views pumped out by numerous publishers – so much so that when Charles I's authority began to slip in England and he lost control of the press, contemporaries talked of English politics being 'Amsterdamnified'.[9] Nevertheless, among all these voices, pro-Orange ones had been loud. Writers had defended the family's position in the state and had advocated the various positions that the princes had taken on issues of the day. Material had ranged from lengthy manifestos and political theory to cheap tracts, verse, ballads, and pictorial material. There was therefore plenty of stuff that appealed way down the social spectrum – even to those who could not read.[10]

Preaching could also be as effective among the illiterate as the literate. As we saw, Protestantism had emerged early as a core element in the Dutch revolt. In particular, that creed's Calvinist brand (with its strict moral discipline, and its particular views on Christian salvation) had taken a central role; and when it did so, the Orange-Nassau family had aligned themselves with the movement. The princes – with the partial exception of Frederick Henry – had defended the role of the Calvinist church and its clergy in Dutch society. They had tended to uphold Calvinist beliefs, especially its characteristic insistence on predestination (the idea that the ultimate fate of souls was predetermined by God, without reference to what people might do to try to live a good life) when this doctrine had been challenged in the early seventeenth century. As we shall see, William III was to follow in this tradition. Calvinism was to be key to his personal faith – if not always his guide in religious policy. In return for this support, Calvinist ministers promoted the Orange image from the pulpit. This further bolstered the pro-Orange press, since published sermons were a major product of the book trade. As both preachers and pamphleteers, the clergy could assure their audience that the Orange-Nassau dynasty was the providentially appointed saviour of the Dutch nation, and of the true faith on Dutch soil.

In all these ways, William III's forebears had channelled considerable advantages down to the child prince. This explains why one of the earliest paintings of him, once he had graduated from infant clothes, placed him firmly in the line of his ancestors. Pieter Nason's portrait, from the very early years of the 1660s, has a young William, about ten to twelve years old, adorned in fashionable court dress (see Figure 4). But he is at the extreme right of the picture, and the rest of the canvas is filled with William I, Maurice, Frederick Henry,

Figure 4 Attributed to Pieter Nason, *Four Generations of the Princes of Orange: William I, Maurice and Frederick Henry, William II, and William III* (c.1664), oil on canvas. SK-A-855. Rijksmuseum.

and William II. They are all in armour, though the ruffs and collars emerging from their breastplates betray shifts in sartorial mode from the later sixteenth century to the mid-seventeenth. Nason's painting is thus one of those slightly creepy images, where dead people of different generations seem to be thriving at the same time, each presented in their prime, and shown interacting with one another. Yet it did important ideological work. William III is situated among his predecessors whose martial attire emphasises their role in the struggle for Dutch liberation. He is also placed among people who had become iconic for a Dutch audience: both because of their leading role in public affairs, and because of their vigorous promotion of their own images.

However, there were serpents in this Orange-Nassau garden. Problems with William's paternal inheritance soured the young prince's position, almost as much the Stuarts' troubles in the years before 1650 had devalued his maternal heritage. One very obvious difficulty was the degree to which the sparkling family image had depended on an active masculine leadership, whose continuity could not be guaranteed. The dynasty had established itself under the headship of a series of adult men, and these men had been able to fulfil the contemporary gendered expectations of effective rule. As males beyond the age of majority, they had been able to lead troops personally on the battlefield, and they had been able to demonstrate the courage and decisiveness that early modern societies associated with elite masculinity. As importantly, their political judgement was not thought to need extensive counsel. Within the assumptions about gender and political authority that dominated the early modern period, men were thought fully rational, and in charge of their emotions, so their decisions could be respected without endless questioning who had advised them, or whose influence they might have fallen under. Given these prevailing worldviews, the family had been particularly fortunate that they had had no gaps in male succession. On the death of each of its leaders, another adult man had been ready to step up to headship of the clan and nation, though there had been a close shave with William II in 1647 who had been only twenty when taking on the job. This was another dimension of the Pieter Nason painting. The picture presented William III as heir to a series of self-assured men. His relatives gazed from the picture with the confidence their gender afforded. They held symbols of masculine authority (William I wielded an imperial baton); they were all set to take martial action – already being in full armour; and most of them sported a beard – that quintessential, if too often preposterously styled, symbol of biological maleness. So, although modern viewers might think the new prince looked somewhat foppish in his pleated and lace-trimmed costume at the edge of the painting, he was in the company of magnificent specimens of manhood. This allowed him to share in their commanding stares at the viewer.

Masculine mystique was thus crucial to the charisma of the Orange-Nassaus. Indeed, one important member of the family, William I's eldest son, Philip William, had been written out of the clan's history because he had been taken hostage to Spain, and so had not been able to play any manly role in the struggle for national liberation.[11] Yet this heritage of masculinity posed a serious challenge in 1650. For the first time since its leadership of the Dutch revolt, the family had no powerfully masculine successor. When William II died there had been no heir at all for ten days, and then the clan's head became a babe in arms. William III was biologically male, of course; but he could not perform any of the standard presentations of maleness. There could be no displays of courage, authority, calm reason, self-reliance, physical strength, or presence – and definitely no beard – from a newborn boy. Worse, with the old prince's demise, influence in the family passed to two women. The leadership of the dynasty came to be shared between Mary Stuart, William's mother, and his paternal grandmother, Amalia van Solms. In reality, both of these people were impressive and determined, but within contemporary assumptions about gender and power, women could only ever be flawed rulers. Females were, everyone knew, too swayed by passion, too unsuited to analysing complex political situations, too incapable of the sort of personal military action expected of leaders. And then, almost instantly, these two particular women fell out over the raising of the new prince and recruited rival factions to advance their causes. This simply confirmed the prejudice that female headship brought indecisiveness, influence-driven intrigue, and division. William III may thus have inherited a powerful family image; but it was one that had been cultivated by active males, and his succession as a baby catastrophically dropped that ball.

Yet even when headed by adult men, the Orange-Nassaus had suffered limits on their power. Most importantly, for all their pretensions to quasi-monarchical status, they were not the royal Dutch dynasty. As the Netherlands were a republic, there was no such thing. Instead, in a fiendishly complex constitution, ultimate authority in the nation lay with the 'states' of each of the provinces (Holland, Zeeland, Utrecht, Gelderland, Overijssel, Friesland and Groningen), which were parliament-like assemblies, constituted by representatives of the nobles, and also of the 'regents', the governing magistrates of Dutch cities. In the richest and most influential provinces – Holland, Zeeland, and Utrecht – these regents were dominant because it was revenue from their urban communities that paid for government. The states of each province controlled its affairs. The assemblies approved each province's budget, set its policies, and appointed its stadhouders. At the federal level, above the individual provinces, sovereignty lay with a 'states-general'. This was another assembly, staffed by representatives from the provincial states, which coordinated policy between those units (though whether it needed unanimity to act – and how far, and in what areas, its authority overrode that of individual provinces – was endlessly debated). In particular this body tried to agree foreign and military policy, and appointed the captain- and admiral-generals who commanded the republic's land and naval forces.

These arrangements certainly gave real influence to the princes of Orange. As we saw, they were, by convention, stadhouders of the majority of the provinces, and they were usually captain- and admiral-generals of the wider Netherlands. The stadhouderships, as was mentioned, brought the right to appoint some of the city magistrates who were represented in the provincial states. Meanwhile, the military offices bestowed considerable power over patronage and military strategy; and in addition, the head of the dynasty chaired a council of state which advised the states-general. Yet, despite all this, the constitution distributed influence well beyond the Orange-Nassau family. Decisions were ultimately taken by bodies which the princes did not control. Within the states-general, the voice of the province of Holland was by far the loudest, because it contributed over half the republic's tax revenue. Nothing could therefore be done until its representatives had been squared. Within Holland, and by the same fiscal logic, the regents of the city of Amsterdam had most sway. Amsterdam was far and away the richest urban centre in the whole republic: its monetary contribution was vital to the viability of the whole Dutch project, so it had an effective veto on public affairs. And crucially, Amsterdam enjoyed a peculiar autonomy. The city had won the right to choose its own magistrates, and to send its own choice of representatives to Holland's states, without interference from the province's stadhouder. The writ of William's clan, with its traditional offices, thus ran widely, but did not penetrate all the most important political units in the commonwealth.

Worse than these technical limits on Orange-Nassau power – perhaps even worse than the need to understand how such a Byzantine system actually worked – was the suspicion of the dynasty in Dutch political culture. William's ancestors might have been lionised as the celebrity founders of the nation, but that nation had been born in struggle with a (Spanish) monarchy – indeed its official founding had been the act of abjuration in 1581, which formally renounced loyalty to that Crown. Consequently, anything that began to look monarchical was viewed askance. As Netherlanders built national myths alongside political institutions, they imagined themselves heroes of republican ideals. They were, they boasted, the descendants of the Batavians. The Batavians had been a tribe of free Teutons from the classical period who, the Dutch fondly conceived, had governed themselves in free citizen assemblies, and had defied the attempts of Roman emperors to bring them under the authority of their autocratic regime.[12] Similarly, the Dutch were sure that the horrors the duke of Alba had inflicted on the first rebels had been typical of the sort of oppression that kings always meted out to their subjects: these atrocities were fostered in the national memory in textual descriptions and pictorial prints of pornographic violence. When the Dutch were not comparing themselves to Batavians, they thought they were a new Venice (that Mediterranean polity that had governed itself without monarchs for centuries); and perhaps the most popular Dutch song of the seventeenth century, the *Wilhelmus* (now the national anthem of the Netherlands), was a lament by William I that any attempt to serve a monarch loyally – as he thought he had tried to do for Philip II of Spain – would be exploited and betrayed by arrogant rulers.[13] In such a culture, it was difficult for the Orange family to present itself as a focus for national unity and loyalty without sparking fears that it was trying to subvert Dutch liberty, and to bring a free republic back under the thrall of kingship. This, of course, was particularly the case because the dynasty's position as rulers of Orange meant the princes were already claiming royal status, if not in the Netherlands itself. The marriage of William II into the Stuart royal house in 1641, and his sister's alliance with Elector Frederick William of Brandenburg in 1646, seemed only to underline ambitions for a place among the crowned heads of Europe.

These tensions had played themselves out at various points in the national history. In 1609, Johan van Oldenbarnevelt, the senior Dutch politician of the age, had signed a Twelve Year Truce with Spain. He had done this, though, against the objections of Maurice, prince of Orange. The political roots of this dispute are complex, and there is no space to explore them in all their subtlety here, but an element of the disagreement lay in the fear that continuing war would enhance the position of the Orange-Nassau family. As Maurice was commanding the military effort, conflict deepened his importance to the republic, and some worried that this would undermine the power of wider elites. In 1618, the dispute came to a head when Maurice staged an effective coup against Oldenbarnevelt's regime. This, perhaps, substantiated the widespread fears of the stadhouders.[14] An even clearer rupture came in the year before William III's birth. After the formal securing of Dutch independence from Spain in the Westphalian treaties, William II had wanted to retain a large army for national defence. Some cities, however, especially those of Holland, led by Amsterdam, were concerned about the costs of this, and about the influence a large military would give the republic's captain-general. The dispute came to focus on whether the individual provinces could disband elements of the federal armed forces. Holland thought they could, and did so; but the prince of Orange mobilised, literally, against this. In July 1650, William had six opposition spokesmen arrested in The Hague, and marched an army of ten thousand towards Amsterdam. Forewarned, the city closed its gates against the captain-general's troops, and a compromise was worked out to avoid a prolonged siege. Yet tensions over the power of the Orange-Nassaus had brought the republic to the brink of civil war. The depth of resentment caused was perhaps encapsulated in a libellous pamphlet which appeared five months after William II's death. Its anonymous author claimed that when the prince's body had been opened for autopsy, the coroner had found the duke of Alba (among other figures of tyranny) hiding inside.[15] Thus, when fanned by crisis, suspicion of Orange-Nassau ambition could associate the family with the very monarchical autocracy it had spent the last eight decades claiming to resist.

Such animus against the princes of Orange suggests there may have been an organised opposition party in the Netherlands. Historians, both Dutch and foreign, have argued about this. Of course, there was no formal partisan organisation, with clear membership, or a coordinated platform of policy. That has only been the stuff of European politics since the nineteenth century. It is also true that the behaviour of politicians was very often driven by local faction, and by manoeuvring between individuals for personal advantage, rather than national issues. For these reasons, insisting on fundamentally polarised

22 *The death of a prince, 1650*

groups in Dutch politics would leave us scratching our heads when statesmen turn out to have worked closely with people who were supposed to be their bitter enemies. Yet some scholars have used these ambiguities to deny any sense that party existed in the Netherlands at all. This surely goes too far. Whatever the complexity of the situation, and notwithstanding a Dutch ability to sink disagreement in common causes, there was a broad division in public affairs. As David Onnekink and Gijs Rommelse have put it, there were 'competing ... clusters of vaguely defined but deeply controversial opinions'. As these scholars have shown, Dutch people disagreed about the constitution of the republic, and about policies on foreign relations, the military, trade, and religion; and as they also show, these disagreements lined up into at least 'rudimentary partisan ideologies'.[16]

On one side of what we can just about call a two-party divide, there were 'Orangists'. These people tended to support a clear Calvinist identity for the republic; they backed a strong army capable of defending the state against external threat; and – crucially for William – they saw a leading role for the House of Orange-Nassau in the state. They argued that the princes had been, and were, essential for national unity, and for coordinating action, particularly against foreign powers. Orangist support had been essential for maintaining the prominence of William's family in the republic and was another potential resource on which he could build. But ranged against such Orangism was a 'Republican' or 'States' alignment. Its adherents wished to limit the power of the Calvinist church; they were suspicious of armies as expensive agents of tyranny; they advocated peace to foster trade (as opposed to the Orangists' tendency to argue for war as a route to security); and – again crucially for William – they worried that an overly powerful Orange-Nassau dynasty would erect a quasi-monarchy in the bowels of the republic, and so subvert Dutch liberty. The existence of this set of ideas posed a genuine challenge for the infant William, in many ways crystalising all his other difficulties. Some historians will argue that this picture presents too neat a polarisation, and too coherent an opposition to Orange-Nassau claims. Perhaps it does. Yet without identifying two broad alignments in Dutch politics, the history of the Netherlands in the seventeenth century is incomprehensible.

One moment in the Netherlands' history that is almost impossible to understand without a reference to a party organised to oppose the Orange-Nassaus is the constitutional revolution of 1650–1. This demonstrated the depth of suspicion of William's family in the republic, and shows the effectiveness, in the right circumstances, of the States-Republican alignment. William II's assertion of his power in the 1650 dispute over army disbandment had left a bitter taste in many mouths. When that prince died, and his family were left rudderless by the lack of an adult male successor, his opponents pounced. Those in Holland who had demanded the right to disband soldiers, and who at least at this moment must be described as the leaders of a States-Republican party, initiated a campaign to seize control from their Orange rivals. They won the argument that Holland should not appoint a new stadhouder. This meant that from now on all cities would be allowed to choose their own governing magistrates, and their representatives in the provincial states. Exploiting dissatisfaction with William II's recent bullying in other provinces, the States-Republicans persuaded Zeeland, Utrecht, Gelderland, and Overijssel to leave their stadhouderships vacant as well; and they then called all members of all other provincial states to a Great Assembly to decide the republic's constitutional future. This body, which met from January to August 1651 in The Hague, decided against appointing a new captain- or admiral-general; it increased the authority of individual provinces to control the army; and it reasserted provincial supervision of the Calvinist church. This was a radical overhaul. Taken together, the decisions of 1650–1 systematically uprooted the traditional sources of Orange-Nassau power. The family had lost its honorific and executive roles in the individual provinces (though its cadet branch hung on to its privileges in Friesland and Groningen); it had lost its federal military posts; and its ally, the church, was to be controlled by states which were now dominated by the States-Republican faction. Perhaps as damagingly, the deprival of offices had curtailed the clan's income. Without the salaries, perquisites, and pensions of public employment, the new prince would have to rely on his own resources. For its advocates, the revolution of 1650–1 represented a triumph of their ideology of 'True Freedom'. This was the notion that the provinces should govern themselves with no remnant of regal sovereignty over them (we remember the stadhouderships had originally been stand-ins for the Spanish king). For the Orange-Nassaus, however, 1650–1 was a catastrophe.

Our survey of the infant William's position within the Netherlands is now complete. But outside this domestic sphere, there were crucial international factors that added to the prince's vulnerabilities, even beyond the sad fortunes of his maternal, British, family. The Orange-Nassaus might be attacked from within the republic, but this was not the sole source of danger. The Netherlands were a relatively small, and pretty exposed, unit of European geopolitics. Other powers wished the new republic ill; and if it were defeated, occupied, or annexed, the standing of William's family would be destroyed.

Since the initial Dutch revolt in the 1660s, the main danger had, of course, been Spain. The old ruling regime in Madrid had wanted to recover its lost Burgundian territories, both for prestige and because they had grown increasingly rich on long-distance maritime trade. As we have seen, this was not all bad for the Orange-Nassaus. They had put themselves at the heart of the Dutch struggle against Spanish hostility and had gained kudos as a result. Their reputation had come through military leadership: war had allowed them to perform their masculine charisma; some of their most important offices in the republic involved command of the army and navy; and they had tended to get most support from those provinces most vulnerable to outside attack (Holland was rather lukewarm in its Orangism, partly because it had no borders with anywhere but another Dutch province). Nevertheless, William's predecessors had fought mainly because they had felt they had had no choice.

24 *The death of a prince, 1650*

If the Netherlands fell, so would they, so they tended to seek the greatest military security they could. When decisions between peace and war were being made in Dutch politics, the Orange-Nassaus had nearly always lobbied for war, believing only more fighting could truly guarantee the safety of the state. They had opposed both the Twelve Year Truce in 1609, and the Westphalian settlement in 1648.

It might be thought that by 1650 the external threat was diminishing, and that William's family might shift its thinking. Spain, it was becoming clear, was a busted flush. Her intervention in the Thirty Years War in Germany had been ruinous, and she had entered her long period of decline: a decline perhaps most dramatically symbolised by her formal renunciation of claims over the Northern Netherlands. Yet part of the reason for Spain's predicament was the rise of France, and this posed a new conundrum for the Dutch and for William's clan. It was true that at the exact moment of William's birth, France was in turmoil. A bewildering – and it sometimes seems rather pointless – series of rebellions, known as the Fronde, had broken out against the French monarchy in 1648, and would continue to destabilise the country until 1653. Yet the French Crown emerged from the rebellions in a stronger position, and the Fronde had been something of a blip in a general recovery in French power. The country had been convulsed by its internal Wars of Religion in the late sixteenth century, but the new Bourbon regime - Henri IV and his successors - had largely healed the rifts and had begun building a modern state, one well able to punch its weight in the European boxing ring. In 1535, France had intervened in the Thirty Years War and had been decisive in that hitherto interminable conflict. The French had rescued the cause of the anti-Spanish and Protestant forces in Germany, which had come close to defeat before France entered the arena, and so had prevented Spain and Austria (the Habsburg powers) achieving hegemony on the continent. The French had brought their enemies to realise a negotiated settlement was the only realistic possibility, so had preserved a geopolitical space for opponents of Habsburg influence.

The Netherlands, and the Orange-Nassaus, had approved all this. They had fought alongside the French; indeed, William II's opposition to peace in 1648 had been based on hopes that France could weaken the old Spanish enemy further. But the growing momentum of France's recovery was starting to create a problem of its own. After 1648, French ambition would be a challenge that would dominate the whole of William III's career. As France advanced, the country emerged as a potential master of Europe. In the phrase used to analyse the threat in English discussions, France might become a new 'universal monarch'. She might become so powerful that the independence of all other nations would be extinguished – perhaps by direct conquest, but at least by overwhelming military, economic, and political influence. Although this was not yet clear in 1650, such a scenario was made more likely by the new French king. Louis XIV had come to the throne as a four-year-old boy in 1643 – and so was not yet exercising power personally when William II died – but his individual courage, and his pride in the face of the humiliations of the Fronde, pointed to a person of considerable resilience and sense of self. In later decades these personality traits would feed into a determined striving for '*la gloire*'. This *gloire* was a perhaps peculiarly French concept, though it was related to the English notion of glory, and it involved the establishment of a spectacular reputation through great actions. Unfortunately for other countries, Louis wanted to secure his eternal fame, not only by building his astonishing palace at Versailles, but also through military victory and territorial acquisition. This spelt serious trouble for the Netherlands.[17] The French king seems to have thought the United Provinces a weak military power; one that he might easily defeat and so gain the reputation he craved. The only barrier the Dutch had against an expansionist France was the land of the now-weakened Spanish monarchs around Brussels; and Louis soon began to cultivate friendships among German principalities to attack the Dutch from the east. In 1650, most of this lay in the future. Yet France was already emerging as a significant potential threat to Dutch, and so to Orange-Nassau, power.

So where did William II's death leave his unborn son? Not all was lost with the break in the Orange-Nassau succession. The family had built a charisma and a reputation in the Dutch nation, and according to some historians, it had established a party in Dutch politics which would uphold their interests. This would perhaps be evident with the young William's christening on 15 January 1651 (Dutch dating). The baptism was a grand occasion in the Groote Kerk of The Hague, attended by a huge crowd which crammed into that church and lined the streets around. In fact, the numerous spectators were so rowdy that the actual ceremony descended into some chaos. Despite this, the family was able to project its claims to status. The baby was attended by soldiers bearing halbards – a privilege technically reserved for stadhouders, an office to which William had not been appointed. Still more controversially, the infant wore an ermine train. This was a rich item of clothing that made claims to royalty. Even political bodies that were turning against the power of the Orange-Nassaus at this point, recognised the continuing purchase of the family in national affairs and bowed to its reputation. The baby was sponsored by members of his family, but also by the states-general, the states of Holland and of Zeeland, and the city of Amsterdam.[18] William might be from a family fallen into misfortune, but he could not be ignored.

Beyond this, though, the situation was pretty dark. The Orange-Nassaus had never had to maintain popularity without an adult male, and often one actively defending the republic on the battlefield, at its head. Instead of such leadership, William's guardians were two squabbling women. If there was an Orange party in the state that might have backed the infant prince's claims, there was just as vigorous an opposition States-Republican grouping. In the months after William II's death, the latter faction seized control, not only displacing rivals from positions of influence, but eradicating the roles the Orange-Nassaus had traditionally played. To do this it had exploited a strong anti-monarchical sentiment in the populace. It had fashioned this sentiment into its creed of True Freedom, a set of beliefs which insisted the Netherlands was a republic with no need of a first family to guide it. Back in the early 1640s, William's family had tried to bolster their standing by marrying into the Stuart royal house. Yet this too had backfired, both because it had increased suspicion of Orange-Nassau ambition and because the Stuarts rapidly got themselves into a position where they could not help their Dutch relatives (in all their sorry history, they were rarely able to help anyone). All this suggests the grandeur of William's christening was far more show than substance. The next two decades would show if his position could be recovered.

Notes

1 Stephen B. Baxter, *William III* (London, 1966), pp.1–3.
2 Marika Keblusek, 'Mary, princess royal, 1631–1660', *Oxford dictionary of national biography*, https://www.oxforddnb.com (Accessed 12/12/23).
3 For more analysis, see Hugh Dunthorne, 'William in contemporary portraits and prints', in Esther Mijers and David Onnekink eds, *Redefining William III: the impact of the king-stadholder in international context* (Aldershot, 2007), pp.263–76.
4 Herbert H. Rowen, *The princes of Orange: the stadholders in the Dutch republic* (Cambridge, 1988), chs.1–4.
5 William Temple, *Observations on the United Provinces of the Netherlands* (London, 1673), p.119.
6 For more on Orange image-building, see Simon Schama, *The embarrassment of riches: an interpretation of Dutch culture in the Golden Age* (London, 1987), pp.65–7.
7 E.P. Richardson, 'The tomb of William the Silent', *Bulletin of the Detroit Institute of Arts*, 21:7 (1942), 62–4.
8 Temple, *Observations*, p.117.
9 Jason Peacey, *Politicians and pamphleteers: propaganda during the English civil war and interregnum* (Aldershot, 2004), p.315.
10 For a sense of this print culture, see Femke Deen, David Onnekink, and Michel Reinders, eds, *Pamphlets and politics in the Dutch republic* (Leiden, 2011), Introduction.
11 Liesbeth Geevers, 'The Nassau orphans: the disputed legacy of William of Orange and the construction of the prince of Orange, 1584–1675', in Liesbeth Geevers and Mirella Marini eds, *Dynastic identity in early modern Europe: rulers, aristocrats, and the formation of identities* (Farnham, 2015), pp.197–216.
12 I. Schlöffer, 'The Batavian myth during the sixteenth and seventeenth centuries', in P.A.M. Guert and A.E.M. Janssen eds, *Geschiedschrijung in Nederland* (The Hague, 1981), pp.84–109.
13 An English translation is available at the official website of the Dutch royal family: https://www.royal-house.nl/topics/national-anthem/music-lyrics-and-customs
14 For more on the dispute, see Jonathan Israel, *The Dutch republic: its rise, greatness, and fall* (Oxford, 1995), chs.17–20.
15 *Op het openen van sijn hoogheyt prins Wilhem* (1650).
16 David Onnekink and Gijs Rommelse, *The Dutch in the early modern world: a history of a global power* (Cambridge, 2019), p.54.
17 For Louis's concept of '*gloire*' see John A Lynn, *The wars of Louis XIV, 1667–1714* (Harlow,1999), pp.27–32.
18 Baxter, *William III*, p.15; Royal Archives, The Hague, account of the baptism 1651, inv. A-16-I-3.

2 Slaughter in the streets, 1672
The Orangist revolution in the Netherlands

He thought he had escaped. On 21 June 1672 (Dutch dating), Johan de Witt, who had led the ruling States-Republican alignment since the early 1650s, had been attacked by a group of knife-wielding men. They had been angry that his management of the Netherlands had failed to prevent a catastrophic invasion of the provinces by France in the months before, and they had been stirred to action by poisonous attacks on the politician from the press and pulpit. De Witt, however, had only been wounded. He had to stop work, and continuing public rage forced him to resign from his public positions some weeks later, but he had been able to retire to his house in The Hague to recuperate. Yet far worse was to follow. Over the summer, the public mood continued to darken. Riots and demonstrations against de Witt's outgoing regime spread from town to town; and his brother and collaborator, Cornelius, was first arrested on charges of treason, and then, after torture, ordered to be banished from the republic. On 20 August, an ugly crowd, which was disappointed at the leniency of Cornelius's punishment, began to gather outside the prison where he was being held. Johan arrived from his home, which was only a few yards away, to help; but he had been summoned by a faked message from his enemies, who wanted to trap the two men together. Once Johan entered the building, his fate was sealed. The prison had no rear exit, and when the city militia turned up – supposedly to restore order – it sided with the mob. What happened next was horrific. The goal's doors were forced and the de Witts were driven out into the street and butchered. Their bodies were then dragged to the prison's gibbet, where they were hung upside down and ritualistically mutilated. The hearts were extracted (soon to be pickled for prolonged public display); easily detachable parts of the corpses (fingers, eyes, toes, genitals) were hawked to highest bidders; and the two men's livers were cooked and eaten in a cannibalistic extirpation of the brothers' power.[1] Much of this was commemorated in prose and in pictorial representations. Since its early days, the Dutch print industry had been practised in publicising, perhaps even celebrating, atrocity.[2]

Of course, this story is distressing. But there is no way to avoid telling it, because it was central to William's political career in the Netherlands. De Witt had been the key opponent of any restoration of Orange-Nassau power in the

DOI: 10.4324/9781003267621-3

decades before his murder; and his removal proved so convenient to William that commentators have ever since debated what role the prince might have played in the street slaughter. It is certain that Orangist words and actions added to public anger. The prince's supporters among the clergy had stirred discontent at the failing government in their sermons; sympathetic printers had done the same in pamphlets; and the prince himself had issued statements suggesting that the de Witts had been incompetent, and perhaps worse. Whether William countenanced or directly encouraged the elimination of his rivals is harder to say. Yet there is no doubt their deaths smoothed a political revolution as complete as the one of 1650–1, and one which completely reversed the effects of those years. In 1672, William effectively regained the power of his ancestors. He was appointed captain- and admiral-general of the Netherlands; he took up the stadhouderships of the five southern provinces; he bathed in popular adulation; in fact, he became so dominant, that he was able to purge the magistracies of Dutch cities, removing those who had resisted his rise. Knowing how this could have happened, and why the old regime proved fragile, is key to understanding the first stage of William's life. Of necessity, the political narrative will be dense. Yet recounting it is essential to grasping the forces that had stood in the prince's way, and how he gradually and eventually overcome them.

Before 1672, there had only been occasional slips in de Witt's grip on power. As a result, and until at least the very late 1660s, William had been consigned to the almost total political helplessness that had been intended by the settlement of 1650–51. De Witt had risen to prominence in the aftermath of that constitutional revolution, which, we recall, had put supporters of True Freedom in charge in the Netherlands. He had been a staunch adherent of that cause, and in the early 1650s had been one of the politicians who had defeated an upsurge in Orangist sentiment which had resulted from the disastrous early months of the First Anglo-Dutch War (1652–4). The origins of this conflict have been disputed (it was either a conflict over trade, or an ideological battle between rival forms of Protestant anti-monarchism), but they matter little here.[3] What is important is that early defeats for the Dutch armed forces led to denunciations of those supporters of True Freedom who had been in office since William II's death, and to calls for the house of Orange-Nassau to be given its traditional leadership role when the provinces were at war. Many in the republic, particularly outside Holland, demanded that the two-year-old William be given the post of captain-general honorifically, with the actual job of commanding the army and navy being performed by his relative Willem Frederick, who was stadhouder of Friesland and Groningen. De Witt, however, proved key to defeating these calls. By 1652, this talented administrator was standing in as Grand Pensionary of Holland, because the formal occupant of that office had fallen sick. De Witt thus became the chief civil servant of the province, managing the business and correspondence of its states, and chairing that body's sessions; and the next year he secured the role officially. Utilising the advantages of this post (which some historians have likened to that of a prime minister – though the fit is not exact), de Witt first quietened Orangist complaints by helping to restore the Netherlands' military fortunes, and then established a political dominance which thwarted William's career for nearly two decades. De Witt was hardworking (his personal motto was *Ago quod ago* – 'I do what I do'); he was an absolute master of political, bureaucratic, and diplomatic detail; he prided himself on a cool and rational analysis of public affairs (he took an abacus into states' debates so he could instantly calculate the financial cost of proposed policies); and he had a rich understanding of the foibles and personal relationships of most of the important players among the Dutch elites. These skills allowed him to unite the forces opposed to the Orange-Nassaus, and to exploit the frequent division and incompetence among his enemies. For perhaps the zenith of the Dutch 'Golden Age' he upheld the principles of True Freedom, and so, as he saw it, preserved the liberties of his country from the wicked Orange-Nassau menace.[4]

Over these twenty years, William had supporters who tried to advance his career, and to restore him to the positions traditionally enjoyed by the head of his family. At moments they had opportunities, and the Orange-Nassaus still benefitted from the advantages outlined in the first chapter. Yet until at least the late 1660s, de Witt was able to outmanoeuvre his rivals, just as he had on coming to office. So: in 1654, basking in the ultimately satisfactory outcome of the First Anglo-Dutch War, the Grand Pensionary persuaded the states of Holland to pass an exclusion act. This barred any member of the Orange-Nassau family from the stadhoudership, or the federal captain-generalcy; and although it caused uproar in other provinces (where Orangist sentiment was stronger), de Witt was able to neutralise this anger. He fermented rivalries among his opponents; he launched a print campaign against the idea that one family should have a special place in the state, centred on his own pamphlet, the *Deduction*; and he suggested that Oliver Cromwell, who had now taken over as a republican Lord Protector of England, had only agreed to peace on condition that William be blocked from offices in the Netherlands.[5] The prince's maternal descent made him a probable agent of Stuart plots to regain the English throne, so it was plausible that Cromwell would have made this demand as a price for ending a draining war. Ultimately therefore the exclusion was accepted, and de Witt's campaign against the Orange-Nassaus continued successfully over the next few years.[6] In the late 1650s, the Grand Pensionary undermined Willem Frederick's position in the northern provinces, and so neutralised efforts by relatives to help William's cause; and from 1660, he stymied another surge in Orangist sentiment when the collapse of the republican regime in England led to the restoration of the prince's uncle, Charles II, to the British thrones. In 1660, many Dutch politicians urged good relations with the new regime in London and wanted to accommodate Charles's desire that his nephew receive proper recognition within the Netherlands. De Witt, however, was able to sidestep this. Although he accepted that the 1654 exclusion should be repealed, he insisted that any appointment of William to high office must be a matter for future meetings of the states once the prince was an adult, and he waited for another turn in the political mood. This duly came when Charles proved intransigent in commercial policy, and the Dutch elites concluded they had gained nothing from placating the Stuarts.

By 1665, England and the Netherlands were back at war. Scholars again dispute why: Charles II's supposed grievances seemed thin, even to many contemporaries.[7] For de Witt these new hostilities presented the brief danger that the pattern of the 1650s conflict might repeat itself. Military setbacks in the early months of fighting led to questioning of the regime's competence, and there were the standard calls for the head of the Orange-Nassau house to be appointed captain-general in wartime, even though William was still only in his early teens. Once again, though, de Witt managed to weather these demands. In 1666, the Grand Pensionary agreed that the prince should be educated as a so-called 'Child of State', to prepare him for an important future role within the republic. This bent to the temporary strength of the Orangist party, but de Witt ensured these gains were largely illusory. He left very vague the exact functions the prince might fulfil when he came of age; and the Child of State arrangements appointed de Witt himself as the young man's chief educator. And soon the balance of military advantage swung back towards the Netherlands, benefitting William's enemies. The Dutch held their own in the campaigns of 1666; and then, in 1667, the English were humiliated at the battle of the Medway. Admiral de Ruyter's fleet sailed up that river, burned large parts of the Royal Navy at anchor, and towed its flagship, the *Royal Charles*, back across the North Sea as booty. The war therefore ended in the lionisation of the de Witts, rather than William. A controversial mural in Dordrecht town hall, which was to be destroyed in 1672, depicted Cornelius laurel-wreathed in glory, a tribute to his part in planning the Medway raid.[8] On the back of all this, Johan de Witt made another move to block any future promotion of William. He drove a 'Perpetual Edict' through the states of Holland. This bowed to the prince's supporters by granting him a place on the advisory council of state and setting a date in some years in the future when he might qualify for some role in the administration, but it was otherwise utterly hostile to their hero. The edict abolished the stadhouderdership of Holland (formally transferring its functions to the states), and it declared that no one who was stadhouder of any other province could be captain-general of the Netherlands as a whole. It therefore destroyed the offices, and the combinations of office, that had always been the core of Orange-Nassau power. De Witt's usual virtuoso politicking got the edict adopted by a vote in the states-general in 1668 (the provinces divided four to three; but, as can be typical of powerful bullies, Holland only insisted on the principle of unanimity when it was in a minority).[9] The Grand Pensionary presented this rout of his rivals as a 'harmony', or compromise, because it offered at least some crumbs to the prince; but fundamentally it left de Witt as influential as ever.

De Witt's skill thus meant William's cause made very little progress before he was eighteen. But Orange-Nassau ambition was thwarted as much by its supporters as his opponents. During his boyhood, William suffered from a series of strong-willed or negligent guardians, whose attempts to advance his interests were not always sustained or well considered, and whose rivalries precluded any coherent strategy to promote their charge. The dominant figures in his infant years were his mother, Mary Stuart, and his paternal grandmother, Amalia van Solms. Both were ambitious for their families, including William; but their approaches and personalities diverged disastrously. While Mary tended to link her son's fortunes to those of the Stuarts, and to make high-handed demands that his status be recognised, Amalia favoured working with other forces in Dutch politics, and saw William's future more within the traditions of the Orange-Nassaus. Early disputes centred on the prince's name and formal guardianship. Initially, Mary had wanted to call her son Charles to stress the Stuart heritage. Amalia, however, insisted on William to emphasise his Dutch descent. This was the right choice, given that the child's most obvious source of immediate support would be Orangist factions in Dutch politics, but it soured relations between mother-in-law and daughter-in-law, and things worsened further in a row over who should manage the prince's upbringing. Mary demanded sole control of William. Amalia, though, countered that someone from his father's side be involved.[10] She was concerned – probably rightly – that Mary would squander family resources trying to help her brother regain the Stuart thrones.[11] Eventually the matter had to be settled in court. Guardianship was split between Mary, Amalia, and Mary's brother-in-law, the elector of Brandenburg. This, however, proved a recipe for continuing bickering, and gave de Witt's province of Holland, which ran the tribunal that imposed the settlement, considerable influence over Orange-Nassau affairs.

Tensions might have eased with the death of Mary from smallpox in early 1661. But her will again attempted to exclude Amalia. It named new guardians for William. These, though, were Mary's brother (by now restored as Charles II) and her mother, Henrietta Maria (who had a record of unsuccessful plotting as the wife of Charles I). The will was a continuation of Mary's promotion of her English family's interests, but it was unwise and counterproductive, as so many Stuart expedients were. At first, Charles II used his new guardianship to press the Dutch to have William promoted to the Orange-Nassaus' traditional offices in the Netherlands. Soon after, though, he lost interest, having no real concerns for anyone's interests but his own.[12] De Witt, meanwhile, was outraged that Mary's will had been drafted without consulting him, and that it had no place for the states of Holland in the arrangements. He therefore refused to have anything further to do with settling the prince's position. This blasted Amalia's potentially more productive attempts to cooperate with the province (she had been open to granting some influence to Holland in the raising of William in return for an expectation that he would play a significant role in the republic); and as a result, the Orange-Nassaus remained deeply divided and without official recognition of their infant head. The family was now left to bring up William as a private citizen, with no government acknowledgment of him as a person of any importance. Amalia's approach came closer to being adopted in 1666 with the Child of State scheme, but the

Orange-Nassaus had lost half a decade with their factionalism and incompetence before this happened; and, as we have seen, that Child of State settlement did little to undermine the influence of the Grand Pensionary. Through to the late 1660s therefore William might have reflected that with the sort of friends he had, he did not really need enemies.

This rapid survey of William's cause down to 1668 suggests more or less complete stagnation. In terms of concrete political advances, this is broadly true. De Witt bestrode all; while William remained a youth with far more claim to power than power itself. However, not all was lost. To start, the inherent strengths of the Orange-Nassaus (which were outlined in the last chapter) remained very much in play during these years. There has been no space for a detailed narrative of public affairs in these two decades – and trying to provide such a thing would have made a complex story even more confusing – but de Witt's dominance was not the result of easy or settled control. Even the quick summary of the period just given made it clear that the Grand Pensionary had to struggle ceaselessly to contain Orangist forces. In particular, he had to field almost constant calls from provinces outside Holland, and sometimes from rivals within Holland itself, that William be made stadhouder or captain-general – either immediately, or once his childhood was over. De Witt also had to negotiate the surviving charisma of the house of Orange-Nassau. There were moments when even his republican regime needed to exploit or accommodate the symbolic power of William as a potential national figurehead. For example, in 1660, when there were hopes of good relations with a restored Stuart government in England, and Charles II was making his way back to London through the Netherlands, the young William was invited to lavish public, and publicly funded, feasting with his uncle in The Hague.[13] Similarly, in 1666, William was used in a morale boosting visit to the fleet in the middle of the Second Anglo-Dutch War. On this occasion, the sailors were given full strength beer to toast the young prince. This might have temporarily dulled their battle-readiness, but William's clan was an icon of past military success, and the opportunity to cheer him was designed to deepen naval determination to defeat the English.[14]

A second reason for Orange-Nassau hope was William's personal upbringing. Although his childhood was not happy, and records of it are not extensive, it became clear the prince's early experiences, and his education, were creating a quite remarkable young man. It is worth underlining that William's political triumph in 1672 came when he was only twenty-one years old. In that first moment of real opportunity, he demonstrated that he had already acquired a set of skills and a focus, and a strong sense of status and destiny, which played a large part in his success. Key to all this, perhaps, was a profound self-belief. By the time he came of age (indeed through his whole career), William was convinced he had a right to a high position in the world, and that he had a God-given mission to advance the causes dear to him. In later life, this bred a reputation for cold arrogance and closed-off self-reliance. But it was, perhaps, essential to his survival in his first two decades, and it was certainly at the heart of the drive and the ambition which would sweep him to power in the Netherlands.

Where had this self-confidence come from? For all this author's sniping at William's childhood guardians, some of it certainly originated with them. Given that, at first, de Witt had not wanted to be involved in the prince's education (he feared intervention would bestow an importance on the child which the Grand Pensionary did not wish him to have), William's upbringing was largely controlled by his family until 1666. His mother and grandmother may have squabbled about what was best for him, but both were determined that the prince they were raising would be someone of great substance. In this resolve Amalia was perhaps driven by her own relatively lowly origins. Although a member of a noble German family, Amalia had only married into the far more elevated Orange-Nassaus after catching the eye of Frederick William in the early 1620s. She had only been in The Hague and moving in his circles because she served as a lady-in-waiting at the exiled court of Elizabeth, the queen of Bohemia (who had been chased off the throne in Prague in the first episode of the Thirty Years War). Some disparaged Amalia's marriage as an unequal match, and she tried to counter the distain by securing high status for her progeny. She had lobbied for the marriage of her son with Mary, a daughter of an English king; and she arranged that her daughters were united with various German princes, including the powerful and prestigious elector of Brandenburg. William's mother, meanwhile, had a strong pride in her own status as a royal Stuart. Indeed, it is possible her disputes with Amalia were embittered by her sense that her rival was well beneath her in Europe's aristocratic hierarchy. Such sensitivity to rank can only have been heightened by the humiliation of the Stuarts' displacement from their British and Irish thrones in 1649, and the failure of Mary's own efforts to reverse this catastrophe. Thus, for different reasons, both William's grandmother and mother insisted on his high standing: it would have been surprising if these attitudes had not rubbed off on the child himself.

The physical setting of the prince's upbringing may well have underlined an exalted view of his status. He lived in splendour of the Binnenhof until he was eight, and he had his own household from 1653. Financial shortages meant his staff was not as extensive as those employed by the heirs of European royalty, or even by many aristocratic families; but numbers expanded in his early years and came to include – alongside the usual compliment of domestic servants and pages – a coachmen, an architect, a picture keeper, and a fountain and grotto builder (essential for the fashionable young gentleman of late seventeenth-century society). By 1656, William had eleven horses in his stables, and a wardrobe budget of over three thousand florins a year. He could also admire the insignia of the Order of the Garter, one of the continent's most prestigious chivalric clubs, which were granted to him by his Stuart uncle when he was three.

In addition, early portraits were commissioned to express the family's pride in their young heir. We discussed those stressing the Orange-Nassau heritage in the last chapter: other pictures portrayed him as a young warrior in armour;

or on horseback (an early modern symbol of command and control, since riding required the mastery of a stronger, but less rational, beast); or proudly displaying his Garter regalia.[15] And the prince was expected to advertise all this magnificence to those outside his household. Both at the Binnenhof and at his residence in Leiden, where he was sent in 1659 to benefit from the instruction of university professors, his daily schedule included times for receiving visitors; and he dined at tables laid out for guests, whether these came or not. He was also required to engage in public appearances. These included those arranged by the city of Leiden (which had always leaned Orangist in politics) to welcome the young prince. His early days in the town were marked by a whole series of speeches and deputations from the locality.[16] Later, the prince's appearances would include participation in a courtly and semi-chivalric order 'L'ordre de l'union de la joye'. This was organised by members of his household circle; it staged various entertainments at its social meetings; it incorporated members of the Dutch elites; and it thus provided William with something of the sort of cultural leadership that royal courts would expect to enjoy.[17]

William's sense of his own importance would also have been bolstered by the formal content of his schooling through to his mid-teens. This was planned to include stress on the Orange-Nassaus' role in Dutch history, their unique bond with the Dutch people, and the possibility of a future role leading the state.[18] And another dimension of the prince's education – his religious instruction – perhaps did even more to augment his self-belief. From the age of five, William was tutored by Cornelius Trigland, a minister from The Hague. Trigland's job was to instruct the prince in the Calvinist faith, and the clergyman had a lasting effect. The boy continued to seek counsel from his spiritual mentor even after his formal religious schooling ended, and William remained a regular communicant in the Dutch Reformed (Calvinist) Church. The prince thus grew up with a profound belief in Calvin's account of salvation; and an attachment to the simple sermon-led worship that marked Protestantism in the Netherlands. Yet beyond these preferences, this religious education gave William a real sense of mission. This stemmed from Dutch Calvinism's attachment to the lessons and stories of the Old Testament, and from the role of rulers within that scripture.

Reformed Christians in the Low Countries saw a close analogy between their own position and that of the Jews as described in the Hebrew Bible. Just like the Jews, Netherlanders felt they were a people of God, trying to protect the true faith in the face of multiple enemies.[19] This gave the Dutch a profound sense of providence: they thought that God had a plan for human history; and that they, like Israel, would be rewarded and punished in earthly affairs according to whether they promoted or hindered this plan. This worldview gave a crucial role to people in authority. Jewish rulers had been a mixed bunch, morally; but each had been held responsible for the sins or virtues, and thus for the rewards or punishments, of their people. The Bible showed that Israel's judges, and then later its kings, had been great influences on the people, and that God had treated them as individual embodiments of the whole nation.[20] Thus, those Hebrew leaders who had ruled righteously had brought blessings to their subjects, but those who had transgressed had seen their people suffer. As Trigland explained in a 1666 book, and as countless sermons from other clerics elaborated, such a view of Jewish history had direct lessons for contemporary rulers.[21] Men in power must emulate the best of the kings of Israel. They must rule as righteously as kings David, Solomon, or Josiah; and this meant standing at God's side as they commanded their nations, exemplifying divine mercy and justice, and protecting the true church in their dominions.

Such talk must have given the young William a heavy sense of duty. If he came to exercise the traditional roles of his family, he believed he would be responsible for the providential wellbeing of the whole Dutch nation. But it also gave him a mission in which he could feel he had God's blessing. In his eyes, the divine plan must surely be that he accede to those traditional ancestral roles. Heaven had bestowed power on successive heads of the Orange-Nassaus so that they could fulfil divine purposes: William must, it seemed, follow that pattern. Domestically, this would mean he should come to lead the Dutch so that he could govern them according to divine law. Indeed, books published by supporters urged him to follow the example of the English boy king Edward VI, who had modelled himself on Old Testament monarchs as he had reformed the faith of England in the mid-sixteenth century.[22] Internationally, the providential vision of rule dictated that William must play a large part in defeating God's enemies in Europe. Kings such as David had launched military campaigns against heathen neighbours of Israel who threatened Zion; and by the end of William's teenage years, this foreign dimension to his divine duty had come to mean (to him at least) that he must rally the continent against Louis XIV of France. Louis had revealed himself as a persecuting Catholic, determined to spread his intolerant perversion of the faith as he expanded France's borders, and to crush the resistance of the true worshippers of Christ both at home and abroad. He was thus a close parallel of the pagan kings who had surrounded the Jews, and whom righteous rulers had mobilised to defeat. This sense of heaven-bestowed mission to lead the Dutch, and to stop French hegemony in Europe, shaped the rest of William's life. These were not modest goals, and they did not dictate a modest personality.

Ironically, further elements of William's self-belief may have been fostered by his great foe, de Witt. Several aspects of his Child of State scheme (that 1666 adoption by the Grand Pensionary of the task of raising the prince) forged a greater sense of self-confidence and self-reliance in his charge. First, implementing the scheme had involved purging William's household of people who were suspected of disloyalty to the regime of True Freedom. The teenage prince had been heartbroken at the loss of his courtiers (he took to bed for two weeks), but the purge seems to have matured him.[23] He realised that he must now depend largely on himself, and he recovered to make a dignified speech to his new tutors, which insisted on his rights and interests.[24] Second, the purge cemented a lifelong friendship. Hans Willem Bentinck, a minor aristocrat from

Gelderland, who had served William as a page since 1664, survived the clear-out. This was probably because Bentinck was still a boy himself (he was only a year older than the prince), and so was unlikely to engage in any anti-government intrigue. The survival of one familiar face perhaps created a bond between the two youths, which was to be a considerable psychological support to William for decades to come and bolstered his sense of the rightness of his position.[25] Third, the Child of State arrangements meant frequent meetings with de Witt. The Grand Pensionary came to see the prince weekly to check on the progress of his education in his role as chair of the committee managing his upbringing; and these encounters helped to teach William to manage his emotions. He knew de Witt was his greatest political enemy, but also knew he had to maintain diplomatic relations in the short term, and so became practised at hiding his true feelings. Fourth, the Grand Pensionary took his duties as educator seriously. As well as checking on general progress, de Witt discussed the practice and principles of politics with his pupil. He used concrete examples of the problems that could arise in statecraft, and talked through how he, and others, had solved them.[26] In later life William said he had learned a lot in these sessions. Direct instruction by one of the supreme politicians of the age had inculcated skills and lessons on which the prince could draw as he began to advance his own career. De Witt had thus – both deliberately and unintentionally – shaped someone who would have the drive and mental resources to overthrow him.

A last dimension to consider, though it must remain speculative, given the thin records of William's childhood, was William's teenage masculinity. In the first chapter, we saw how the death of the prince's father created a crisis for the Orange-Nassaus. They had, for the first time since the revolt against Spain, failed to provide an active male who could serve as the head of the family. Yet, of course, his father's demise was also a crisis for William himself. His predecessors had provided such models of ideal masculinity (martial, decisive, authoritative; at least in their popular imagery) that – without diving too deeply into questionable and usually evidenceless psycho-history – the young man must have felt a need to prove his manhood. This was probably compounded by physical challenges. Although healthy enough as an infant, William came to suffer medical and bodily disadvantages which prevented him meeting expectations of male vigour and impressive appearance. He grew to be only five and a half feet tall. His adult face was not conventionally handsome. His back was hunched. He suffered from asthma, which often gave him a hacking cough; and early instructions for his education urged his minders to be aware of his less than robust constitution.[27] These problems perhaps combined with other hobbles on William's full manhood. He was still in personal and political tutelage until he was 1668 (not least to strong-willed women in his early years); he had been effectively emasculated by de Witt in public affairs; and, as an unmarried adolescent, he was unable to perform standard male tasks such as household headship. All this may well have created a real sense of inadequacy in his gender role and might have pushed him towards passionate assertions of masculinity in all the arenas that were open to him.

There are glimpses of this possible process in William's youth. We know that he picked up a love of hunting very early, which stayed with him his whole life. The mastery of a horse, the courage, and the energy that this activity required were standard expressions of masculinity in the early modern world.[28] We also know that he idolised his governor through to the age of fifteen, Frederick Nassau of Zuylestein. Zuylestein was an illegitimate son of the prince's grandfather, who had a military career, and who looked dashing and manly enough in a portrait by Jan de Baen. Armour, moustache, confident gaze – all the accoutrements of masculinity were there.[29] William's attachment to Zuylesteing may have been a crush (we will examine his sexuality later), but it may also have been rooted in a resolve to emulate a model of full manhood. Again, we know that the young prince interested himself in military technology and tactics. This was certainly practical – he was preparing himself for an expected role as a leader of Dutch forces – but that role was also quintessentially masculine. Being on the front line and directing and inspiring troops were almost impossible for women in the seventeenth century, and so were definitive marks of maleness. If a concern to demonstrate masculinity had been important to William, it combined with other aspects of his upbringing to make him ready to exploit a change in political atmosphere from the late 1660s. Believing he was destined for great things by God and family history; self-reliant and politically skilful; and perhaps desperate to prove himself a man, the prince leapt at his chances as these began to present themselves from his late teens.

The background to the change of fortune was the increasingly obvious threat to the Netherlands from Louis XIV's France. By the mid-1660s, it was becoming clearer and clearer that the French king had hostile designs towards the Dutch, and deeper and deeper questions were asked about the effectiveness of de Witt's response to this. The first real shot in France's campaign was a 1667 tariff list that imposed swinging taxes on exports to France, including on goods vital to Dutch trade and prosperity, such as cloth, fish, ceramics, and produce from colonies in the East Indies. That same year, French troops entered the Spanish Netherlands, trying to enforce Louis's claim that the territories around Brussels had come to him as an inheritance via his wife. At this point, it was not clear how far France's ambitions for expansion really went (Louis was perhaps just seeking a defensible border, or simply desired military *gloire*, with no clearly worked out geopolitical goals), but this aggression raised the alarming possibility that Europe's emerging superpower would gain a common border with the Dutch republic, the Spanish buffer having been absorbed.[30] De Witt had some success countering this danger by allying with England and Sweden to threaten Louis in halting his troops, but the French monarch's actions were palpably weakening his position. The Grand Pensionary had been unable to do anything about the tariff list; and he soon failed to block France's next moves. Louis engaged in energetic colonial expansion in the Netherlands' spheres of influence overseas, and he built links with states on the Dutch eastern border (especially the bishop of Münster, who had his eyes on lands in Groningen, Gelderland, and Overijssel). Worse, even de Witt's old friends in Dutch politics began to question his competence and strategy. The Grand Pensionary had tried to maintain good relations with Louis and wanted to negotiate solutions to international tensions. Yet the elites in Holland's cities, who hitherto had supported True Freedom, were now stung by French attacks on their trade and interests. They came to demand more energetic action against France, and they also complained about de Witt's neglect of the Dutch army. The Grand Pensionary had expected to find allies to fight any land war, but his diplomacy was failing, and the republic looked dangerously isolated and militarily unprepared. From 1671, it seemed likely the Netherlands would not only face a full-scale invasion by France, but that this would be coordinated with a land attack from Münster and Cologne, and a naval blockade by the English royal navy (Charles II, always with an eye on the main chance, had broken his alliance with the Dutch, and thrown his lot in with the French). De Witt's geopolitical approach thus lay in ruins. William could seize his opportunity as the Dutch political nation began to look to him as a potential saviour.[31]

The prince's first move came in the autumn of 1668. It was modest. William had probably learnt political caution and restraint from de Witt's lessons in statecraft: his early career was marked by relatively limited demands which would not alienate moderate opinion, nor offend the republican sentiments which jostled with admiration for the Orange-Nassaus in many Dutch souls. Under pretence of a hunting trip, the prince travelled to Middelburg, the capital of Zeeland. Once there, he accepted not the province's stadhoudership – for which some pro-Orange forces had been agitating – but instead the much more lowly post of 'First Noble'. This gave him a vote in the provincial states; and the new voice broke a deadlock between the cities represented in that body and meant that Zeeland would back the prince's advance from this point on; but the advance had been deliberately limited. Weeks later, in late October, William's guardians (Amalia, Charles II, and the elector of Brandenburg) handed him direct control of the Orange-Nassau estates. This was a symbolic recognition by the prince's relatives that he was coming of age (William would be eighteen on 14 November – Dutch dating); and it flew in the face of de Witt's insistence the prince would not reach maturity, until the young man was twenty-three; but it could also be read simply as a private matter of managing family property, and so one that was difficult for the Grand Pensionary to protest against.

The prince's advance accelerated in 1670 as Louis's hostile intensions became ever clearer. In that year, William took up the position on the council of state which had been offered as part of de Witt's 1668 'harmony'. He thus tactfully, but also strategically, withdrew his earlier objections to the compromises the Grand Pensionary had suggested, so that he could begin to exercise influence at federal level. Mobilisation by supporters in Holland, and elsewhere, ensured the prince would have the casting vote on that advisory body. Then, in November, William travelled to visit his relatives in England. This gave him some early diplomatic experience and enhanced his symbolic power, but did so without making direct demands in Dutch politics. A series of ceremonies and receptions during his four-month stay in London underlined William's status as a member of the Stuart royal house, and indeed reminded all that he might one day inherit the English throne, given that Charles II had no legitimate children, and that the daughters of the king's brother, James, were in poor health.[32]

By the time the prince returned to the Netherlands, the French threat was becoming palpable. In response, a campaign to have William appointed captain-general was gaining ground. The prince himself was active in encouraging local agents to advocate this promotion; but he again avoided overplaying his hand. The captain-generalcy was a role he could expect to come to exercise under the 1668 harmony, so that, in pursuing it, he could not be accused of unwarranted or illicit ambition. De Witt resisted the appointment for months, hoping to have strict limitations placed on any promotion. Yet by February 1672, as French forces gathered on Dutch borders and as Netherlanders increasing turned to their traditional saviours in the Orange-Nassau family, the Grand Pensionary had lost. Again, William exercised prudent restraint. He accepted being made admiral- and captain-general for only one campaigning season, and he acquiesced to a ban on his issuing orders to the navy without clearing these with the leaders of the fleet. However, the prince himself recognised he had no experience of maritime command, so that control of ships was best left to others; and the term limit was something of an empty gesture towards de Witt's supporters. The states-general declared that on William's twenty-second birthday, which would fall at the end of the 1672 season (for which he had already been installed as the republic's military commander), he could secure the captain-generalcy for life.

So far, William's ambitious drive, and his political skill, had been abetted by Louis XIV. The danger posed by the French king had created fertile conditions for the prince's advance within the Netherlands. From the spring of 1672, however, France imperilled everything. If William were to enjoy the position marked out for him by providence and clan destiny, there would have to be a viable Dutch republic for him to lead. But Louis's invasion proved so devastatingly successful that that seemed in doubt. The Netherlands came so close to being wiped off the map of Europe in 1672 that, in Dutch history, the year has gone down as '*het rampjaar*' or 'year of disaster'. It is important to understand why this did not result in disaster for William himself. How did it in fact lead to an almost unequivocal political triumph – albeit one marred by the massacre of de Witt?

The success of Louis's forces was terrifying. In May, the French king led his army through the Spanish Netherlands to cross the Maas river just north of Maastricht, and so cut that southernmost Dutch town off from the rest of the republic. As he did this, Louis's ally, the bishop of Münster, declared war on the provinces, along with another bellicose priest, the archbishop of Cologne. The German clergy invaded from the east, capturing Overijssel and besieging Groningen city by early July: the use of offensive artillery in this action earned the bishop of Münster his Dutch nickname 'Bommen Berend' (which translates as 'Bombing Bernard'). Meanwhile, once the French were over the Maas, they swept through Dutch garrisons on the Rhine in the Duchy of Cleves and crossed into the Netherlands proper just south of Arnhem in Gelderland. Louis had therefore encroached from an unexpected direction, evading Spain's territorial buffer in the south, and bypassing defences which had been established along the Ijssel river to protect the Dutch homeland from the German side. As a result, the republic's forces went into desperate retreat. Those which had been deployed along the Ijssel were evacuated towards Amsterdam, some of them in boats across the Zuider Zee; but the French chased them all the way. By mid-June the vanguard of Louis's forces was at Amersfoort, on the eastern edge of the province of Utrecht, and under a week later they had captured Utrecht city itself. They were soon celebrating Catholic mass in the cathedral there. Holland was only saved by opening sluices and inundating its so-called 'Water Line'. This was a set of floodable fields which ran all the way from the Zuider Zee to the river Waal, and which acted as a natural defensive moat. By July, Holland was one of only three provinces not largely occupied by Louis or his allies (remote Zeeland and Friesland were the others); and the French king was, no doubt, already planning the later glorifications of his triumphs in the paintings that would grace his palace at Versailles.[33]

During this catastrophe, William, the new captain-general, had not been able to do very much. The army he had taken charge of in the spring of 1672 was understrength, ill-disciplined, and badly scattered across too many garrisons. When the prince got to the front along the Ijssel in April, he found fewer the half the men he had been expecting and he was forced into recruiting untrained peasants. The troops were also badly underequipped. Gunpowder and the sort of large artillery that might make a real difference in battle were in particularly short supply. For all these reasons, morale was non-existent, and officers were openly saying that the defensive line could not be held. Once the French crossed into the republic, William had to agree with these mutterings. He retreated to try to protect the western provinces, leaving Gelderland, Overijssel, and Groningen alone to face their fates, but he soon found even the west hard to defend. He had wanted to make a stand at Utrecht. However, the city leaders and population were terrified of a siege (and early modern sieges could be notoriously brutal for urban populations), so they refused to allow him to enter or fortify their town. William therefore had to abandon yet another province and slunk behind the Water Line to Holland. It was a miserable start to his military service.

That this debacle did not end William's career – indeed had the very opposite effect – was the result of a number personal attributes, many of which we have seen rooted in the circumstances of his upbringing, and many of which would resonate in later parts of his career. To start, William's application to his job as captain-general meant it was hard to pin responsibility for defeat on the prince himself. As soon as he was appointed to the role, he threw himself into the work. He certainly felt the pull of his ancestors' zeal as military leaders; he may have wanted to display his masculinity in a military capacity; and, as the campaign wore on, the struggle against Louis may have assumed the commitment of a religious crusade for him (the French king seemed determined to relegate the true Calvinist faith, assigning the chief church in every town he captured over to Catholic worship). William therefore laboured for the army in a way that helped to absolve him of blame for its capitulation. He was tireless in the job, getting little sleep between his frequent visits to the troops, and his furious efforts to make good their undersupply. Similarly, in an approach that would become characteristic of all his later campaigns, he led from the front itself. He camped among his men, and ensured he was always in as much physical discomfort and danger as they were. William also showed courage in wanting to engage the enemy rather than constantly falling back. He was ordered to withdraw from the Ijssel by his political masters in the states-general, and did so only reluctantly; and we saw that it was not his choice to retreat behind the Water Line – he had wanted to stop and fight at Utrecht. Later traditions have him resolving to 'die in the last ditch' to save his homeland (and inventing that phrase as he did so); but even if he never said those exact words, they do express something of his dedication during the *rampjaar*.[34]

William could thus be judged to have done his best in most unpromising circumstances on the military front, but it was in the civil sphere that the real explanation for his success lies. Raised with the pride of the Orange-Nassaus, William was certainly ambitious for the traditional roles of his family within the Netherlands (perhaps for more than these); but skills learnt from de Witt, and from the failures of his relatives' too obvious promotion of the family's claims in a polity with strong streaks of republicanism, were also key to his success. He channelled popular Orangism in 1672, and he was able to harness public opinion to his advantage – but he avoided appearing too personally ambitious for his promotion, and so blunted any backlash against his advance. It was an approach which would not only triumph during the *rampjaar*, but as we shall see, was repeated in 1688–9 as William secured the Stuart thrones.

In the summer of 1672, the public mood in the Netherlands was bewilderment, turning rapidly to incandescent anger. The people, especially those in the cities of Holland and Zeeland, could not understand how their prosperous and puissant nation had been humbled so quickly; and they began looking for scapegoats. Unfortunately, but perhaps inevitably, fury was unleashed on de Witt and his regime. The Grand Pensionary had been in power for most of the previous twenty years, so he must have expected to be blamed for the national humiliation; but the policies he had followed meant that he was genuinely responsible for some of what happened. As the French threat had escalated from the mid-1660s, de Witt had been too willing to try to work with Louis and to try to find compromises, so he had not acted with enough urgency against the peril the republic faced. He appeared not to realise the scale of the danger the French king posed, he did not understand Louis's determination to secure military victories over an enemy even if he had no real cause for war, and he only dimly glimpsed French contempt for the Netherlands. De Witt also, certainly, had skimped on the army. He had believed that the nation's chief defence lay in its ships, and that the landward provinces should arm themselves against attack, with little help from federal money or expertise. It was therefore a force ultimately under de Witt's command that had been so unprepared in the spring of 1672. The Grand Pensionary's diplomacy had also broken. Though he had constructed the Triple Alliance of 1688 between the Netherlands, Sweden, and England, and though this has faced down Louis's ambitions for a while, the success had been fleeting. England drifted into Louis's sphere of influence (Charles II had perfidiously signed a secret treaty with France in 1670 and would join in the French declaration of war in 1672); and Louis was able secure his alliance with Münster. Perhaps more culpably, de Witt's Netherlands had been too slow to mobilise support from Spain (who had interests in the southern Low Countries), from Austria (who did not welcome any further increase in French power), or from German Protestant states (who saw Louis's eastward push as a geopolitical and religious threat). As a result, the Netherlands had faced invasion virtually alone.[35]

De Witt had been neither unpatriotic nor systematically incompetent. His investment in the navy may have diverted funds from land troops, but it paid off. In early July 1672, Admiral de Ruyter fought a battle with the English Royal Navy at Sole Bay, which may not have been an unequivocal victory, but damaged England's fleet enough, and sufficiently dented English confidence, that Charles II's forces played no further real part in the war. De Witt also did what he could to work with William to supply and re-enforce the forces on the eastern border; and once the scale of Louis's threat was clear, the Grand Pensionary did secure some, admittedly late, military help from both Spain and Brandenburg. The prince of Orange would later benefit from alliances with the Spaniards, Austrians, and Protestant Germans; but it had been de Witt who had laid the foundations for this collaboration. Yet in the summer of 1672, none of this counted for anything. With French troops occupying most of four provinces, and the other three cowering behind flooded fields, the Dutch public wanted punishment for guilty men. This spelt a wholesale purgation of de Witt's regime.

Protest began at Dordrecht, but it soon spread throughout Zeeland and Holland, not only to cities with traditional Orangist sympathies, but even to those which had been bastions of True Freedom. Anger was fuelled by the scale of defeat, but also by rumours of treason among the elites who had supported de Witt, and by disgust at what the states-general seemed prepared to give away to Louis to secure peace. At points there was talk of the Netherlands paying Louis's war expenses, accepting a punitive tariff regime, and surrendering all its territories outside the seven provinces proper (this included Maastricht, substantial lands on the eastern border, and the 'Generality' in North Brabant, which had formed a defensive buffer along the border with the Spanish Low Countries). What was most noticeable and radical in the unrest was the mobilisation of the lower classes of people. Crowds were composed of ordinary workmen and artisans; of women; of peasants coming into the cities from fields that had been flooded to block the French; of fishermen left unemployed in the wartime dislocation; and – most dangerously for the personnel of the old regime – of armed militiamen from the local forces that had been raised to resist Louis. Action took violent and coercive forms, aimed particularly at those who had run towns under the regime of True Freedom. Riots targeted symbols of the government's power; the houses and persons of those who had supported de Witt were attacked; and mobs surrounded or occupied town halls, hoping to force changes of policy and postholders. As we saw, would-be assassins wounded de Witt himself in late June and forced him to resign his offices soon after.

There was no doubt that William gained from this popular movement, and that his supporters were fanning it. The positive demand of the mobs, beyond their fury at the Grand Pensionary and all his works, was for the prince to be made stadhouder of the southern provinces, with the same powers as his ancestors had enjoyed. Such a platform showed the populace turning to the Orange-Nassaus in time of war, as they had in the past; and it was a call for a government as clearly different from the one that had failed as could be imagined. William therefore benefitted from popular Orangism in a time of crisis; but his allies were careful to re-enforce this trend. In particular, the clergy of the Calvinist church, who had been long-time friends of the princes of Orange, denounced de Witt. They presented the French invasion as divine punishment on a regime that had not defended true faith; and they constructed William as the heaven-sent saviour of God's chosen people. Much mob demonstration thus began with firebrand preaching. Similarly, an Orangist press sprang into action. Through the summer, pamphlets poured out that accused the de Witt regime of treason; that called for retribution against those who had allowed the French to invade; and that insisted that only the elevation of the prince could save the republic now. The tone of many was poisonous. For some writers, de Witt had plotted against William's interests, and indeed his life, since the prince had been born: one claimed he would cheerfully have smothered the baby in its cradle. Many pressed for the execution of the Grand Pensionary; or had the Devil crying out for his soul from hell.[36] In this atmosphere, it was unsurprising that de Witt himself was physically attacked.

William's cause was therefore being advanced by propagandists and rioters over the summer of 1672; but the prince was careful to do little to seem to promote it himself. Under the terms of de Witt's late 1660s harmony, William had sworn an oath not to seek or accept stadhouderships, and until popular pressure to reverse his exclusion became overwhelming, he did nothing to openly break this promise. As the unrest unfolded, William concentrated on his role as military leader. He kept his head down organising defences along the Water Line, rather than putting himself at the head of the people's demands. In fact, initially, and in so far as he took a role in domestic politics, he posed as a supporter of order and the existing authorities. So, he went to Gouda to persuade the peasants who had invaded that city to leave and cease threatening the local magistrates. When the leaders of Dordrecht begged William to come to their town to try to restore order, he made no acknowledgement of the pressure to promote him when he visited on 29 June. He simply accepted dinner from the city's magistrates and inspected their fortifications. A crowd which stopped his coach as he was leaving asked if he had been promised Dordrecht's support in a bid for Holland's stadhoudership. He had not, but he said he was perfectly satisfied with this. He only went further to accept his family's old posts when the crowd took him back into the city and barricaded the magistrates and prince in an inn until documents were signed supporting promotion.[37] Even when Orangist forces were triumphant, William held back. He refused to accept the old offices of his family until he had been assured that he had been absolved of his solemn promise not to accept these posts by the authority (the states-general) that had imposed that oath upon him.

William thus at least performed reluctance to lead a *coup d'état*. But the popular mood ensured that that *coup* came. Overijsel, Gelderland, and Utrecht were occupied, and in no position to make decisions about their future constitutions; Groningen and Friesland were fighting for their lives, and anyway already had stadhouders (the junior branch of the Orange-Nassaus); but Zeeland and Holland could move to appoint William to his family's roles – and did so quickly. Zeeland acted first. That province had always been more Orangist than Holland; it was now swayed by William's recent appointment as its First Noble; and it was facing rioting in its cities which it hoped could be calmed by acceding to the mobs' demands. Zeeland's states offered its stadhoudership on 2 July. The position in Holland was more balanced, with cities such as Leiden calling for rapid capitulation to Louis, rather than face the horrors of continued fighting under William. However, popular action had left the allies of de Witt (who himself, to be fair, opposed any abject surrender to France) holed up in fear in many places, and the generally chaotic situation demanded a rapid settlement. The provincial states therefore voted to award William their stadhoudership the day after Zeeland had done, and he took up the office under a week later.

Thus, William had triumphed despite shows of loyalty to the existing regime. He had gained what he wanted despite every appearance of resisting his own advance and had let popular pressure sweep him to power. This both legitimated what had happened and strengthened the new stadhouder's position. The prince could claim the people's mandate (which for some was equivalent to heaven's) and over the next months it was partly local action in individual cities that removed de Witt's supporters from their posts in urban government and ensured men loyal to the prince ruled.

What had happened in 1672 had been astonishing, but it was partly a result of William's upbringing. The prince accepted offices he felt were his by family right, and to which he believed had been called by God. Yet he had behaved with a guile, a willingness to exploit popular sentiments, and an ability to conceal his own feelings and ambitions, which had been learnt from his dealings with de Witt. At the same time, the events set patterns for the future. William would make the defeat of Louis XIV the central mission of his life. Not only had the French king tried to destroy the Netherlands – the prince's ultimate power base; and revealed himself the enemy of reformed religion - William's spiritual pole star; but he had established William's political image and narrative. The new stadhouder had risen by opposing the French. This therefore became his brand, his purpose, and his validation in Dutch and other eyes. After 1672, the prince would always be most politically powerful (both in the Netherlands and in the Stuart realms once he came to rule them) when Louis's threat seemed most pressing. Moreover, the *rampjaar* prefigured William's whole political style. In the future he would repeatedly dissemble his real objectives in order to secure them more securely; he would work with popular opinion to secure his ends – sometimes using it as a tool to overawe resistance from elites; he would exploit agents in pulpits and the press to stir up a zeal in his cause; and he would stress that the focus of his life was service – to God, and to his people – and that his personal comfort and glory would always be sacrificed to that. William was only twenty one in 1672: but the man was pretty nearly fully formed.

This chapter started with the horrific murder of Johan de Witt, and the Grand Pensionary has been as much its hero as William has been. We must therefore end with a deeper assessment of the prince's role in that massacre: not only because this will further illustrate conditions in 1672, but also because it is, potentially, the greatest stain on the prince's reputation from any point in his career. Obviously, William was not on the streets of The Hague when the de Witts were dragged from the gaol and their bodies were dismembered. Mobs have a rationale and logic of their own that even people they admire cannot control. But William clearly gained from the final destruction of the leaders of True Freedom, and we have to ask how much blame he bears for the public mood that drove the crowd.

On first taking up the stadhouderships, William issued orders for calm, and published a letter absolving the existing governors of the cities of treason.[38] He therefore seems to have attempted to disperse the demotic gatherings that had brought him to power; but he soon changed his approach and appeared to stir more agitation. He did nothing to bridle the outpourings from the press and pulpit that called for the highest punishments on de Witt. These voices were independent, and perhaps William could not have done much to silence them; but he did not even try, and this looks like dishonourably deniable action at a distance. Worse were the prince's initiatives and omissions in his new offices. In late July, he refused to endorse an edict drafted by the states of Holland that aimed to counter disorder, even though maintaining civic peace was a stadhouder's main duty. At around the same time, when the states-general investigated the terms for the truce that had been offered to Louis, the prince accused the chief negotiator, Pieter de Groot, of trying to sell the country to the

French, and this generated such popular anger that the diplomat had to flee Dutch territory. When de Witt wrote to William from his recovery bed after the first attack, asking the prince to clear his name so that he might suffer no more attempts on his life, William at first refused, and then printed a letter saying he did not know the details of the charges against the Grand Pensionary and was too busy to comment on them.[39] Finally, in the days before the murder, William encouraged the publication of a letter from Charles II. This said the English king had joined Louis's attack on the Netherlands because of the arrogance of de Witt's government, and so made the old regime the prime cause of the republic's isolation, its invasion, and the sufferings of its people.[40] Further damning material comes from the day of the massacre itself, and afterwards. Some of William's close friends and allies were in the mob, including his old governor Zuylestein; and those who perpetrated the deed suffered no real punishment. In fact, one William Tichelaar, a surgeon who had masterminded of the ruse to get the de Witt brothers together so they could be slaughtered in one swoop, was given a government job, and was then granted a pension by the stadhouder when he was fired from that post.

All of this suggests a high degree of culpability on William's part, and constructing a defence is not easy. It is true there is no evidence of the prince advocating, or directly organising, the killing. As the historian Stephen Baxter noted, there is no other point in his career where he seemed to countenance murder – he even warned his great enemy Louis of assassination plots.[41] It is also possible, as Wout Troost has suggested, that the hostility to de Witt was driven by those in William's entourage, rather than the prince himself. People such as Gaspar Fagel, who took over as Grand Pensionary of Holland, may have been hoping to exploit popular anger to cement their grip on power.[42] Again, it must be acknowledged that, for all his precocious skills, the stadhouder was still young and inexperienced when de Witt died, so the situation may have slipped out of his hands; and we must recognise that the popular mood was so dark in the summer of 1672 that it might have been pointless to try to control the anger, and foolish to oppose it. The prince may thus have resolved that it was safer to try to shape popular rage, rather than try to suppress it: this might explain the apparent change of direction after his initial appeals for order. Yet such arguments read like pleas in mitigation after a guilty verdict has been established beyond all reasonable doubt. William had played with, and failed to channel, forces that would result in high crimes against humanity. Perhaps the best that can be said is that the new stadhouder could not avoid a world in which such miscalculations might happen. As we shall see in the rest of the book, exercising authority in the Netherlands, and increasingly in the Stuart realms, was no longer a matter of simply issuing directives from courts. The public, the press, the pulpit, the presentation of power to wide audiences, and often vicious partisanship had all come to matter deeply, and had to be negotiated. That lesson, like so many others from the *rampjaar*, would resonate through the rest of William's life.

Notes

1 Herbert H. Rowen, *Johan de Witt: Grand Pensionary of Holland, 1625–1672* (Princeton, 1978), ch.41.
2 Jill Stern, 'Poison in print: pamphleteering and the deaths of Concini (1617) and the Brothers De Witt (1672)', in Femke Deen, David Onnekink, and Michel Reinders eds, *Pamphlets and pamphleteering in the Dutch republic* (Leiden, 2011), pp.121–42.
3 The older commercial view, put well in J.R. Jones, *The Anglo-Dutch wars of the seventeenth ecntury* (London, 1996), was challenged by Steven Pincus, *Protestantism and patriotism: ideologies and the making of English foreign policy, 1650–1668* (Cambridge, 1996).
4 See Rowen, *Johan de Witt*, chs.7–9.
5 Johan de Witt, *Deductie, ofte declarative van de staten van Hollandt ende West-Vrieslandt* (The Hague, 1654).
6 Jonathan Israel, *The Dutch republic: its rise, greatness, and fall* (Oxford, 1995), pp.722–6.
7 For satire of Charles II's justification of war, see [Andrew Marvell], *The second and third advice to a painter* (Breda, 1667), p.15.
8 The painting had been by Jan de Bean, but now only survives in prints and engravings, such as *The republican triumph of Cornelius de Witt* (1670) – reproduced in Israel, *Dutch republic*, plate 20 – or in smaller copies such as the *Allegory of Cornelius de Witt* at the Mauritshuis museum in the Hague.
9 Israel, *Dutch republic*, pp.791–2.
10 Marika Keblusek, 'Mary, Princess Royal', *Oxford dictionary of national biography*, https://www.oxforddnb.com (Accessed 23/04/23).
11 *Mercurius Politicus*, 37:603.
12 For Charles's approach to the Netherlands in his early years as king, see John Miller, *Charles II* (London, 1991), pp.84–8.
13 Stephen B. Baxter, *William III* (London, 1966), pp.25–6.
14 Israel, *Dutch republic*, p.772.
15 Adriaen Hanneman, *Portrait of William III at the age of four* (1654) – in the Rijksmuseum, Amsterdam (displays the Garter sash); Pieter Janssen, *Equestrian portrait of William III* (1655) – original now lost but engraving reproduced in F.W.H. Hollstein, *Dutch and Flemish engravings and woodcuts, 1450–1700* (Amsterdam 1981), vol.15; after Abraham Ragueneau, *Portrait of William III as a boy* (1661) – Mauritshuis museum in The Hague.
16 For this whole period of William's life, see Baxter, *William III*, pp.19–25.
17 For the Orange court during William's boyhood, see Olaf Mörke, 'William III's stadholderly court in the Dutch republic', in Esther Mijers and David Onnekink eds, *Redefining William III: the impact of the king-stadholder in international context* (Aldershot, 2007), pp.227–40, section I.
18 'Instruction que j'ay en oudre de faire pour M. de Zuylestein' [Sent to Leiden, 1659], reproduced in Theodoor Jorissen ed, *Mémoires de Constantin Huygens* (The Hague, 1873), pp.163–74.
19 Simon Schama, *The embarrassment of riches: an interpretation of Dutch culture in the Golden Age* (New York, 1987), ch.2.
20 For further exploration of these ideas, see Tony Claydon, *William III and the godly revolution* (Cambridge, 1996), pp.132–3.
21 Cornelius Trigland, *Idea sive imago pincipis christiani* (The Hague, 1666).
22 Frits Broeyer, 'William III and the Reformed Church of the Netherlands', in Mijers and Onnekink eds, *Redefining William III*, pp.109–24, at pp.111–12.
23 N.A. Robb, *William of Orange: a personal portrait* (2 vols, London, 1966), I, 150.

48 *Slaughter in the streets, 1672*

24 Baxter, *William III*, p.41.
25 David Onnekink, *The Anglo-Dutch favourite: the career of Hans Willem Bentinck, first earl of Portland, 1649–1709* (Aldershot, 2007), p.11.
26 Rowen, *Johan de Witt*, pp.674–5.
27 'Instruction', p.171.
28 For connections between horsemanship and attributes considered masculine, see Lucy Worsley, 'Reining Cavaliers', *History Today*, 54:9 (2004), 9–15; Andrew Graham-Dixon, *A history of British art* (Berkeley, 1999), p.71.
29 The painting is in a private collection, but a monochrome image could be viewed on Zuylestein's Wikipedia page, at least on 5 December 2023.
30 Richard Wilkinson, *Louis XIV* (Abingdon, 2007), pp.124–8.
31 Rowen, *Johan de Witt*, chs.34–8.
32 Details of William's visit to England are provided in Baxter, *William III*, pp.55–6.
33 Peter Burke, *The fabrication of Louis XIV* (New Haven, 1992), pp.75–83.
34 The classic sources for the quote were published some years later: [Daniel Defoe], *Jure divino: a satyr* (London, 1706), book XI, 13 – footnote; Gilbert Burnet, *Bishop Burnet's history of his own time: vol one* (London, 1724), p.327.
35 Rowen, *Rohan de Witt*, chs.35–6.
36 For examples of this material, see *Waerschouwinghe aen all edelmoedige en getrouwe inwoonderen van Nederlandt* (Amsterdam, 1672); *Geneesmiddelen voor Hollantsqualen* (Antwerp, [1672]); *Dortse en Haagse Woonsdag en Saturdag* (1672); and other material summarised with short passages translated into English in Stern, 'Poison in print', pp.132–4, and Rowen, *Johan de Witt*, pp.853–4.
37 Baxter, *William III*, pp.76–7.
38 W.P.C. Knuttel ed, *Catalogus van de pamfletten-verzameling berustende in de Koninklijke Bibliotheek* (9 vols, The Hague, 1889–1920), pamphlet 10144.
39 Rowen, *Rohan de Witt*, p.856.
40 Wout Troost, *William III, the stadholder-king: a political biography* (Aldershot, 2005), p.85–6.
41 Baxter, *William III*, p.84.
42 Troost, *William III*, p.85.

3 An invitation, 1688

Dutch politics and the path to the invasion of England

The letter was so treasonous that it had to be signed in code. It was sent to William from England on 30 June 1688 (British dating); and it invited the prince of Orange to come over to that kingdom, bringing an army with him.[1] In this way, the writers hoped, William could resolve a situation in the Stuart realms that they thought had become desperate. This invitation would rapidly lead to a Dutch invasion, and to William becoming monarch of England, Scotland, and Ireland.

The authors, who have gone down in history as the 'Immortal Seven', were a group of elite English conspirators, who had been in contact with the prince for some months, and had been consulting with him on what to do about the rule of his uncle, James II. King James, a Catholic, had come to the throne in 1685 on the death of his brother Charles II, and had rapidly made himself unpopular with his Protestant subjects. He had used royal power to overturn restrictions on his coreligionists which had been imposed by parliamentary statute and thus could not, most people thought, simply be repealed by the king's will. In doing this, James had raised fears of 'popery' and 'arbitrary power'. These were the twin demons that haunted the English political imagination in the seventeenth century. Catholicism and absolutism were everything the nation believed that it stood against: they were the forces that seemed to have sunk so much of Europe in darkness, without liberty or godly faith. By the early summer of 1688, James's perceived campaign to advance the paired monsters had looked terrifyingly near completion. He had used his prerogative to declare free worship for Catholics, and their right to hold public office; he had bolstered his regime with a large standing army – much of it in Ireland and staffed by adherents of the Roman Church; and his wife had, he claimed, just given birth to a son who would now displace his Protestant daughters in the royal succession, and who would be raised according to his political and religious principles. For his opponents, the prospects were so dire that the authors of the letter – who included leaders of the church, the military, and the landed nobility – were prepared to beg a foreign power to invade. It was a last throw of the political dice, and it was entirely understandable that they signed with numbers, not their names.

DOI: 10.4324/9781003267621-4

In order to explain why alarmed Englishmen looked to William in their distress in 1688, we have to survey his life from 1672. After all, the prince's situation in the *rampjaar* had itself looked pretty hopeless. It had seemed unlikely that he would ever be in a position to help anyone. Although he had just advanced to the offices traditionally held by his family, he was leading a shattered country, which was still in danger of obliteration by French forces. Yet, over the next sixteen years, he had became not just the salvation of his own country, but the potential saviour of peoples well beyond that rump of his homeland which was all he had at first controlled. The rest of this chapter will try to explain this astonishing turnaround.

Obviously, the first dimension to William's revival had to be a reversal of military fortunes. This came remarkably quickly. Within eighteen months of Louis's invasion, William had been able to rally the Netherlands' forces sufficiently to expel the French from the territories of the republic. This was a notable achievement which would establish the prince's reputation. It is true that much of the success was due to the inherent strengths of the Dutch state (particularly the ability of its navy to neutralise any threat from the sea); to a geopolitics which ensured the Netherlands rapidly gained international friends; and to considerable luck. Yet William's own leadership was also important, and this was rooted in qualities we have already seen in the young Orange-Nassau. Crucial here was a boundless dedication to any task the prince set himself. From his accession as stadhouder of Holland, just as from his earlier appointment as captain-general, he worked backbreakingly hard to organise, mobilise, and motivate, his troops. Along with the bureaucratic competence of the Dutch governing class, and the support of military subordinates like Field Marshall Georg Frederick Waldeck, this created a modern army in a state which had recently neglected its land forces. William also remained prepared to share his soldiers' dangers and hardships, as he had proved from his first command on the Ijssel. Despite pleas from the states-general to attend to his own safety, he led his men from the front – prominent and vulnerably recognisable in his garter star and armour; and he warned English diplomats that they must never think fear was part of his character.[2] Such displays of masculine bravado no doubt inspired the dedication of William's soldiers, and accounted for much of his popularity with a wider public.

The revival of the Netherlands also owed much to that patriotic commitment to the national cause which the prince had inherited from his family, and which had perhaps also rubbed off from his education by de Witt. William refused to surrender even at the darkest moments of 1672. He resisted the demands of Louis's negotiators, and turned down peace terms suggested by Charles II, even though these would have advanced his own individual position. Envoys sent from London in the summer of the *rampjaar* offered to end the war if the Dutch would accept humiliation. They had to disgorge considerable territory, pay a large indemnity, and accept the elevation of the House of Orange to hereditary sovereignty over the Netherlands. This last provision was included to end the long Dutch experiment in republican government – something which had offended Charles's monarchical soul; and it was designed to tempt William away from his compatriots with even higher office than he had recently gained. Yet the prince rejected it. He told the envoys that 'he liked better the condition of stadhouder which they [his countrymen] had given him, and that he believed himself obliged in conscience and honour not to prefer his interest' over the duties of that role.[3] How deep this loyalty to the Netherlands' constitution really ran is debateable (the prince would explore the idea of sovereignty later in his career, as we shall see), but he was, at least, smart enough to understand that positions gained in defiance of public opinion in open polities such as the Dutch provinces were probably not worth having. It was an insight that consolidated his support in Holland in the face of French armies in 1672, and it would later shape his behaviour as king of England.

William's personal qualities were therefore vital to the salvation of his homeland, but so was diplomacy. Louis's near total triumph in the Dutch war alarmed all the European powers not in league with him; and this gave the new stadhouder opportunities to secure military allies. The Spaniards were worried about the advance of their old French adversaries, and they knew France's domination of the United Provinces would weaken their hold of the Spanish Netherlands. The Austrians tended to support their fellow Habsburg rulers in Madrid, and were concerned that France's alliances and conquests along the Rhine would challenge their leadership of Germany. German Protestant princes feared the destruction of a Dutch republic which had helped protect them against Catholic rivals in the Thirty Years War; and they fretted that Louis might use his strengthened position to interfere in their part of the world, and to attack their faith (as he had done in those provinces in the Netherlands he had captured). The wind was therefore set fair as William looked for friends abroad; and his conviction that the Dutch would get aid if they could only hold out against their invaders, was vindicated. At first, help was somewhat indirect and informal. For example, the Spaniards allowed their troops to be employed as Dutch auxiliaries even during Louis's first invasion, and a joint force from Austria and Brandenburg patrolled the eastern bank of the Rhine from the summer of 1672. This did not intervene immediately in William's conflict with Louis, but it did ensure French troops had to keep one eye over the river, distracting them from a final blow against Holland; and it caused the bishop of Münster to abandon his occupation of Groningen province, fearing this force might be used against his own territories. By August 1673, such action was consolidated into a definitive alliance, when the Habsburg powers agreed to mobilise against France. In May 1674, the Diet of the Holy Roman Empire declared war on Louis, bringing most of the German states into the conflict on William's side.

This international support allowed the prince of Orange to turn the tide in the Netherlands. His first action demonstrated the boldness that often marked his military command. In November 1672, he left the defence of the Water Line to subordinates and launched an unexpected attack on French positions way to the south – first around Maastricht, and then in a siege of Charleroi. Unfortunately this campaign illustrated the prince's paucity of decisive victories throughout his career as much as his habitual energy (he failed to link up with Austrian troops on the Rhine as he had hoped, and had to withdraw from Charleroi as he lacked the equipment needed to overcome its battlements), but the unexpected strike did show that Dutch forces could still be dangerous, and it unsettled their adversaries. It is true that momentum stalled over the winter of 1672–3, a season that had to be dedicated to the defence of Holland. There was a constant danger that the flooded land, which was that province's main barrier to invasion, would freeze and allow passage to the French. This nearly happened in the days after Christmas, and the Dutch were only saved by a near-miraculous warming of the weather. Similarly, there was little opportunity for William to take action in the spring and summer of 1673. These had to be spent improving the army and finalising international alliances. Yet by early September the captain-general was ready to move again. He attacked French positions at Naarden, capturing the town in the first serious reverse for Louis, and moving the front line closer to Utrecht. In October, he again marched out of the republic itself, meeting up with Austrian forces in the Rhineland territories of France's ally, the bishop of Cologne. Leading his troops in the very heat of battle (an action that sparked censure from the states-general who begged him to be less personally reckless in future) William successfully stormed Bonn, the de facto capital of that ecclesiastical state.[4] In a parallel development, Admiral de Ruyter (whom the prince had appointed deputy admiral-general of the republic, despite his earlier close association with the de Witts) won a series of naval engagements with the English through the course of 1673. This removed any danger of landings on the Dutch coast and helped turn public opinion back in London against the war. As a result of all these actions, the republic's integrity was restored. The French realised their armies would be in danger of being cut off if there were further successes for their enemies along the Rhine, and they withdrew their forces from Utrecht late in 1673. At the same time, Münster, Cologne, and England abandoned all claims on Dutch territory, and broke with France to make peace with the Netherlands early in 1674.

Underpinning this astounding military triumph was William's power within Dutch politics. In 1688, the Immortal Seven would look to the prince, not only because he had restored the Netherlands' freedom to act in international affairs, but because these Englishmen believed he had enough authority within the provinces to mobilise their resources to counter James. We must therefore investigate how the prince established his domestic power after 1672, and so looked capable of making an impact in the Stuart realms.

At the core of William's Dutch dominance were the traditional Orange-Nassau offices. Once regained in the *rampjaar* crisis, these gave the prince multiple sources of influence. The roles as admiral- and captain-general brought William control over military strategy and a good deal of patronage to reward supporters. The seat on the Council of State gave him a voice in many areas of public policy. The stadhouderships of Holland and Zeeland bestowed a right to speak at the states-general as well as the provincial states; they brought the means to maintain public peace and justice in those provinces; and they included considerable sway over the appointment of city magistrates. Such privileges were augmented during the expulsion of French forces, in gratitude to William for leading that liberation. As the provinces of Utrecht, Gelderland, and Overijssel were released from occupation, the prince was appointed to their stadhouderships; and – in quite a break with the republican ethos of the Netherlands – he was rewarded with more permanent tenure in all his offices. At various points in the first years of the war against France, supporters in provincial estates succeeded in having William's roles made lifelong, and even hereditary in his male line. There was therefore intended to be no repeat of the stadhouderless period from 1650 to 1672, when the Orange-Nassaus had been excluded from their birthrights.

All this was a considerable foundation of formal power. Yet William's influence came to extend well beyond his official posts. He built networks of allies and clients in the Netherlands which spread control beyond the technical prerogatives of his stations. A large part of this came from patronage within the Dutch towns. In 1672, disgust and anger at de Witt's regime meant the Orangist party had an opportunity to purge their opponents at local as well as national level. Seizing control of the provincial states in Holland and Zeeland, William's allies granted the prince rather more than a stadhouder's traditional rights to select names for town magistracies from lists provided by the cities: he was awarded an extraordinary, one-off, power to remove those deemed responsible for the catastrophe of the *rampjaar*; and he was allowed to appoint people not on the submitted lists, even men who were not from the towns concerned. Similar provisions were made over the next months in the other provinces as they were freed from the French and readmitted to the union. As a result, William found he could sack over a quarter of Holland's magistrates and replace them with people more congenial; and there was wholesale remodelling of city governments in Zeeland, Utrecht, Gelderland, and Overijssel as well. This gave the prince considerable supervisory authority in the towns; perhaps even more importantly, it ensured he had legions of reasonably loyal lieutenants in the key political units of this highly urbanised society, and that he controlled the cities whose delegates dominated the sovereign provincial states.[5]

William also exploited networks of supporters by building structures staffed by friends, which shadowed or bypassed the formal machinery of Dutch government. An example was foreign affairs. Technically, relations with other powers were controlled by the states-general, which met every day to consider them, but – under William – policy was in fact decided by a small committee of the prince's confidants, which communicated its thoughts to the official body only when the general shape of an approach had been decided. Similarly, the republic's diplomatic corps was supplemented by a small team of William's favourites, whom he sent on missions to other courts, seeking alliances, conveying information, and floating proposals. Arguing that this method brought benefits of speed and secrecy, the prince often only reported the results of these initiatives to the states-general, or to its official ambassadors, once agreement had been reached with foreign rulers. Again, William retained control of military affairs in his personal circle. He planned campaigns with this small number of people; he made appointments to senior military positions after discussing these with his friends (though in law he should have consulted with the states-general in exercising this patronage); and he instructed his appointees to report back to members of his cabal rather than to the republic's formal military command. All these networks skirted the traditional elites of Dutch society. They tended to be staffed by people from the rural eastern provinces, rather than the leaders of Holland's cities who had led the country under de Witt.[6]

Obviously, this style of government depended on close working relationships with a small number of key individuals. This suited William's personality. Having grown up with the intrigues of his enemies swirling around him, to say nothing of the plots of his divided family, he trusted very few people. This deepened his natural – and rather glum – introversion, and his tendency not to suffer fools at all. As a result, the prince was reliant on a handful of allies who had proved their loyalty and usefulness. William placed an almost unbreakable faith in this tiny cast of characters, and the list of those in whom he had confidence grew only very slowly through the decades. It was a trait that would lead to criticisms of running a secretive and introspective regime once he was king of England, but in the years after 1672 it provided him with solid sources of advice and support in Dutch politics.

One key ally was Gaspar Fagel. Although this Haarlem politician seems to have started life as an opponent of Orange-Nassau pretensions, he hitched his star to William in the *rampjaar*, and was appointed Grand Pensionary of Holland, to replace Johann de Witt. Once in post he proved a fantastically capable operator. Fagel ran networks of correspondence for the prince, he masterminded Orangist propaganda and intelligence campaigns, and he managed relations with the formal sovereigns of the republic, through his influence in the states of Holland and the states-general.[7] Of at least equal importance was Hans Willem Bentinck. As we have seen, Bentinck had been a page in William's boyhood household, and remained a close personal friend till a rupture between the two men in the late 1690s. The correspondence between these individuals was constant (it is still a crucial source for the prince's life and career); Bentinck nursed William through a near-fatal brush with smallpox in 1675; and their association was so intimate as to later spark accusations of homosexual relations from hostile forces in England. We will consider the truth of these later; but what is certain is that Bentinck was at the heart of those close and informal circles on which William's rule depended. Bentinck held command in the prince's military campaigns, he advised on foreign relations, he served as an unofficial emissary to other countries, and he ultimately helped to build the conspiratorial contacts with Englishmen which would result in the invitation from the Immortal Seven.[8]

Thus far, this survey of William's success after 1672 has tended to mirror our account of the power of the Orange-Nassaus in the whole history of the Dutch republic. Both rested on masculine military action, the formal authority of offices, and the help of supporters. But we remember that William's family had also relied on a charisma established through court-centred display, and a reputation built by popular polemic. William was to follow his ancestors' example in these areas too. To take the court first: we saw that the very young prince of Orange assembled a household around him, which though constrained in size by financial shortages, and his political powerlessness, had allowed him to appear with a reasonable entourage, and had served as the focus for self-presentation and hospitality. After 1672, this household expanded and came to resemble the stadhouderly courts of his predecessors. William's construction of informal groups of confidants to lead his government was anchored in this household: many of the key figures he relied upon gathered around him every day and had offices within his court structure. For example, Bentinck held a series of court posts, whilst other close advisors served in roles such as chamberlains (who oversaw the organisation and financing of William's household), personal servants (if the actual service was sometimes somewhat honorific), and masters of William's stables. This entourage meant the prince's residences were impressively full of powerful people. These courtiers also staffed household ceremony; they made William's progresses around the country considerable spectacles (and William travelled extensively within the territories of the republic); and – interestingly – they ensured key members of the Dutch elite were tied into the stadhouder's regime. The courts of earlier princes of Orange had tended to be occupied by members of the wider European aristocracy. William, however, employed his close allies from the Netherlands. The new prominence of people from the eastern provinces which marked his entire regime was most notable at court.[9]

As well as finding positions for allies, courts had always been centres of ideologically charged artistic patronage; and William preserved this tradition as well. Once the prince had become stadhouder and captain-general, the production of formal pictorial portraits continued, though they now had to stress different themes. In the 1670s and 1680s, pictures of William were produced by a series of artists, including ones of substantial reputation such as Peter Lely (who had flourished at Charles II's court in London); Willem Wissing, a pupil of Lely's; and Caspar Netscher, who was the most sought-after portrait painter in Holland of his age. Themes within these images included William's martial prowess (he was often presented in armour, posing before battlefield scenes); authority (often conveyed by the subject's grip on a general's baton, which was a symbol associated with Roman emperors); and chivalric status (in his infancy, William had been portrayed with the ribbon of the Order of the Garter – now he appeared with the full regalia, including the star).[10] The historian Hugh Dunthorne has called the pictures from this stage of the prince's life 'disappointing'.[11] The artists concerned certainly lacked the panache of the previous generation of European court painters, which had been led by Van Dyck,

Rubens, and Velázquez; and one could argue that the images of William produced after 1672 were formulaic, and so dull. However, formulas were how elite portraits conveyed messages in the early modern era; and even Dunthorne admitted a Lely piece from around 1677, which came to be much copied, succeeded in creating an air of command (see Figure 5).

Another noteworthy dimension of William's artistic patronage was his building of residences throughout the Netherlands. The Orange-Nassaus had always had their rooms at the centre of power in the Binnenhof, in The Hague; and Prince Frederik Henry had built new houses close to the capital at Honselaersdijk, Nieuburch, and ten Bosch, in the 1630s. William used all these spaces, but he also constructed major new residences of his own, outside the province of Holland. The first was at Huis Soestdijk in Utrecht. William purchased a simple farmstead here, and the provincial states then augmented this with the gift of lands around the property. Over the next four years, the architect Maurits Post put up an elegant and impressive mansion on the site (perhaps rather more elegant, if less impressive, than it became with the addition two wings in the

Figure 5 Peter Lely, ***William III, prince of Orange*** (c.1677), oil on canvas. Royal Armouries Museum.

nineteenth century). In 1684, William bought Het Loo in Gelderland and again benefitted from provincial gifts of the surrounding estates. A new palace and gardens arose very rapidly: work was largely complete within two years. This residence became the prince's main rural retreat, and was in ambition, if not close style, the model for his architectural patronage at Hampton Court and Kensington once he was king of England.[12] Het Loo is still a Dutch national treasure. Handsome and substantial, it has been associated with generations of the Orange dynasty since William's day.

These new edifices were more than pleasant dwellings, however. They performed important ideological functions. They showed the stadhouder's wealth, taste, and magnificence (perhaps in the gardens as much as the buildings – these were fitted with fabulously expensive waterworks and were designed according to latest fashions). The houses also gave William a real and symbolic presence in parts of the republic less used to seeing the Orange-Nassau family than Holland and Zeeland; and they were a site for strengthening ties with the elites. Conceived as much as hunting lodges as palaces, the estates allowed the prince to invite (selectively) leading players in the polity to his favourite sport. As the historian Olaf Mörke has put it, this established William as 'the crucial patron of a highly privileged social body, controlling hunting as a social as well as political event'.[13] Architecture was also, of course, a vehicle for iconographic messaging. At both Het Loo and Soestdijk, the virtues of the chief inhabitant were celebrated in garden statues, murals, inscriptions, paintings hung on the walls, tapestries, and so on. In your author's favourite example, the bell atop Het Loo had a Latin version of the second half of the verse Romans 8:31 moulded into its rim: 'If God is for us, who can be against us.' This seems as succinct a presentation of William's providence-based self-confidence as can be imagined.[14]

William used print propaganda as much as he employed artistic patronage at his court, and this was probably more important, as it reached a far wider, though less elite, audience. The burst of Orangist polemic that had been seen in 1672 was not sustained at that intensity, but the *rampjaar* press campaign prepared the ground for a steady production of tracts and pamphlets supporting the prince over the next years. Some of this came as very substantial work. For example, in 1675, Petrus Valckenier's tome *Verwerd Europa* (*Europe in turmoil*) put a massive and detailed case for an anti-French foreign policy.[15] As we shall underline, this was the core of William's political position in these years, and Valckenier hailed the prince's diplomacy as the saviour of the state. Much Orangist material, however, was shorter, cheaper, and more populist than this sort of doorstopper. Ephemeral pamphlets and one-sheet broadsides sang the praises of the prince, celebrating the wisdom of his foreign policy, his battlefield courage, his patriotism, and his proud lineage. Within this output an important theme was the stadhouder's supposed reprise of William I's role as 'father of the fatherland'. If the earlier prince of Orange had founded the republic, authors now suggested his latest successor had effectively refounded it by saving it from the French.

58 An invitation, 1688

Pulpits and printed sermons joined in. Religious works deployed political arguments for Orange-Nassau rule (for example, claiming the prince had preserved Dutch liberty), but they still included thick slices of providentialism and biblicism. In clerical polemic, as perhaps in his own mind, William was a new David, or a heaven-sent successor to earlier princes of Orange. He had protected and purified the true religion, and God's blessing was evidently upon him.[16] Another genre of print publicity came in the form of petitions. Especially in the aftermath of 1672, the Orangist party tried to show it had popular support by publishing demands of city or provincial governments, incorporating lists of those who supported its agenda.[17] Pictorial stuff was important too. The official oil portraits of William from this era may have been dull, but they served as models for engravings and woodcuts which might be far more easily afforded, and which could be displayed in homes or taverns as marks of popular loyalty to the prince. Some material was sophisticated, going beyond simple portraiture to provide rich allegorical or historical interpretation. For example, Romeyn de Hooghe's 1675 'Wonderful Mirror of Orange' framed a central picture of William with narrative strips telling a story of his life and highlighting both his triumph over his early misfortune and his recent military victories.[18] All this material was designed to exert Orangist pressure on the political leadership of the republic. Ordinary folk may have had little formal power in a constitution that reserved day-to-day influence for urban oligarchs and landed nobles; but 1672 taught these elites that street opinion mattered.

So far, we have built up a picture of a regime that derived its authority from a considerable range of sources. This is important, and we will analyse the combinations in more depth soon. However, before we do, we also need to note a paradoxical source of strength. This was that the prince proved able to learn from political mistakes. He could still make such mistakes – and serious ones – because, despite all we have just said, he never achieved absolute dominance in the Netherlands. Although the Orangists had purged their enemies from the town magistracies in 1672, formal power remained in the provincial states and the states-general in which urban elites were represented; and the interests, the objectives, and the political visions of these groups could diverge from those of William, even among those who had supported him in the *rampjaar*. The regents thus remained a significant locus of autonomous influence, and potential opposition. Angering them could still be costly; and the prince found he had to keep learning how to work with them.

The first rupture between William and the established political class came over the sovereignty of Gelderland, early in 1675. As a province, Gelderland had a slightly different position to the other parts of the Netherlands. It had originally been a duchy, rather than a mere county, within the late medieval Burgundian state (the lands that had passed to Spain early in the sixteenth century, some of which then revolted to form the Dutch republic). It had therefore been recognised as higher in status – though not in practical power – than the other provinces of the Netherlands. After Gelderland had been rescued from French occupation, its reconstituted government – which was more influenced by landed nobles than was the case in the western maritime parts of the country – wished to reward William in a way that would assert the province's traditional cachet and also perhaps underline its aristocratic nature. Consequently, the Gelderland states offered the prince of Orange, not their stadhoudership, but instead a sovereign dukedom. William was flattered and was minded to accept, but his ambition was swept away by hostile reaction in the other provinces. Many regents in Holland, Zeeland, and Utrecht feared that making William duke of Gelderland would be the first step in Orange-Nassau suppression of their hard-won republican constitutions. They might support William as stadhouder, and as captain-general – within the existing state structures, but this proposed promotion in Gelderland was going too far. Although the states in Holland and Utrecht accepted the prince's elevation, substantial minorities in both bodies were opposed. Zeeland, meanwhile, voted outright to protest. It thus became clear that there had been a public relations disaster. The prince had alienated vital segments of Dutch society with which he would have to work. All that William salvaged was the stadhoudership of Gelderland, and some lessons recognising the limits of his power. Mercifully, he had been smart enough to await reaction elsewhere before accepting the dukedom and sensible enough to decline it as soon as that reaction came in.

Later divisions between William and the regents centred on the vigour with which Louis should be opposed. The prince had made his reputation resisting the French, so he tended to be associated with that cause, and the years after 1672 gave him ever greater grounds for Francophobia. Despite his setback in 1673, Louis remained aggressive on his eastern border, though historians have debated whether his motives were expansionist, defensive, or simply silly (a position the man himself came to endorse on his deathbed, admitting that he had loved war too much).[19] The French king also showed increasing signs of anti-Protestant bigotry. Life for his Calvinist subjects – whose freedom of worship was supposed to have been guaranteed by the Edict of Nantes in 1598 – was made harder and harder as Louis's reign extended, until that edict was repealed and full-scale persecution began in 1685. For William, a committed member of the Dutch Reformed Church, this suffering called for a resolute response.

The prince was also the victim of what must have seemed deliberate slights. Louis's expansion absorbed many of the Orange-Nassaus' ancestral lands, causing some significant loss of individual revenue; and then in 1673 the French occupied the city of Orange (they were to do this repeatedly until they formally annexed the town in 1713). This was a deep personal wound. As we saw, sovereignty of Orange was the thing which had given William equality of status with the other crowned heads of Europe. The town's absorption into France threatened to reduce him to a glorified civil servant in a republican, and middle-ranking, state: this perhaps explained his interest in the dukedom of Gelderland – a new sovereignty might have compensated for the loss of the old one. For all these reasons William cheer-led a robust policy towards Louis in Dutch politics. But not all the regent class were convinced. In a repeat of tensions between Dutch cities and earlier generations of Orange-Nassaus, the urban elites fretted about the costs of war and the disruption to trade that poor relations with neighbouring states could bring. Amsterdam, in particular, took up its traditional role opposing hostilities and calling for settlement as soon as the basic security of Holland looked secure. The result was a series of struggles within the republic: many of which William lost.

The prince might have strengthened his political position with military success. Yet after the triumphs of 1673, the war with France settled into a stalemate. Indeed, towards its end, in 1678, it became a series of losses to Louis. Poor coordination with William's Habsburg and German allies, and a seeming lack of commitment from them, meant that French positions on the Flanders border and along the Rhine remained viable, and that France continued to be a real threat. Thus, in 1674, William's plan to invade France itself from the Spanish Netherlands was thwarted by a bloody battle at Seneffe, in which the prince lost his baggage train; and although he did manage to winkle the French out of their last toehold on Dutch territory at Grave, this may ultimately have weakened his position within the republic, since it led some of his compatriots to think the conflict should end, war objectives having been largely achieved. The military effort in 1675 had to be largely defensive, as the Spaniards provided few troops, and William's ally Brandenburg was distracted by a separate war with Sweden on the Baltic. The year 1676 saw the situation darkening with French advances into Spanish territory and the failure of William to retake Maastricht (which Louis had stormed in 1673 in his only major victory of that year). Things got even worse in 1677, as the French took a series of key towns south and west of Brussels, including Valenciennes, Cambrai, and St Omer. There was now a real danger that Spain's entire holdings between France and the Dutch would be overrun. The threat only increased in 1678 as Louis captured Gent and Ypres.

This run of failure bred anti-war sentiment in the Netherlands and stoked conflict between the regents and William. As early as 1675, leading politicians from Amsterdam and other cities in Holland started pressing for a settlement, and the military situation on the ground meant peace negotiations started in earnest in 1677. In that year, and the next, the advances by Louis raised a clamour for a truce. Although William was bitterly disappointed that he had not established the barrier to further French expansion that he had hoped for at the start of the conflict, and although he sought help from his relative on England's throne in bolstering his international alliance against Louis, he found military and political practicalities forced him to bow to this pressure. English help did not come, and Dutch cities were reluctant to pay for any further armed action. The 1678 treaty of Nijmegen therefore saw Louis return his very recent gains to Spain, but he retained key fortresses which still menaced Spanish territory.

This pattern – tension between William and Holland's towns over how much to worry about France – repeated over the next decade. After Nijmegen, Louis pursued a policy of 'reunion'. He occupied areas on his eastern border for which he had any treaty claim, no matter how tenuous. As part of this, the French annexed Strasbourg and Luxembourg in the early 1680s, along with a string of less substantial places. William vehemently opposed this expansion, not least because they confiscated more of his private estate. He tried to build international alliances to counter France and lobbied for the Dutch to send troops to the trouble spots, but he still faced stiff internal opposition.[20] A powerful faction emerged, especially in Holland, which was led by the Amsterdam regent Coenraad van Beuningen, and which argued that the disruptions of war were too costly. This group also pointed out that action was pointless when the Habsburg powers seemed unwilling and unable to help defend their own territories (Spain's ability to mobilise to fight was embarrassingly limited, and Austria was diverted by a major Turkish incursion into its Balkan lands, which went as far as a siege of Vienna). Things came to a head over the winter of 1683–4. Amsterdam protested at the states-general's decision to aid Spain and then refused to pay for sixteen thousand new troops. In response, and in an unfortunate echo of his father's actions in 1650, William toured cities more loyal to his cause in an attempt to bully Amsterdam's magistrates; and he accused those regents of treasonous correspondence with the French ambassador. Relations between the prince and Holland's urban elites became truly poisonous, and the republic was paralysed in its response to continuing French aggression.[21]

It might not be entirely clear what this sorry narrative of William's difficulties is doing in a section of this book surveying his political strength after the *rampjaar*. The story must certainly qualify any idea that the prince had triumphed utterly in 1672. Yet the nature of power can be subtle. It can consist in moderation, knowing one's limits, and being able to negotiate. In the end, and for all his troubles, the prince held on to his leading role by compromising with his opponents, and he avoided the sort of rupture with the regents that would have rendered his country a divided nullity in European affairs. So, he turned down the offer of the dukedom of Gelderland even though he had wanted the honour very much. He accepted that peace was the only option in 1678 despite his frustration at its terms. After the dispute of 1683–4 he knew he had to repair relations with Amsterdam – from that point he discussed his thinking with the city's leaders, and ensured they were squared before proposing anything in wider forums. The fruits of the accommodating approach came in a united response to new bursts of French aggression from 1685. When Louis launched aggressive attacks on Dutch trade, and threatened the Rhineland once again, William found he had his country behind him in fashioning a robust response. Generous military budgets were voted from 1686; and when the invitation to intervene in England arrived from London, the nation mobilised to supply the navy and army that would be needed for an expedition.[22]

So: taken all together, we can see why William's career between 1672 and 1688 encouraged the Immortal Seven to approach him as their saviour. Beyond his Protestantism, and his marriage to James's daughter Mary (which we will look at in more detail soon), the prince seemed to have a range of qualities which suited him for the role. He had military experience and had shown competence and courage – if rarely flair – on the battlefield. This, obviously, would be essential in organising an invasion of England. He also had a record of opposing France. This was important to the English conspirators because they saw Louis as the key enabler and inspiration for James's experiment in Catholic absolutism. France was not only a diplomatic supporter of the English regime, but many thought the English king wanted to model his realm on Louis's. James's promotion of royal power, his fashioning of a large state upholding an army, and the advance of Catholicism in his realm all seemed worrying close parallels to how the French monarch ruled his kingdom.[23] William also seemed in tight-enough control of the Netherlands. Although not in absolute command, he did seem to possess the political capital and skills to persuade the regent class that an intervention in England might be wise.

The prince of Orange, then, might have appeared worth approaching in 1688 because he had recovered sufficiently from 1672 to have a good degree control over the Netherlands, and a promising set of political attributes. But of course, those who invited him to England also knew he would want to explore such an intervention. A large part of his interest in the Stuart kingdoms came from his crusade against Louis. For some time (and we will cover this soon) the prince had been hoping to bring the English into his alliance against France. The situation in 1688 created an opportunity to gain influence in his mother's country, and to avoid the potential disaster of England throwing its weight behind France. James, it is true, had tried to be largely neutral in the tussle between Louis and his European enemies. But it was widely assumed that, if things ever came to a crunch, he would back the French king. James and Louis shared too much in their worldviews, not least a deep antipathy to a Protestant Dutch republic that seemed an embodied rebuke to Catholic monarchs like themselves. William therefore feared the sort of Anglo-French union against him that had occurred in 1672; or if that did not happen, he worried about civil war. Reports he was getting from London suggested a nation on the brink of rebelling against the Stuart king. An England plunged in internal crisis could not help against Louis; and the last time the country had thrown off its monarch, in the 1640s, it had led to Cromwell's regime. Cromwell had been anti-Dutch in general, and even more fiercely anti-Orange-Nassaus in particular. William therefore felt he had to intervene in England to save his Europewide cause: by the summer of 1688 the Immortal Seven had been in close enough contact with him to know how he was thinking.

Yet even beyond all this, the authors of the invitation were aware of William's long-standing engagement with their own country, which had started well before James II's accession. From the moment he was born, the prince had been a considerable figure in the Stuart royal house, and he had tried to use this to his advantage as his adult political career matured. These attempts had had limited success. By 1688, a frustration at repeated failures to alter policy in London must have magnified the temptation to intervene more directly in the Stuart realms. William had attempted to entice his uncles to join his anti-French alliance; and as the crisis caused by James's Catholicism had deepened, he had urged them against antagonising the English political classes. Yet the Stuart kings had shown their family's habitual allergy to good advice. As a result, their nephew eventually concluded that he owed little loyalty to relatives who seemed, to him anyway, bent on a course of self-destruction.

William's first attempt to play his Stuart cards came in 1672. Appealing partly to family solidarity, he explored whether Charles would be willing to break his alliance with Louis and make a separate peace. The English king, however, demanded far too high a price, both for himself (he wanted English annexation of a number of ports on the Dutch coast), and for his French friend (Louis was to keep the lands he had conquered). William was bewildered at this lack of Stuart solidarity, and could not understand why Charles 'could find his advantage' in the destruction of a counterweight to France.[24] William responded by changing tack. Instead of continuing to court his uncle, he made contact with opponents of the war in the English Parliament and he launched a print propaganda campaign which advocated settlement with the Dutch. Centred on smuggled-in copies of Peter du Moulin's work, *England's appeal from the private cabal in Whitehall to the great council of the nation* (1673), this aimed to persuade public opinion that Charles's attack on the Netherlands was part of a conspiracy. Men close to the heart of government had joined with the French in a plot to suppress Protestantism in Europe.[25] The polemic hit home. It was rendered convincing by Charles's 1672 'Declaration of Indulgence' that had granted religious liberty to Catholics; by the emergence of the secret that the king's brother and heir, James, had converted to the Roman faith; and by the news that James was going to marry a Catholic princess, Mary of Modena. Coupled with the English navy's poor success in the war, William's rhetoric killed any enthusiasm to fund further conflict in Parliament. Without money, Charles was forced to conclude that 1674 peace which gained him nothing (he was also forced to withdraw his declaration of religious toleration). William's backup strategy in relations with England had therefore been successful – and it heralded key features of his later dealings in the Stuart realms. It demonstrated a willingness to look for support at some political distance from his relatives, and a skill in manipulating print-based popular opinion in London.[26]

Although William's flirting with the opposition in England had paid dividends, he did not at first abandon his attempts to cash in on his connections with the Stuarts. While he was still at war with Louis, till 1678, the prince tried to persuade Charles to ally with him to curb French ambition, or at least to serve as a friendly arbitrator to secure acceptable terms for peace. The English king did make some approaches to Louis, but he refused to break fully with his fellow monarch – partly, probably largely, because the French had been paying him a secret subsidy – and he proved unable to moderate France's demands for any settlement. However, in these years William did gain a new lever in English affairs, and one that would become hugely significant later. On his birthday, 4 November, and during a trip to London in 1677, he married his Stuart cousin the Princess Mary. Mary was James's daughter, and, as things stood, was second in line to the throne after her father.

Charles's motives in agreeing to the match were simple and opportunistic. Since his brother's conversion to Catholicism, and the Dutch propaganda campaign of 1673–4, there had been public suspicion of French popery at his court. The king calculated that Mary's marriage to a staunch Protestant, and the chief opponent of Louis to boot, might calm such hostility: indeed he told courtiers the match was 'the only thing capable' of allaying hostility to the royal family.[27] William's motives, on the other hand, were multilayered, and perhaps emphasise the lack of security the prince still felt, despite his political successes in the Netherlands. Most obviously, he hoped that tying himself more closely to his mother's family would bring him more influence in England and provide more tools for his diplomatic task of detaching Charles from Louis. But there were personal as well as political attractions (if these two dimensions can be separated, given the role of individual image in the foundations of the prince's power). First, a match with Mary emphasised the prince's Stuart heritage: this was perhaps why he had explored it even before becoming stadhouder on that visit to England in 1670–1. Second, marriage into a major royal house enhanced William's status. It gave him a charisma that might compensate for his failure to secure the dukedom of Gelderland, and his fading sovereignty over the city of Orange. For these exact reasons, the match was not popular among the more republican leading opinions of Holland's towns: this was probably why William had not told anyone in the Netherlands why he was travelling to England when he set out to bring back a wife. Marriage also bolstered the prince's presentation as a masculine ruler – to himself as much as any wider audience. He might have shown dashing courage on the battlefield, and decisive leadership in public affairs, but full manhood still required headship of a household, with a wife, and if possible, children. Mary provided that possibility. Fatherhood of the nation would be more real if echoed in fatherhood of personal offspring; and this was perhaps even more important now that key Orange-Nassau offices had been made hereditary. Portraiture understood this. Pictures of Mary produced for and soon after the marriage depicted her potential fecundity, with emphasis on her breasts revealed by ever looser and more impractical clothing.[28]

Whether William was also looking for love and companionship is more debateable; as is whether he got it. Before leaving for London he had refurbished his residences to make them more attractive, indicating a desire to please his new wife; and he actively sought information on Mary's looks, accomplishments, and personality. Yet, as we have seen, the prince was a private and withdrawn figure, who did not welcome newcomers into his inner circle easily, and was perhaps, at this point, gaining most emotional support from old and close male companions such as Bentinck. Lady Temple, the spouse of the English ambassador Sir William, and another friend of the stadhouder at this point, said she knew the prince thought he 'might not be easy for a wife to live with'.[29] Once the marriage was concluded, William treated Mary with some indifference. His cold attitude to her was noted at the celebratory ball; he went straight back to diplomatic and military business when they arrived back in the Netherlands; and he may quickly have taken a mistress. This was Elizabeth Villiers, a daughter of Mary's governess, who had come over with her as part of her household; though the exact nature of the relationship is not certain. Although many historians have asserted William and this courtier were lovers, the evidence is in fact a bit sketchy, being largely composed of politically convenient rumour. Later gifts of lands in Ireland by William to Villiers suggest at least a close friendship; but as with many aspects of the prince's emotional life, his congenital privacy closed his bedroom door on modern scholars as much as contemporaries.[30] For her part, Mary was initially horrified at her union with William. Only fifteen years old; concerned about leaving her homeland; and not attracted to a man who was so short and ugly that her sister Anne christened him 'Caliban'; she reportedly wept for a day and a half on hearing she had been betrothed. Mary wept again for hours on leaving London to head for the Netherlands.[31] It is clear she only made the journey, or, indeed, had agreed to became princess of Orange in the first place, out of a sense of duty that marked her whole life. In time, as we shall see, the partnership of William and Mary became close. A mutual respect eventually bred genuine affection; but in the late 1670s this was all far in the future. The marriage very much a diplomatic, not love, match.

Now that he was united with the Stuarts by nuptials as well as descent, William might have hoped for a strong voice at the heart of family counsels. But he was again to be disappointed. England became no more helpful in resisting France after the wedding than it had been before. Charles followed what the historian Wout Troost has called a 'pendulum policy', seeming to threaten Louis with an alliance with the Dutch, and then swinging back to neutrality, or positive support for the French king.[32] And then the prince's views were largely ignored in the series of perils that engulfed the Stuarts at end of the decade. In 1678, hysterical, but widely credited, rumours of a 'popish plot' began to circulate in London. According to their fraudulent instigator, Titus Oates, this conspiracy aimed to assassinate Charles and replace him with his Catholic brother, and this soon led to calls that James be barred from succession to the throne. From 1679 to 1681, three parliaments were elected whose Commons, at least, voted to exclude the heir from power; so, Charles was forced to dissolve each one to protect the rights of his heir. In this 'exclusion crisis' public opinion was riled and divided. Censorship broke down, and radical pamphlets stoked calls for wholesale constitutional remodelling. Mass demonstrations, petitioning, and election campaigns kept the political temperature high; and polarisation between supporters and opponents of exclusion created a long-term fissure. These years marked the birth of England's bitterly rival parties: the Whigs (pro-exclusion) and the Tories (anti-exclusion).

William's position on all this took a while to emerge; partly because the calculations he had to make were quite complex. He had a loyalty to his uncles, and an attachment to the principle of hereditary legitimacy. He was therefore temperamentally opposed to exclusion, and told an English contact, Henry Sidney, that he thought it an injustice.[33] He also feared that removing Charles's brother from the succession would weaken the claims of that brother's daughter. That daughter was now, of course, William's wife; and he may have hoped that one day he might control English policy through her. A widely canvassed method of excluding James would be for Charles to recognise the claims of the duke of Monmouth, his illegitimate, Protestant, and popular son. If this expedient were adopted, it would divert the Crown from the line that would bring it to Mary. Faced with these considerations, William resisted pressures to go to England, as some urged him to do, in case it suggested he supported the wrong kind of exclusion. Eventually, however, the prince came to believe that the turmoil in English politics was neutralising the Stuart realms as possible allies against France. It might even risk the family being chased again from the throne. William therefore concluded that barring James from the succession would allow calmer conditions, and so engineered the publication of a memorial from the Dutch states-general – to avoid his fingerprints being too obviously on the initiative – arguing that Charles must come to terms with Parliament (which in practice would mean accepting exclusion) for the security of all Protestant Europe.[34] Almost exactly as William began to advocate this line, however, Charles resolved on the opposite course. He began facing the Whig movement down. Aided by Tory propaganda, the court denounced the exclusionists as the sort of troublemakers who had caused civil war in the 1640s. It accused them of various forms of treason and proceeded against their leaders judicially; and it set its face against any further meetings of Parliament. The prince's strategy for dealing with the crisis had been rebuffed.

Initially it looked as if Charles had been right to ignore his nephew. The Whigs were defeated and James retained his position in the succession. Indeed, he came to the throne peacefully, and with some considerable public enthusiasm, on his brother's sudden death in 1685. But soon, the new monarch's approach to rule suggested the family might have been better off listening to William. As we noted at the head of this chapter, James rapidly alienated his subjects by promoting Catholicism and appearing to overturn a constitution which many believed guaranteed their liberties, and the rule of law. It is true that the direction things were going was not obvious in the first months of the regime. James promised to protect the Protestant Church of England and called a Parliament in hopes of advancing his agenda through consent. In these early weeks, William was prepared to support his father-in-law: he congratulated him on his accession and sent troops to help him suppress a rebellion led by the duke of Monmouth, who made a desperate bid for the throne denied him by the failure of exclusion. Yet as James's plan to promote his religion and royal power became clearer, William again became fearful that the Stuarts would embroil England in internal dispute. He worried division would both endanger the Crown he hoped in due course to control through Mary; and hobble the country as a potential ally against France. The prince therefore switched to more confrontational tactics – ones that had worked for him before. Whilst advising the English king to change course, he also made contact with opponents of the court, and launched a campaign of print polemic to win over English opinion.

Key to this policy was the mission of Van Weede van Dijkvelt to London in 1687. Dijkvelt was from William's all-important inner circle, and was sent by the prince to sound out the political situation in England. The envoy had conversations with James in which he urged the monarch to align himself with the Netherlands, rather than with France; and he expressed William's disapproval of the king's religious policies. He stated that although the prince had no objection to James trying to improve the legal position of Catholics, this had to be done in a constitutional way, through Parliament. At this point, William feared that simply extending religious freedom by royal fiat could breed 'disorders which would imperil the monarchy'.[35] The talks yielded little – James was not listening to his son-in-law's advice – so Dijkvelt also advanced another part of his mission, which was to sound out the attitudes of the king's English opponents. Some were noncommittal, but others – of whom the Immortal Seven became the core – welcomed the possibility of a rescue from the Netherlands. From at least the summer of 1687 they formed a conspiratorial network, in touch with William's stadhouderly court, and informing him of the mood in London.

Another dimension of William's involvement was propaganda. The prince not only urged James privately to work through Parliament, and to be mindful of public opinion, but he ensured a much wider English populace knew the thinking in The Hague. In an echo of the tactics in 1673, which had forced Charles II out of his war with the Netherlands, William tried to bully a Stuart uncle to change course by turning public opinion against him. The most important intervention was the publication of a letter from Fagel which made the prince's position on religion clear. While the prince opposed persecution and would allow people to worship outside the Protestant Church of England, he would not support the admission of Catholics to public office.[36] The letter circulated widely in the early months of 1688 and it removed a number of potential fears about what would happen if the prince came to direct affairs in England (perhaps if and when Mary became queen). It also built him a fair degree of support among the English, who came to see his approach as a sensible alternative to royal policy. People were now assured the William would protect the Protestant establishment, but that he would also seek solutions for those who disagreed with it.

Those who could not accept the existing religious settlement included Catholics, but also numbers of 'dissenters'. Dissenters were people who shared the Church of England's Protestantism, but had found it hard to belong to that body since the early 1660s. They objected to the ceremonies and forms of ecclesiastical government (especially the resurrection of the office of bishop) that had been imposed when Charles II had returned to the throne. In another part of the Dutch-inspired press campaign, one of William's contacts, George Savile, the marquis of Halifax, appealed directly to these dissenters. He warned them against accepting the freedom to worship outside the church, which James was offering them alongside his own coreligionists, and which was threatening to divide the Protestant cause in England. Savile cautioned that the dissenters' protections would mean nothing once the king had established the principle that he could change the law at will. The proffered liberty thus was a trick to win temporary support: in his famous phrase dissenters were 'to be hugged now, only that you may be the better squeezed at another time'.[37]

All this manoeuvring was, no doubt, putting William in a frame of mind to intervene more directly in England. Historians have debated exactly when he decided this was his best move. Any sane assessment of the risks involved in amphibious military action would push the date towards the later end of the range of possibilities. The prince would surely have wanted to wait for as long as possible to see if the crisis in England could be resolved in his favour by any means other than a seaborn invasion. William's close confidant, the exiled clergyman Gilbert Burnet, gave no indication that a decision was made before May 1688 in his later account of that year. In May, the prince promised Admiral Russell, who had been sent over for consultations by James's opponents, that he would do something – and this seems the most likely timing for the final resolution to invade. It was only by this stage, as Russell stressed, that the English were losing all non-desperate options to save the faith and liberties.[38] James was now well into a campaign to pack Parliament with his supporters by altering the franchises in the boroughs that elected most MPs (so the legislature no longer looked like a bulwark of Protestantism that could stop the monarch); and he was flexing his muscles with the Church of England. He demanded that his Declaration of Indulgence for Catholics be read from all its pulpits, and he then arrested seven bishops, and charged them with sedition, when they led a widespread refusal by the clergy to advocate what they thought was an unconstitutional act. Substantial sections of the English ruling classes were openly defying their king by this point. Many among the nobility, gentry, and town elites had refused to cooperate with James's attempts to engineer a friendly legislature when he had formally asked if they would; and declarations of support for the detained bishops flooded in.[39] With all this going on, William concluded that he needed to act soon, or the situation in England might descend into chaos.

Any final doubts in the prince's mind must have been stilled by the birth of a son to James in June. In many ways this was an unexpected – and troublingly convenient – event for the king. His wife had had multiple pregnancies since the marriage in 1673, but these had tragically resulted in miscarriages, or children who died very young; and there had been no new prospects of offspring for four years. The birth was thus a surprise. Perhaps the queen's 1687 pilgrimage to St Winifred's Well in Denbighshire to pray for a child had paid off, but some among James's opponents assumed court shenanigans. Despite clouds of witnesses to the contrary, rumours circulated that the baby of a common miller had been smuggled into the royal birthing chamber in a warming pan. Absurd conspiracy theories were a speciality of late seventeenth-century politics in England; and this one ramped up discontent with the king.[40] Yet even without such suspicions of fraud, the birth raised political tension by blasting the comforting prospect of Mary acceding to the throne. English people could no longer hope that James's rule might be a temporary interlude, and that he would be replaced by his Protestant daughter in the reasonably near future. William's Stuart loyalty kicked in long enough for him to congratulate his father-in-law on his son; but he later acknowledged, and the letter of the Immortal Seven berated, that this had been a mistake.[41] Once James's son had arrived, it was probably that a showdown between ruler and people was coming in England. William knew he would have to be present in the country, and bring force with him, to shape the outcome of the growing crisis. Preventing an attempt to alter the succession with a low-born baby would have been a convenient excuse for this intervention.

We have now seen why the letter of 30 June 1688 was sent. A key section of the English elite had become desperate and saw a saviour in William. Here was a man they knew was interested in intervening, and whom they thought had the political resources to make an intervention work. But there may, just possibly, have been something more. The authors of the letter may have had a shadowy sense that William was a new kind of ruler, one more appropriate for new times. He had, as we noted, rested his Dutch power on multiple foundations. Some were characteristic of traditional, deferential, and hierarchical societies. William had claimed a providential mission, and so, in a sense, a divine appointment to his role. He had built a courtly charisma, displaying his magnificence in personal appearance, entourage, and architectural patronage. He established a masculine reputation for battlefield courage; he ran policy with a small group of advisers from his household; and he traded on a heritage of loyalty to one of the great aristocrat families of Europe. All of this would have been at home in any medieval or renaissance polity. Yet, at the same time, William was comfortable with more open, decentralised, and demotic systems, of the kind which the Netherlands definitely was, and which the Stuart realms had perhaps become. By the later seventeenth century, England in particular had come to mirror important elements of Dutch political society. Whilst there was no equivalent of the Netherlands' dominant regents, English local government was dependent on a gentry class, and on urban leaderships, whose views the monarchs could not ignore (as Charles I had found to his very high cost). Whilst the Parliament in Westminster was not sovereign as the Dutch provincial states were, this representative body did have to be squared if the court wanted to raise taxes, and it had perhaps grown more confident in the face of the Crown's severe financial difficulties. Certainly, popular politics was not quite as free as in the Netherlands (for example, press censorship was supposed to operate during most of the Stuarts' time on the throne), but the English population was highly literate, politically engaged, and contentiously divided – especially over religion. There had been periods – notably the early 1640s, and during the exclusion crisis – when controls had broken down and a vigorous open public debate had ensued.

Thus, to the Immortal Seven, William might have seemed a good bet. Since the prince was used to Dutch politics, he could well be someone who would understand how to operate England's emerging political culture, and he had already demonstrated many of the skills that might be needed. He had become adept at political negotiation and alliance-building with other influential forces in a state. He had come to know when to compromise and retreat in the face of opposition. He understood that that he needed wider public support and had employed campaigns of propaganda to secure this: he had, indeed, already used print polemic in England itself, and highly effectively, in 1673 and 1687. Given that the seven notables were opposing a ruler with none of these characteristics, they might have warmed to someone with a very different style. James seemed to want a centralised and authoritative government; and ignored the popular element of the English polity. He overrode the people's representatives in Parliament to pass his own laws and attempted to overawe any resistance with his army. The prince of Orange was nothing like this, at least after political disasters in the Netherlands had proved that he could lose support dramatically if he threw his weight around. This may well have been an attraction. But whether or not William's approach to public life figured in the calculations of the prince's English contacts, it would still be crucial. The prince's hybrid experience of rule would, as we are about to see, be key to his successes in the Stuart realms.

Notes

1 The text is reproduced in Andrew Browning ed, *English historical documents, 1660–1714* (London, Eyre and Spottiswood, 1953), document 39, and is also available online at https://www.englishhistoricaldocuments.com
2 N. Japikse ed, *Correspondentie van Willem III en van Hans Willem Bentinck* (5 vols, The Hague, 1927–1937), II, i, 115–16.
3 Quoted in Baxter, *William III* (London, 1966), p.88.
4 Japikse, *Correspondentie*, II, i, 309–10.
5 These changes are well covered in Simon Groenveld, 'William as stadhouder: prince or minister?', in Esther Mijers and David Onnekink eds, *Redefining William III: the impact of the king-stadholder iniInternational context* (Aldeshot, 2007), pp.17–38.
6 Groenveld, 'William as stadhouder', at pp.24–5.
7 For an appreciation of Fagel's role, see Elizabeth Edwards, 'An unknown statesman? Gaspar Fagel in the service of William III and the Dutch republic', *History*, 87:287 (2002), 353–71.
8 David Onnekink, *The Anglo-Dutch favourite: the career of Hans Willem Bentinck, first earl of Portland, 1649–1709* (Aldershot, 2007), chs.1–2.
9 For William's stadhouderly court, see Olaf Mörke, 'William III's stadholderly court in the Dutch republic', in Mijers and Onnekink, *Redefining William III*, pp.227–40.

10 There is a complete chronological list of all known portraits of William at https://www.npg.org.uk/collections/search/personExtended/mp04834/king-william-iii?tab=iconography
11 Hugh Dunthorne, 'William in contemporary portraits and prints', in Mijers and Onnekink, *Redefining William III*, pp.263–76.
12 For the limited stylistic influence, see Simon Thurley, *Hampton Court: a social and architectural history* (New Haven, 2003), p.167.
13 Mörke, 'William III's stadholderly court', p.235.
14 I am grateful to the curators of Het Loo, for taking me up on to the roof to discover this.
15 Petrus Valckenier, *Verwerd Europa ofte polityke en historische beschrijving der waare fundamenten en oorzaken van de oorlogen en revolutiën in Europa* (Amsterdam, 1675).
16 Matthijs Wieldraaijer, 'Good government and providential delivery: legitimations of the 1672 and 1688/9 Orangist revolutions in Dutch sermons', *Dutch Crossing*, 34:1 (2010), 42–58.
17 Michel Reinders, '"The citizens come from all cities with petitions": printed petitions and civic propaganda in the seventeenth century', in Femke Deen, David Onnekink, and Michel Reinders eds, *Pamphlets and pamphleteering in the Dutch republic* (Brill, Leiden, 2011), pp.97–119.
18 Romeyn de Hooghe, *Orengien wonderspiegel* (Amsterdam, 1675).
19 For a clear exposition of the confusions in Louis's objectives and strategy, see Richard Wilkinson, *Louis XIV* (Abingdon, 2007), pp.129–38.
20 The manoeuvrings were complex; and have been hugely simplified and summarised here. A clear exposition can be found in Wout Troost, *William III, the stadholder-king: a political biography* (Aldershot, 2005), ch.7.
21 There is a clear and concise account of tensions with Amsterdam in Troost, *William III*, pp.166–71.
22 The story of the turning of Dutch sentiment is well told in Jonathan Israel, 'The Dutch role in the Glorious Revolution', in Jonathan Israel ed, *The Anglo-Dutch moment: essays on the Glorious Revolution and its world impact* (Cambridge, 1991), pp.105–62.
23 The parallels are emphasised in Steven Pincus, *1688: the first modern revolution* (New Haven, 2009).
24 Report from English envoys to William, 18 July 1672 (Dutch dating), reported in Wouter Troost, *Sir William Temple, William III, and the balance of power in Europe* (Dordrecht, 2011), p.44.
25 Other key works included: *An answer to his majesty's declaration of war* (London, 1673) and *A relation of the most material matters handled in parliament* (London, 1673).
26 The classic study is K.H.D. Haley, *William of Orange and the English opposition, 1672–4* (Oxford, 1953).
27 Remark by earl of Ossory, reported in John Miller, *Charles II* (London, 1991), p.240.
28 For more on the iconographic dimensions of this paragraph, see Catriona Murray, 'An inflammatory match? Public anxiety and political assurance at the wedding of William III and Mary II', *Historical Research*, 89:246 (2016), 730–50.
29 Cited in K.H.D. Haley, 'The Anglo-Dutch rapprochement of 1677', *English Historical Review*, 73 (1958).
30 Rachel Weil, 'Elizabeth Villiers, countess of Orkney', *Oxford dictionary of national biography*, https://www.oxforddnb.com (Accessed 25/04/23).
31 Tony Claydon and W.A. Speck, *William and Mary* (Oxford, 2007), pp.107–11.
32 Troost, *Sir William Temple*, ch.6.

33 R.W. Blencowe ed, *Diary of the times of Charles II, by Henry Sidney* (2 vols, London, 1843), II, 120.
34 *An intimation of the deputies of the states general* (London, 1680).
35 Conversation with James II's envoy to William, the marquis d'Albeville, quoted in John Miller, *James II: a study in kingship* (London, 1976), p.176.
36 *A letter writ by Min Heer Fagel, pensioner of Holland* (London, 1688).
37 [George Savile], *A letter to a dissenter* (London, 1687).
38 Gilbert Burnet, *Bishop Burnet's history of his own time: volume one* (1724), p.746.
39 The best coverage is William Gibson, *James II and the trial of the seven bishops* (Basingstoke, 2009) and Peter Walker, *James II and the three questions* (Oxford, 2010).
40 The best coverage is Rachel Weil, *Political passions: gender, the family and political argument in England, 1680–1714* (Manchester, 1999), ch.3.
41 William's acknowledgement was tacit: his manifesto for his invasion of England raised questions about the legitimacy of James's son even after the prince had sent congratulations – William III, *The declaration of his highness William Henry, prince of Orange of the reasons inducing him to appear in arms in the kingdom of England* (The Hague, 1688).

4 A coronation, 1689
William and the Glorious Revolution in England

It was a new phrase. When William and Mary were crowned king and queen of England and Ireland in Westminster Abbey on 11 April 1689 (British dating), they took an oath before the congregation and their people. This was traditional – but the exact wording of their promises to their subjects had changed. In the past, incoming rulers had sworn they would, in some vague sense, uphold the 'rightful customs' of the realm. Now William and Mary solemnly stated that they were to govern 'according to the statutes in parliament agreed on, and the laws and customs of the same'.[1] There were a number of remarkable things about this. First, the oath implied a new basis of monarchy. To an extent never made so explicit before, the offices of kings and queens were now described as defenders of an authority that derived from the representatives of the people, not solely from royalty itself. The point was driven home by the attendance of the entire House of Commons at the ceremony. This was an innovation: previously only the Lords had gone to the crowning as of right. Second, the promises were made by two people. William and Mary were both deemed to be regnant monarchs. This was a formal sharing of royal sovereignty between a royal couple that had never been seen before. Third, and perhaps most extraordinary, was the fact that a coronation ceremony was happening at all. The former king, James II, was still alive, though he had fled to France. This succession was therefore highly unorthodox and would remain extremely controversial. To understand these novelties and peculiarities, we must tell the astonishing story of William's life from the end of June 1688 to the spring of the following year. We need a narrative of what has gone down in history as the 'Glorious Revolution'.

When the prince of Orange had received the secret invitation to intervene in England in June 1688, he was already making preliminary plans to assemble an expeditionary force with which to cross the Channel. Exactly what he was hoping to achieve remains elusive to historians. He had certainly come to the view that James could no longer be left to govern the Stuart realms unsupervised. The king's policies were building such a head of opposition that England might lapse into anarchy, and anarchic lands could be no help in the grand struggle with Louis. But did the prince want more? Did he, at this stage, wish to overthrow his uncle and become king of his family's realms? Unfortunately,

DOI: 10.4324/9781003267621-5

we simply don't know. He certainly showed no hesitation in advancing to the throne once James's regime collapsed – as we shall see, it soon did – so it is highly possible this had always been his aim, and there are other glimpses of an early monarchical ambition. His secretary, Constantijn Huygens, was sent seals by Bentinck bearing the coat of arms of England just before the prince set sail, which is certainly suggestive; and Huygens recorded speculation in the prince's circle about what would happen if he became the English ruler.[2] However, there is no direct evidence of William's resolution to take his uncle's position before the winter of 1688–9. His private correspondence is silent on the issue; and during the expedition memos were circulating among his entourage weighing the merits of a number of different outcomes.[3] And in many ways this was understandable. Quite a range of scenarios would have achieved William's underlying aim of recruiting his uncle's kingdoms for the crusade against France. The prince's objectives would, of course, be most cleanly realised if he managed to seize the Crown. Yet he might also get what he wanted by forcing his appointment as James's regent, or his wife's appointment as a regent; or if a Parliament called under the protection of Dutch soldiers passed measures to curtail James's power and redirect foreign policy. Given all this, it is possible that William made no final decisions about whether to try to become monarch until the best option became obvious. That would have to wait the outcome of his enterprise, and a better sense of how the situation in England played out.

There was far more clarity about William's position in the Netherlands. Whatever his motives in launching an invasion, he had very few resources of his own. If he were to gather the many tens of ships, and the tens of thousands of soldiers, which he would need to give himself a chance of success, he would have to rely on the logistical and financial support of the Dutch state. Fortunately, William's mature political approach to politics in the Netherlands, and external circumstances, delivered this. The prince's more conciliatory dealings with Amsterdam since 1684 had won him increasing sympathy from that often hostile, but absolutely key, city; and then, from 1685, a spectacular campaign of self-sabotage by an arrogant Louis delivered Dutch opinion into William's hands. The French king's first mistake was to persecute the Netherlanders' coreligionists. The revocation of the Edict of Nantes, which ended toleration of Calvinists in France, upset not only William, but outraged Dutch society very widely. Many French Protestants fled to the provinces with heartbreaking tales of cruelty that elicited deep indignation and a full programme of public relief. This unforced error was then compounded by economic hostility. In 1687, Louis barred the import of Dutch herring, unless preserved with French salt; and he reverted to a tariff list of 1667, a move which doubled the taxes on exports of fine cloth from the Netherlands, and damaged multiple other industries as well. The Dutch saw this as initiating a vicious trade war, not to say an act of bad faith because lower customs had been part of the peace treaty of 1678. And to compound all, Louis resumed what looked like territorial expansion on Dutch borders. Making fictitious claims to the German Palatinate and threatening to impose a pro-French candidate as the next archbishop of Cologne, the French king sought to increase his influence on the middle Rhine (in fact he began a full-scale invasion of the area in the early autumn of 1688). The events of 1672 had demonstrated how much trouble Cologne could cause the Netherlands if it fell into the wrong hands, and how important holding the area upstream on the great river was.

Louis's interventions therefore looked like a pressing threat – and one which William exploited fully in the battle for Dutch public opinion. Explaining quite why France's king behaved so unwisely is a job for historians of that country (from outside it looks a lesson in the dangers of narrow advice and believing in one's own invincibility, which could profitably be learned by many regimes). What is certain is that Louis cemented Dutch backing for William's expedition. The international situation had given the prince material for a polemical blitz, which included a published speech to the states-general a few days before he headed towards embarkation, and a flood of pamphlets produced by allies in the press.[4] This convinced most Dutch politicians and people that intervention in England was necessary. Both in assembly debate, and public discussions, any counter-case was virtually silent.

The logistical support provided by the federal government, and other sources, was impressive, and it demonstrated the fruits of William's courting of the Netherlands' elites and populace over the preceding years. The exact size of the force that was assembled in the summer of 1688 has been debated by historians, but it is likely the prince gathered twenty-one thousand land troops (largely crack Dutch regiments, but also English, Scottish, and French Protestant volunteers). These were supplied and equipped with a thoroughness and professionalism that was unusual in seventeenth-century warfare: the entire cost (met by grants and loans from the states-general and some leading citizens) came to seven million guilders. The soldiers were accompanied by a substantial store of artillery, and perhaps five thousand horses, and they were conveyed by a fleet of around five hundred ships and boats. This was four times as many vessels as joined the famous Spanish Armada of 1588, and it was the largest amphibious operation in western history to this point.[5] Contemporary prints of the expedition suggest a sea groaning with ships, with masts behind masts stretching back to the horizon: the fleet was certainly so large that it was easily visible from the English shore when it sailed up the Channel.[6] William's own contribution to this effort was his usual hard work in military preparation, and his determination to see a task through. When his ships first set sail in late October, they were driven back by a storm and lost many horses, yet Huygens noted that whilst the prince was downcast by this setback, he kept courage and announced he would try again as soon as the winds were favourable.[7]

William therefore showed the sort of dashing courage that had been central to successful rule in Europe for centuries, but, as we have seen, he was also a new kind of leader. As at earlier points in his career, the prince made use of ideological, as well as directly coercive, tools. The expedition was accompanied by a print propaganda campaign which was as carefully planned as the ones in 1672 (which had brought the prince of Orange to power in the United Provinces); 1673 (which had broken English enthusiasm for the war against the Dutch); and 1687 (which had turned opinion in England towards the idea of intervention from the Netherlands). At the heart of the effort was a manifesto for the expedition. William's *Declaration of reasons ... for appearing in arms in the kingdom of England* had been drafted by Gaspar Fagel, and it had then been translated it into English, and edited down to a racier style, by Gilbert Burnet. Burnet was an exiled Scottish clergyman who had become close to William and Mary after arriving in the Hague in 1685, and who would be appointed both the prince's chaplain during the invasion and then bishop of Salisbury, in reward for his efforts. In his version, the *Declaration of reasons* became a rhetorical masterpiece. Choosing the ground for intervention with passion, but also huge tact, it avoided alienating any of the groups that would need to be onside if William were to avoid serious resistance.

First, while complaining about the advance of Catholicism in James's England, the manifesto did this solely on the grounds that the king's policies were illegal in English law. It did not suggest there was anything evil about the Roman faith per se, so it dodged offending William's vital Catholic allies on the continent: Spain and Austria. Second, while charging that the court was responsible for the recent discontents in England, the *Declaration of reasons* blamed evil counsellors round the king, not James himself, and it stated that William's expedition was aimed at them, not their sovereign. This reassured English people nervous about the removal of monarchs after the experiences of the 1640s and 1650s: the prince, it seemed, was not demanding the king's abdication or a trial for his crimes. Third, William made it clear he was acting as prince of Orange, and as a concerned member of the Stuart family: the Netherlands were not mentioned at all. This avoided sparking anti-Dutch xenophobia in England at the prospect of a foreign invasion (a risk since the wars between the two nations of the mid-seventeenth century), and it underlines how important the separate sovereignty of Orange was in William's self-presentation. Fourth, while appearing to endorse the Whigs' long-standing warnings about granting full royal power to James, the manifesto also made an appeal to Tories. Not directly attacking the king was a sop to them (William did not embarrass the party by parading the catastrophic results of their choices in the exclusion crisis); and almost all the evidence in the publication for the malice of false counsellors involved the harm being done to the Church of England. Such an ecclesiastical pitch resonated with Tories; as well as supporting hereditary legitimacy in the last years of Charles II's reign, this group had become zealous defenders of the church. The *Declaration of reasons* also made Tory-friendly arguments as it raised the possibility that James's son was a fraud. Fanning the preposterous warming pan myth was outrageous, and it involved a U-turn on William's part, since he had very recently welcomed the arrival of a new Stuart. Yet Fagel and Burnet clearly thought these were prices worth paying. Questioning the legitimacy of the baby prince might turn Tory attachment to hereditary monarchy away from James's heir, since Tory principles only bound folk to support the *genuine* offspring of rulers. Finally, the manifesto stated that 'our Expedition is intended for no other Design, but to have a free and lawful Parliament assembled as soon as possible' and that William would support everything such a body would resolve for 'the Peace and Happiness of the Nation'. This might please everyone. Delaying consideration of what exactly should be done about England's problems until a freely elected and uncoerced Parliament could meet, left everyone with all to play for. No one need oppose William because they feared his triumph would end their preferred solution to the future of James; to the succession to the throne; to the position of the church, Catholics, and dissenters; or whatever else they fretted about.[8]

The manifesto was logistically as well as rhetorically brilliant. It was not only cleverly worded; it was efficiently distributed. At the most official level, it was sent, translated into various languages, to other European capitals to explain why the Dutch were invading England. This was largely why it had been so careful to avoid denouncing the beliefs or practices of Catholics. More demonically, sixty thousand copies were printed secretly – in English – by specially commissioned presses in The Hague, Rotterdam, and Amsterdam. Once they were ready, Hans Willem Bentinck again demonstrated his value to the prince by organising the smuggling of these works into England and Scotland: piles of the manifesto were concealed at locations across the Stuart realms for release once the expedition had landed. Copies were also sent, free of charge, to English printers so that they could join the campaign for mass production; and remarkably, a printing press was included in the military equipment of the Dutch invasion force. Once landed, this press was set up at Exeter, the first major urban centre captured, and it churned out yet further editions – along with other Williamite polemic. In fact, the tract was such a success that several historians have suggested it set the ideological meaning of the prince's actions in the public mind. It won him considerable support, if it was not, as we shall see, entirely to his later convenience.[9]

With the publicity and military machines in place, William had only to wait favourable weather. When this came, on 11 November (Holland's dating), it proved so advantageous that it became known as a providentially 'Protestant wind'. A stiff easterly breeze allowed the Dutch fleet to sail out of its ports and along the Channel, but it bottled up James's navy in the mouth of the Thames, unable to engage its enemy. A few days later William's armada had reached Torbay, in Devon. This was chosen for the landing after another fortunate meteorological development: the wind swung to a south-westerly, aiding navigation into those sheltered waters. On board, there seems to have been a debate about when exactly to put ashore, alongside the general relief at the expedition's luck. The prince was keen to set foot in England on 4 November (English dating), because it was his birthday (according to the calendar used in the Stuart realms), and he had felt – always with an eye to public opinion – that this might suggest that fate and heaven approved his enterprise. Yet he was persuaded to wait until the next morning. His chaplain Burnet, with an even keener sense of how things played with the English, suggested that arriving on 5 November would have even greater resonance. The fifth, of course, was the anniversary of the frustration of Guy Fawkes' Gunpowder Plot of 1605, a day which had taken off as a popular thanksgiving over the intervening decades, and had become of symbol of the nation's preservation from popery.[10] If the prince lost the tussle on dates with Burnet, he perhaps gained gentle revenge as he paddled on to Brixham beach. In earlier theological discussions, he and his chaplain had disagreed over how tightly God controlled the universe. William, as a staunch Calvinist, had insisted that the deity left no real role for human decisions in the course of events or the fate of souls, whilst the cleric had thought there was more space for people's will and action in such matters. Meeting Burnet during the disembarkation, the prince jokingly asked what the chaplain thought now. Did the expedition's astonishing success not prove a Protestant God had left nothing to chance? This story shows William with more of a sense of humour than most of his contemporaries reported; but it also underlines his conviction that his career had a grand purpose.[11]

Conviction would certainly be needed over the next couple of weeks. The fortune that had followed the fleet along the Channel was not fully shared by the army that advanced from Devon towards London. The weather was terrible, the roads in the west country were worse, and the force got bogged down, literally and metaphorically, in a slow march eastwards. More worryingly, there was a lack of practical support from the English. The conspirators who had invited William had promised rallies of armed men from the local population to join the Dutch, and mass defections from James's army. Yet in truth the reenforcement was disappointing. Some people, such as the west country Tory Sir Edward Seymour, did join the camp, and a trickle of officers came over from the king's soldiers. This, however, was not the decisive flood the prince had hoped for. Meanwhile, James managed to mobilise a large number of his troops to march towards Salisbury Plain. There, it seemed, a pitched battle would have to be fought, and one that looked worryingly evenly matched. The only bright spots for William in his early land campaign were short detours to admire gardens and picture collections in stately houses he passed; news of risings against James in the north, and in garrison towns such as Plymouth and Portsmouth; and considerable popular adulation. Ordinary people cheered the prince all the way from Brixham to Wiltshire; and he was happy to put on a spectacle for them. He rode into Exeter in an elaborately staged and exotic procession that included 'two hundred blacks brought from the plantations of the Netherlands in America' who were all dressed in white as a guard of honour.[12] Such comforts, however, could not compensate for the fear of a coming showdown. By mid-November the expedition had gone reasonably well, but it had not yet triumphed, and much uncertainly and violence seemed to lie ahead.

But then luck, or fate, or (William would insist) providence, intervened again – and quite spectacularly. James joined his troops outside Salisbury, but once he arrived in his camp, he appears to have suffered some kind of psychological breakdown. He was afflicted by a nosebleed that lasted two whole days, and on 23 November (English dating) he ordered his army to retreat back to London. Quite what caused this spectacular loss of nerve can be never fully known. James had had a military career and had served in the thick of naval battles in the 1660s and 1670s, so he was not pusillanimous by nature. Perhaps he had been unnerved by the desertions from his officer corps to William's camp. Perhaps his morale had been destroyed by signs of his unpopularity among his subjects over the summer of 1688. Perhaps the prospect of close members of his family working against him had destroyed his faith in the future. Whatever the reason, the king's collapse transformed William's prospects, especially as, on getting back to Westminster, James bundled his wife and infant son out of the country for their safety and would soon implement plans to try join them in exile in France. The prince's path to the English throne was now clear. If taking the Crown had been only one possible objective of the expedition when it set out, it now looked like the optimal way to command the resources of the Stuart realms in the great struggle with France, and so kingship became William's clear objective from this moment on. The prince's earlier reluctance to do or say anything overtly against James's position as king rapidly gave way to a barely disguised willingness to remove him. When James's first attempt to leave the kingdom was foiled, and he was brought back to London, there was considerable consternation in William's camp.[13] The prince demanded that his uncle be removed from Whitehall, and then sent him to Rochester, from where he was encouraged to escape by boat to Paris.

At this point it is worth pausing the onward rush of events to consider William's position, and the calculations he would have to make to gain what he wanted. The prince was now the only effective power in England. He might therefore have simply marched on London and seized the Crown: that was, after all, the way quite a number of kings in history, from William I to Henry VII, had come to rule the country. Yet everything in the prince's Dutch past screamed that this would be a mistake. William had seen that authority rooted in public approval was far more impressive than power exercised without it, and he doubted the English would take well to a foreign conquest. The prince had come to lead the Netherlands on a wave of popular approbation; but he had seen himself weakened each time his ambitions had gone beyond what general opinion would bear. He had failed to become duke of Gelderland, and he had to curtail his crusades against France, when the people turned against him. It was true that England was a monarchy, not a republic as the provinces were, so the balance between its individual leader and the people would be different. A king need not, perhaps, be so constrained by others' opinions as a stadhouder. Yet William knew the Stuart realm well enough to understand that kings could be blocked if they ignored or alienated their subjects – indeed he had exploited this in his own interventions in English life, with his propaganda campaigns of 1673 and 1687. He therefore realised he had to be cautious, and that any coercive usurpation would be unpopular.

This was especially true because his own manifesto for the expedition had disavowed any intent to replace James. William's *Declaration of reasons* had been a masterpiece in the art of building support in the circumstances of the autumn of 1688; but now, as winter approached, it was becoming an obstacle. The prince had to be careful not to go against his own promises in what would look like a hypocritical or opportunistic manner. In this situation, he drew on his political experience to engineer his advance without too obviously promoting himself. As he had done in 1672, he held back whilst waiting for circumstances, and the representatives of the nation, to elevate him to the highest office. Here was a new kind of leader indeed.

Key to William's strategy over the cold months of 1688–9 was to at least appear to defer to Parliament. He had called for a freely elected and uncoerced meeting of that body in his manifesto: now he worked to present all political developments as the result of the deliberations of the nation's representatives. Of course, it was impossible to summon an actual Parliament in the winter of 1688–9, at least not quickly enough to resolve the crisis caused by the James's flight. Before a legislature could meet, writs would have to be sent out to convene it by someone whom everyone recognised as king (and there was no such person yet), and the somewhat lengthy process of electing members of the House of Commons would have to unfold. Yet William overcame these difficulties by working with groups and bodies that were as close to a Parliament as could be organised in the chaos, and which he could claim had granted him valid authority to act. The first of these was a provisional government that had established itself in London when the king first left the capital on 11 December (this, and all subsequent dates in this chapter, according to the English system), which consisted of all the members of the House of Lords who could get themselves to the Guildhall in the City. The Lords were only half a Parliament, but that had to be good enough in what the group itself described as a 'great and dangerous conjuncture'.[14] Wanting forces of order to enforce its decisions, this provisional government vowed to work with William to secure the objectives of his *Declaration of reasons* – which centred on the gathering of a free legislature – and this would involve him coming to the capital. The prince was therefore invited to London, and was able to occupy the royal palace at St James's on 19 December, without this appearing to be a conquest.[15]

William's parliamentary way of proceeding continued once he arrived at the seat of government. Rather than do anything on his own authority, he consulted with groups closely associated with the two traditional chambers of Westminster. On 20 December he called a meeting of the House of Lords, which debated the constitutional future of England for the next three days. This meeting was divided because James was still in the country after his failed first flight, and this stoked some reluctance to remove him from the throne. William therefore tried to chivvy the Lords along by calling another parliament-style gathering, this time an irregular and informal session which encompassed everyone who had served in the House of Commons during Charles II's reign (members of James II's 1685 Commons were deemed too compromised to have a role), alongside the elected members of London's City government. This, and the king's finally successful departure to France, broke the logjam. Over Christmas, both meetings addressed the prince, calling on him to summon a 'convention', which would be constituted exactly as if it were a Parliament, and which would decide the constitutional future of the kingdom. Both also granted William executive authority until that body met. Elections for the lower house of the convention – conducted as if to a regular Commons – took a month; the convention convened in the palace of Westminster, the traditional seat of the two chambers, on 22 January 1689.

So, William had hidden his ambition. He had worked with representatives of the English nation to stage the free Parliament he claimed had been his only objective. Yet as in 1672, the underlying strength of the prince's position carried him forward without him having to make open demands for promotion and allowed him to claim his advance rested on public consent. When the convention met, it was technically free to choose between a number of possible settlements. However, any solution that did not meet William's hopes to gain the Crown were impractical. In the late winter of 1688–9, decisions had to be made quickly to meet a number of pressing challenges. Disorder was one. The danger of this had been demonstrated during the 'Irish night' panics of December, when, for a few days, rumours of Irish Catholic troops wandering the countryside and slaughtering inhabitants had convulsed London and other places in counter-rioting. Ireland itself was another potential threat. Its majority Catholic population had rallied round James's viceroy in Dublin, the earl of Tyrconnel, who had declared continued loyalty to the exiled king, and offered him a base from which he might reconquer England. Louis was a third problem. Welcoming James to his country, he had thrown his weight behind his fellow monarch's restoration. This became a central plank of French foreign policy: if it, or the aims of the Irish, were achieved, this would bring doom to English politicians who had cooperated with William. In this situation, the prince was the only protector of those in the convention. His Dutch troops were occupying the south-east of England, but he would not have to use them in any direct bullying to get what he wanted. He could simply threaten to withdraw his army and leave the ungrateful English to their fates. Everyone knew this, and in the end, it forced them to do as William wanted. As with the taking of power in the *rampjaar*, the prince could stand at arm's length from the ugly business of seizing control.

On a more positive note, perhaps, William gained additional strength from the sort of courting of public opinion he had practiced in the Netherlands. His constant deference to parliament-like bodies was part of this; but a wider propaganda campaign, which had opened with the prince's *Declaration of reasons*, was sustained through the winter. There were further pamphlets arguing the merits of his case. Some were run off the printing press he had brought with him; some were produced by sympathetic commentators and publishers in England; and several were written by Gilbert Burnet, who effectively acted as head of communications, as well as chaplain, for the expedition.[16] This allowed

William some flexibility of polemic to respond to events. For example, when James promised to remove many of the grievances cited in the original Orange manifesto as the Dutch invasion neared, William issued an additional declaration denouncing the king's initiative as a series of fake and opportunistic concessions.[17] Yet print was not the whole story. A major effort was put into ensuring discipline in the Dutch army – 'that no disorders should be committed' – and guaranteeing that it paid for all local supplies.[18] This avoided alienating inhabitants of places the troops marched through, and any unfavourable stories about its conduct. William also used public presentation and ceremony: not only in his entries to towns along his invasion route, but once he got to London. Over the winter of 1688–9, the prince regularly reviewed his troops; dined in public; and attended the Chapel Royal. According to the diarist John Evelyn, these appearances were appreciated, and resulted in a great press of people wishing to see their hero.[19] Preaching also played a part (useful when one's publicity chief was a cleric). Burnet gave a sermon from the pulpit of Exeter cathedral a few days after the prince's landing and published an address he had given from the chapel of St James during William's first days in the palace. Both interpreted the Dutch advance as a providential salvation of the true, Protestant, religion.[20] And then on 31 January 1689, a national thanksgiving was held. This summoned the whole population into its churches to hear more sermons, and used a specially composed form of prayers which praised God for making William the 'glorious instrument' of delivering the nation from popery and arbitrary power (this was probably the first time the word 'glorious' was used in connection to the events of William's arrival). Public celebration of William's presence in the country suggested the publicity campaign had worked, as did considerable advances for the Whigs (who were more willing than the Tories to bend the succession toward the prince) in the elections to the convention. Thus, William may have had a security hold over the men who would formally decide his future; but they would also have felt the pressure of popular mood.

Notwithstanding William's huge advantages when the convention met, it would stage surprisingly open discussions about England's constitutional future. Some of those present at Westminster, particularly among the Tory majority in the Lords, were wary of removing a king for the second time in forty years, and worried about the implication that monarchy in England was becoming elective. They therefore resisted the simplest way forward: they refused simply to declare that James had lost the Crown, and that William could now take it. In the early days of the convention the Lords rejected the resolution of the Whig-leaning Commons that James's misgovernment had broken an original contract with his people, that he had therefore forfeited power, and that the throne was now vacant. The Lords' challenge, however, eventually crumpled in the face of Commons insistence on their position, and rumours from St James's that William was becoming impatient, and might indeed retire back to the Netherlands if a settlement favourable to him did not emerge. A similar fate awaited proposals to make William a regent for his uncle. This would avoid fully removing the old monarch, but it was now absolutely unacceptable to the prince; and most people acknowledged that it would cause confusion. Regencies were good solutions if monarchs were absolutely incapable of exercising power (because infants, mad, or medically incapacitated) – but that was not the situation early in 1689. James had fled, but he still claimed to be king, and had set up a court in France. If he were to issue rational-sounding orders that countermanded what William as regent was doing, the fact that everyone still recognised him as the monarch would confuse which instructions people were supposed to obey.

Another solution that was floated was to make Mary queen on her own. This failed, but only by three votes in the Lords (partly, because the prince again made his views known, saying that 'he was so made, that he could not think of holding anything by apron-strings').[21] Yet the closeness of the decision demonstrated that many looked to Mary, rather than William, as a more hereditarily secure future for the English monarchy. She was at least James's daughter, and if one assumed the king's recently born son had been a fraud, she remained his legitimate heir. These were powerful claims, which were to be acknowledged in the final settlement – so to understand the failure of the campaign to make Mary queen, we must do more than simply state that William rejected it. We have to follow a slight tangent and update our coverage of the relationship between the prince and princess of Orange.

At first the marriage, as we noted, had not gone well. Mary had dutifully travelled to the Netherlands with her new husband in 1678 – but he largely ignored her; and then two miscarriages meant there were no children to bind the couple. The stadhouder and his wife also quarrelled over religion. William was disappointed that Mary did not join the Dutch Reformed Church, but instead worshipped with Anglican chaplains according to the rites of the Church of England. However, despite this inauspicious start, the union slowly began to work. Mary proved useful in the public presentation of William's rule. She was popular with the Dutch – compensating, as she later would in England, for her husband's dour and private demeanour with a far more outward-facing approach to the public and political nation. Her memoires claimed 'my inclination leads me to a retired, private life', but if this was so, she convincingly pretended otherwise.[22] In response, William came to respect his wife's help in dealing with his countrymen; and she came to respect his dedication to public service, and his opposition to persecuting Catholicism as he battled Louis XIV. And then at some point after 1685, Gilbert Burnet sorted out a misunderstanding between the couple (or so he claimed). William hoped that Mary would enable him to control England if she inherited the throne, but exactly what authority he would have was not clear. If Mary became queen by inheritance, he would not be king, and she could rule as well as reign, in the style of Elizabeth I. Such a prospect would not only undermine William politically, but for a man who spent so much effort asserting his manhood, it would be almost literally emasculating. He would be playing second fiddle to a woman and would not be leading his own household as complete males should. We can perhaps see William's insecurities in this sphere in his 'apronstrings' comment when rejecting the idea that Mary should be sole monarch at the time of the convention. Yet Burnet said he had been able to resolve most of the concerns. Discovering Mary had not realised her husband would not automatically have power if she acceded, he persuaded her to promise formally she would invest William with full monarchical authority if she came to the throne.[23]

Whether or not the Burnet story is true (and this character was so fond of magnifying his significance in historical events, that there must be some doubts about its accuracy in all details), the notion of a reconciliation between William and Mary by the time of the 1688 expedition chimes with all the other evidence we have. Mary was distraught at the danger William faced in braving the invasion of England, and even though this expedition was aimed at her father, the princess of Orange's loyalty was unequivocally with her husband. She expressed anguish in her diary about the divisions in the family, but she acknowledged that God and religion had determined the choice between her duties as daughter and wife. She also seems to have come to share her sister's adamant conviction that the warming pan story was true.[24] In her eyes, James had tried to trick her out of her rights to the throne. This perhaps explains her complete cooperation with William's plans in 1688–9, which – apart from entertaining his ally the elector of Brandenburg while he was on campaign – largely involved staying in the Netherlands through the winter. Obviously, it would not have been sensible for her to join the military expedition in November, but Mary did not go to London even in late December or January, by which time William was in pretty secure control of England. She stayed away because her husband ordered her to, and to avoid becoming a rival focus of loyalty or lobbying among the English as they decided their constitutional future. She thus did all she could to deflate arguments for her sole elevation to the throne. In fact, she did not embark for her old country until a political settlement had been reached, when her husband had secured the position he desired, and when she might become useful, rather than a problem, in building support for the new regime.

With alternatives fading away, the convention agreed, by mid-February, that James was no longer king, and that William should replace him. As a sop to those championing Mary, she was made a regnant queen alongside her husband in a novel form of 'joint monarchy', but to avoid any future confusion, William was vested with sole executive authority. In a sense, the deliberations that arrived at this arrangement had been a charade. The prince's desires, and his power to secure them, had been too strong for any substantially different result. Yet in fact William's choice to proceed through the convention had been highly useful to his cause, since it established his rule on a solid basis of public approval. Working through the body assembled at Westminster, the prince had stayed true to his manifesto's word. Although he had gained a promotion to the throne that his *Declaration of reasons* had not mentioned, he had – more or less – organised that free Parliament which his pamphlet had demanded to resolve the crisis facing the nation. The convention also created an impression of elevation by consent. The politicians gathered at Westminster may, in reality, have had little room for manoeuvre, but the formal process for deciding the future of the monarchy had been an open debate of options, and a final choice of William, by the representatives of the people. All this was a firmer foundation for a new regime than any coup or conquest would have been – and this was particularly important given that the new king wished to lead his new realm into war with France. Conflict would be bloody and expensive; its leader would have to be thought of as legitimate as possible. William may have demonstrated explicitly that he understood all this. According to Gilbert Burnet, the prince had puzzled people with his silence as the convention deliberated, but he had explained to a delegation from the House of Lords that he would not infringe their 'full freedom of deliberating and voting in matters of such importance'.[25]

One further area where William strengthened his position by following his manifesto was over the 'Declaration of Rights'. When the convention met, some members moved that this was a moment, not only to decide who would be monarch, but to define and limit the monarchy's prerogatives to avoid the sort of abuses James had perpetrated. This gelled with the Whigs' ideals (they had long been suspicious of court power), and the Tories were attracted to the idea of enclosing William within constitutional fences, if they were going to have to accept him as king in violation of their hereditary preferences. The suggestion was therefore taken up, and a Commons committee began work drafting a list of powers which monarchs could no longer exercise (or according to its wording, that rulers had never been permitted in England). Items included raising taxation without parliamentary consent; refusing to consult the legislature for long periods or interfering with its elections; suspending the operation of statute; inflicting cruel or unusual punishments; and so on. William was not entirely happy about this. Now he was in a dominant position, he hoped to secure the full traditional power of English kingship, and some of what was proposed seemed to cut deeply into that. Pressure from St James's got a few clauses dropped (monarchs were not to be forced to call annual elections, or to lose their powers to sack troublesome judges) but the logic the prince had followed over the deliberations on the future of the Crown bound William here too. Any pressure to block the Commons' initiative had to be modest. James's stretching of the royal prerogative had been deeply unpopular, so William needed to respond to that mood to retain support. Similarly, the prince knew that many of the suggested restrictions on royal authority were modelled on the list of wrongs he had put at the heart of his own manifesto: in fact, those who suggested the limitations explicitly stated they were trying to implement William's *Declaration of reasons*.[26] Just as with his campaign to gain the Crown therefore the prince had to be careful not to undermine his own words with overly obvious attempts to control what the convention was doing. As a result, a Declaration of Rights accompanied the offer of the Crown to William and Mary. This was read out to the couple in a ceremony at the Guildhall on 13 February which established the new regime, and it included much of the list the Commons committee had discussed. In his reply, William did not explicitly promise to obey the terms of the convention's statement, but he did say he would 'endeavour to support' the 'Religion, Laws, and Liberties' it was trying to preserve, and that he would concur with the Lords and Commons 'in any thing that shall be for the Good of the Kingdom'.[27] Despite continued private grumbling, he did not block the Declaration of Rights becoming a full and binding statute later in 1689.

All this was a remarkable story. William had gambled for huge stakes when deciding to intervene in the Stuart realms, but he had emerged triumphant. The term 'Glorious' applied to the revolution that had unfolded referred certainly to English relief at the removal of a popish king, and the ending of a perceived threat to ancient liberties, but it captured the sense of astonishment that things had gone so well and so bloodlessly (in England, anyway, as we shall see, things would be different in Scotland and Ireland). Contemporary commentators talked of events that seemed 'miraculous', 'unexpected and unlook'd for', 'strange', and 'unexampl'd in the records of time'.[28] Yet if the revolution had seemed unprecedented, it had strong echoes of William's earlier seizure of power. As during the *rampjaar*, the prince had become unassailable by courting public opinion, but had made few overt demands himself. In both cases, he had benefitted from the military collapse of the old regime, but had waited to be appointed to, rather than seizing, power. Once again, he had emerged from a crisis in a strong position to lead a nation in a struggle with France, enjoying not only formal authority, but a good deal of popular backing. From his success in 1672, he had learned a new style of leadership: one that might be built around his own advantages, but which also sought support among a width and depth of political participants, and which rooted its legitimacy in consent.

This new style was embodied in the coronation with which this chapter started, but it would shape William's whole reign in England – and to some extent in other Stuart kingdoms as well. William may have been a conqueror, using force to get what he wanted, but he also realised he needed partnership. Certainly, with his wife, who commanded the support of many Stuart loyalists: why he accepted the novelty of a joint monarchy. But also partnership with the political classes in his new realms. This was why he had staged his accession as a parliamentary process, and why he was willing to declare in his coronation oath that it was his chief duty to uphold laws 'in parliament agreed on'.

Notes

1 The act requiring the new oath is available at https://www.legislation.gov.uk/aep/WillandMar/1/6/data.pdf
2 Rudolf Dekker ed, *The diary of Constantijn Huygens Jr: secretary of stadholder-king William of Orange* (Amsterdam, 2015), pp.49, 52.
3 See, for example, the note by Gilbert Burnet reproduced in R.W. Blencoe ed, *Diary of the times of Charles II by the honourable Henry Sidney* (2 vols, London, 1843) II, 288–91.

4 *Redenen van afscheyt van sinj Hooghe Mogende hebben bewogen on Syne Hoogheydt, in person near Englelands overgaende* (The Hague, 1688): translated summaries of the key material appear in David Onnekink, *Reinterpreting the Dutch Forty Years War, 1672–1713* (London, 2016), ch.4.
5 Jonathan Israel, 'The Dutch role in the Glorious Revolution', in Jonathan Israel ed, *The Anglo-Dutch moment: essays on the Glorious Revolution and its world impact* (Cambridge, 1991), pp.105–63.
6 Edmund Bohun, *The history of the desertion* (London, 1689), p.35 – reported sightings of the fleet from the Kent coast, half-filling the strait of Dover. For pictorial material see, for example, Romagne de Hooghe, *The landing of William III and his army at Torbay* (Amsterdam, 1689).
7 Dekker, *Diary of Constantijn Huygens*, p.50.
8 William III, *The declaration of his highness William Henry, prince of Orange of the reasons inducing him to appear in arms in the kingdom of England* (The Hague, 1688).
9 For the centrality of the declaration, see Lois G. Schwoerer, 'Propaganda in the revolution of 1688–9', *American Historical Review*, 82 (1977), 843–74; and Jonathan Israel, 'General introduction', in Israel, *Anglo-Dutch moment*, esp. pp.13–18.
10 Gilbert Burnet, *Bishop Burnet's history of his own time: volume one* (London, 1724), pp.787–8.
11 Burnet, *Bishop Burnet's history ... vol one*, p.789.
12 *A true and exact relation of the prince of Orange, his public entrance into Exeter* ([Exeter], 1688).
13 Burnet, *Bishop Burnet's history ... vol one*, p.799.
14 'The declaration of the lords spiritual and temporal in and about the cities of London and Westminster, assembled at the Guildhall, on the 11th of December, 1688', printed in Robert Beddard, *A kingdom without a king: the journal of the provisional government in the revolution of 1688* (Oxford, 1988), p.71.
15 See 'The proceedings of the Lords Spiritual and Temporal from their first meeting at the Guildhall, London, from the 11th December to the 28th following, 1688', reproduced in Robert Beddard, *Kingdom without a king*, pp.66–169.
16 See, for example, [Gilbert Burnet], *An enquiry into the present state of affairs* (London, 1689); [Gilbert Burnet], *An enquiry into the measures of submission* (London, 1689); Gilbert Burnet, *A sermon preached at the Chappel of St James before the prince of Orange, 23 December, 1688* (London, 1689).
17 *His Highnesses additional declaration* (The Hague, 1688).
18 John Whittel, *An exact diary of the late expedition* (London, 1689), p.46.
19 Julie Farguson, *Visualising protestant monarchy: ceremony, art, and politics after the Glorious Revolution*, (Woodbridge, 2021), pp.60–1.
20 The Exeter sermon only survives in summary – Whittel, *Exact dairy*, p.48; 'The expedition of the prince of Orange for England', in *A complete collection of papers, in twelve parts: relating to the great revolution* (London, 1689), part 3, pp.1–8 at p.6; Burnet, *A sermon preached at the chappel of St James*.
21 Burnet, *Bishop Burnet's history ... vol one*, p.820.
22 R. Doebner ed, *Memoires of Mary, queen of England, 1689–1693* (London, 1886), p.11.
23 Tony Claydon and W.A. Speck, *William and Mary* (Oxford, 2007), p.115.
24 Doebner, *Memoires of Mary*, p.3; and more widely, Claydon and Speck, *William and Mary*, pp.117–21.
25 Burnet, *Bishop Burnet's history ... vol one*, p.820.
26 See the contributions to Commons debates on 29 January by Lord Falkland, Sir William Williams, and Hugh Boscawen reported in Anchitel Grey, *Debates of the House of Commons* (10 vols, London, 1769), IX, 29–31.

27 *The declaration of the lord spiritual and temporal and commons assembled at Westminster, concerning the misgovernment of King James, and filling up the throne* (London, 1688 [1689 modern dating]).
28 *The speech of Sir George Treby* (London, 1688), p.2; Simon Patrick, *A sermon preached at St Paul's Convent Garden on the day of thanksgiving* (London, 1689), p.7; E.S. De Beer ed, *The diary of John Evelyn* (6 vols, Oxford, 1955), VI, 600; [White Kennett], *A dialogue between two friends occasioned by the late revolution of affairs* (London,1689), p.1.

5 A triumph in Ireland, 1690
The establishment of William's regime in the Stuart realms, and the start of the war with France

They finally clashed. William had not had to fight James during his invasion of England in the late autumn of 1688, because the old king had retreated from Salisbury. Yet less than two years later, the two commanders would lead armies to battle with each other. The encounter occurred on 1 July 1690 (British and Irish dating), just inland from the town of Drogheda, in County Louth, in eastern Ireland; and on the banks of the river that gave its name to the battle: the Boyne. Troop numbers on the two sides were similar. Each king had forces of just over twenty thousand men, though William's were perhaps more experienced and better trained. His soldiers included substantial numbers of professional Dutch, Danish, and French Protestant troops who had seen action in earlier continental wars, whilst James's ranks were mostly filled with local Irishmen. William's objective in the fight was to get to the south bank of the river, and the heat of the action centred on a ford at the hamlet of Oldbridge. Fighting for this was intense. William lost key commanders in the tussle, but he was eventually able to prevail, partly because he had opened the day's action by sending a feint attack which appeared to threaten a different crossing point upriver. James had fallen for this diversion, directing a large proportion of his forces to a place where local geography meant they could not engage the enemy. Once William had forded the Boyne, his path on to Dublin was open. The battle was his first clear and significant victory in open warfare (as opposed to town sieges); it has lived in Irish memory, as triumph or disaster, ever since (the terrain is now excellently and impartially presented in a fine visitor centre); and it meant the prince of Orange was secure on the thrones of all three Stuart realms.

Of course, the first part of an explanation of the victory on the Boyne must be why William had had to fight at all, at a place supposedly within his own dominions. The short answer is that his accession was not universally welcomed. The change of regime in England may have been subsequently celebrated as a 'bloodless revolution', but the process in Ireland, and Scotland, had been anything but peaceful – and even among the English, William's elevation to the throne had faced opposition. England's transfer of power had been the smoothest among the three kingdoms, but significant groups had nevertheless refused to abandon allegiance to the old king. Some politicians – for example, the earls of Rochester and Clarendon – declined to swear loyalty to the new monarchs; and this resistance was shared by around three hundred members of the clergy, including prominent figures such as William Sancroft, the archbishop of Canterbury. In addition, large numbers of the officers in James's old army resigned rather than serve the incoming regime. Some of these men led mutinies in the early months of 1689, and those who did not headed to France to help James try to regain his thrones from a troublesome underground of holdouts in London. It is true that many of those who protested against William and Mary's elevation had also been horrified by the exiled monarch's rule. Often, too, they were motivated by individual scruple rather than hatred of the new Dutch regime. Having sworn to obey one king, some found it hard to revoke solemn promises before God. As a result, only a minority of those concerned about the revolution actively plotted its reversal – but even so, the Jacobites (as supporters of the displaced monarch were known) worried the authorities in England, and opposition to William was far more serious in the other Stuart realms.[1]

In Scotland, Jacobitism had deep roots. Although the kingdom probably had no more Catholics than England as a proportion of its overall population, there were whole communities in the Highlands who followed the old faith; prominent members of the nobility adhered to Rome; and all these people had obviously been sympathetic to James's religious policies. Some Scots also had an attachment to the legitimate line of the Stuart family, viewing this as the continuation of the ancient succession of the kings in the north (the Stuarts had come to rule England only in 1603, after generations as monarchs of the northern kingdom). Again, religious disputes made many nervous about a Williamite future. As the prince of Orange had marched towards London, crowds of radical Protestants in Scotland had attacked churches and ministers of the episcopalian ecclesiastical establishment, particularly in the south-west around Glasgow, and there had been calls for a return to the Presbyterian settlement that had obtained in the 1640s and 1650s. This terrified those who supported the church as it had been restored under Charles II, and who associated the radicals with political subversion. Consequently, although historians have challenged the traditional picture of a country quiescent in the face of James's rule, the old king had had promising sources of support north of the border; and it had taken all of William's tact and political experience to become king.[2]

In 1689, Scotland was still constitutionally separate from England. It had therefore had to take its own decision about what to do when James fled from Whitehall – though as the revolution had unfolded among the English, the Scots had borrowed some of its patterns. By early January, many leading Scottish politicians had made their way to London, gravitating to William, whose influence was visibly magnifying by this point. On 7 January, the prince asked those who had come south for their advice on what should be done in Scotland: after three days deliberation, they offered him executive control of the kingdom, and asked him to convene a constitutional convention – as in England, constituted as if it were a Parliament – to decide a future settlement. This convention met in Edinburgh on 14 March; but initially there had been a balance of opinion on whether James had lost the throne. Those who thought he had were matched by a vigorous Jacobite block. At this stage, however, William's standard strategy of at least pretending to defer to the representatives of nations, reaped rewards.

The prince had already sold his expedition to Britain with a Scottish manifesto, which – like his *Declaration of reasons* to which it appeared as an appendix – had called for a free Parliament to salve the nation's ills. On 16 March, the newly convened convention opened and read two letters, and the reaction to these again underlined the importance of the Dutchman's habitual deference to national opinion. The first epistle, from William, was diplomatic. It defended the Protestant faith but left future decisions about Scottish government and church to the country's legislature. The other, from James, demanded continuing loyalty, and threatened all who had forsaken their 'natural allegiance' to him with dire punishment.[3] James's message was such an inappropriate and bombastic performance that his supporters in the convention were demoralised, and numbers left. This allowed a vote that the old king had 'forfaulted' the Scots Crown, and Scotland followed England in offering the throne to William and Mary on 11 April. Over the next months, William showed further tact accepting a 'claim of right' as part of his accession to the throne (this document limited the powers of monarchy rather more than the English 'Declaration of Rights' had); and by allowing a wholesale remodelling of the church, or kirk. Although the new king himself had hoped for 'comprehension' (a compromise ecclesiastical settlement, which would have allowed diverse strands of Scottish protestant opinion to participate in the kirk), he gradually surrendered his preferred solution as demands for the wholesale abolition of episcopacy and of ritual in worship proved too strong. He consented to the loss of bishops in July 1689, to the establishment of a thoroughgoing system of Presbyterian ecclesiastical government in 1690, and to a gradual exclusion of those ministers who had supported the structures of the old church over this period.[4]

William thus gained control in Scotland, but the new regime had been applauded by only part of the nation; and it was not fully settled. One of those who had left the convention, John Graham of Claverhouse, the viscount Dundee, raised troops loyal to James in the Highlands. By 27 July, Dundee was ready to sweep down towards Edinburgh to challenge the new Williamite government, and won a battle at Killiecrankie, allowing his forces to follow the river Tummel as it threaded its way out of the mountains. Fortunately for William, Dundee himself was killed in the encounter, and his troops were turned back less than a month later at Dunkeld – but this did not end the unrest. Pockets of resistance and minor skirmishes continued in the north of the country through to the early 1690s; Jacobite plotting became a regular pastime among discontented sections of the Scottish nation; and – after the initial brilliance of his letter to the convention – William was to prove a rather less capable ruler of Scotland than he was elsewhere. He never went to his northern kingdom; the factions that dominated Scottish politics seemed to bewilder him; he put trust in inappropriate deputies; and, early in his reign, he made proposals for a union between the two British realms, without preparing the ground anywhere near sufficiently – in the English Parliament, anyway.[5] As a result, by the end of 1689, there was vigorous opposition to his policies in Scotland. An awkward squad in Parliament, nicknamed the 'Club', protested at everything the king's ministers tried, and this group flirted with both Jacobitism and Jacobites as it used legislation to chip away at royal power. William's ability to work with politicians was remarkable – but it worked best when he was among the people he was dealing with. He neglected Scotland, so it became hard to manage.[6]

William thus had his troubles in both his British kingdoms, but these paled compared to events in Ireland, where Jacobitism was the strongest. James's rule had been popular among the majority Irish population because they shared his religion, and because he had begun to remove the legal disadvantages under which they, as Catholics, had previously suffered in a land that had been dominated by an English-backed Protestant government. The old king had also appointed a capable viceroy in Dublin: Richard Talbot, the earl of Tyrconnel. Tyrconnel was a Catholic, and when James's power collapsed in Britain, he rallied the Irish administration and people in support of the now exiled monarch. Constitutionally, Ireland was a subordinate kingdom of England. William's elevation in London should thus have made him ruler of Ireland automatically, but Tyrconnel had ensured that, in fact, the new king's writ ran almost nowhere. The English administration was recognised only in a few places in Ulster, where a Protestant population (largely settled from Scotland earlier in the seventeenth century) was strong enough to hold out against the Dublin regime. One such place was (London)Derry, whose resistance to Jacobite forces in a siege from April to August 1689 has gone down in Ulster Loyalist mythology. Yet this later commemoration was of a stubborn survival against the odds. The city was almost alone in its struggle, underlining the scale of Jacobite control. The movement in favour of the old king received a further boost when James himself arrived in Ireland on 12 March. The old king had recovered some political poise after his meltdown the previous autumn, and he accepted Louis XIV's military help in an attempt to use Ireland as a springboard for a reconquest of Britain. It was not clear how serious the French ruler was in this enterprise, since his supporting army was quite small, but Louis knew having James back in one of his realms would, at the very least, be a distraction to William.[7]

William's response was characteristic; if not initially very successful. He wanted to go to Ireland himself in 1689, to land among the Protestants of the north, and to lead a conquest of the last of his Stuart realms. But his ministers in England would not hear of it. They worried about the personal danger to their new ruler and demanded that he stay in London to settle English affairs.

The king acquiesced, recognising a clash of considerations here. He itched for the sort of courageous campaign that had often marked his career. It would have fulfilled his providential role; gelled with the brand on which his propaganda had traded; and perhaps met his need to perform his masculinity. Yet by now, William was also clear his power must lie in consent as well as charisma, and he had perfected the art of bowing to others when necessary. Therefore, instead of personal command William stayed in London and sent Frederick Herman de Schomberg, an experienced general in his service, to lead a force which landed at Belfast Lough on 13 August. This made some early progress because of earlier separate actions by Protestant forces. William's navy had helped to break the siege of Derry, and local troops had relieved those who had been defending Enniskillen against the Jacobites. These victories had encouraged a general retreat by James's armies from Ulster. Soon, however, a battalion of troubles prevented any further advance. In orders from London, William urged aggression, and he would probably, himself, have taken risks to take the fight to the enemy. It was his style. Schomberg, however, knew his master's past military gambles had not always paid off, and as he explained in a series of somewhat self-justifying letters back to England, a forward policy was impossible. Many of the soldiers had fallen sick. The army suffered incompetent, and probably corrupt, provisioning, so it was short of shoes, carts, beer, coats, and decent horses. A landscape of bogs was hard to move through (Schomberg exclaimed that 'a country such as this was never seen'); and many officers lacked training or motivation. Those of the artillery were unequivocally damned as 'ignorant, lazy and timorous'.[8]

By the start of 1690 therefore William was facing considerable challenges in all his new realms. Yet, at the same time, he had been building the foundations on which his victory at the Boyne would rest. The triumph in Ireland was not just the result of one day's tactical brilliance. It was possible because of a solid base of political support in Europe, and particularly in England, which had allowed him to mobilise his army. As with William's popularity during the revolution, that support was partly raised through skills rooted in the prince's Dutch experience. From 1689, however, he had another set of resources. He exploited the traditions, the charisma, and the authority, of the English monarchy – to which he was now heir. Thus, both Orange-Nassau and Stuart inheritances led to the Boyne. The mix between the two traditions was not always comfortable, but it was ultimately successful. William found an effective blend of conventional and imaginatively innovative uses of English royal authority.

As we saw, the most obvious way in which William unlocked his new opportunities was through his wife. James's elder daughter had been kept out of the country during the revolution itself for fear of becoming a distraction. As an alternative focus for English loyalties, Mary might have complicated the prince of Orange's path to the throne. Yet once that danger had passed with William's accession; and once the power of Mary's hereditary claims to the English throne had been harnessed to the new regime in the joint monarchy; the new queen took an iconic role in the regime's propaganda. Her prominent presence reminded audiences that this was a traditional Stuart and English government, for all that it was also a revolutionary and Dutch one. So, Mary sat alongside her husband at the ceremony in the Guildhall, in which they were offered the Crown in February 1689. She was also a full participant in the coronation on 11 April. Ceremonially this was largely conservative (for all the changes in the oath sworn by William, and the need to adapt proceedings to crown two full monarchs at once), so it stressed that members of the ruling Stuart family were being elevated to the throne according to the ancient forms of English monarchy. Traditional royal iconography was also adapted to depict shared rule, so that the queen might lend hereditary legitimacy to the king. Medals coined to celebrate the coronation showed the royal couple in mirrored profile; engraved double portraits were commissioned and seem to have found a popular audience; and state oil paintings were produced in 'pendant' form – these were separate images of the two monarchs, but they were complementary in format and were designed to be hung together.[9]

William therefore borrowed legitimacy from Mary, but he exploited the charisma of Stuart monarchy in his own right. His first deployment of this was controversial, but it demonstrated a will to assume the full authority of an English king. Once William and Mary had been elevated, the convention that had appointed them declared itself to be a Parliament. This would attract some adverse comment (it was not the capacity in which the body had been instituted), but it avoided the delay of new elections at a time of desperate uncertainty. On 18 February, the new king went to address the convention, partly to encourage this conversion to a legislature – and he did so in full regalia. He wore his crown, the robes of state, and all the accoutrements of his new headship of the Order of the Garter. This, too, was criticised because William had not yet had his coronation, and some objected that such royal garb should not be donned before this had happened. The new king, though, clearly thought an early ceremonial assertion of his authority as a Stuart monarch was worth the sniping.[10] His choice of clothes and accessories connected him symbolically to the traditional powers of kingship, and it is important to remember how extensive this power was. The revolution's Declaration of Rights may have chipped away at corners of royal prerogatives, but the core was very much intact. A king was still head of state, and chief executive; he appointed all ministers and office holders; he set national policy in almost all areas of government action outside taxation; he was supreme governor of the Church of England; he was commander in chief of the armed forces; and he managed foreign relations – including decisions over war and peace.

William also took up an English monarch's traditional role as protector of Protestantism. This was something his predecessors had stressed, partly because it had augmented their constitutional claims to authority – which had sometimes been rather dodgy – with a divinely awarded commission to advance true faith. Monarchs in a potentially weak position, such as Edward VI (because a boy), Elizabeth (because a woman), James I (because a foreigner), and

Charles II (returning from exile), had posed as God's champion on earth, albeit in rather different ways. William followed their example. In fact, his Protestant self-presentation had begun during his invasion. For all that his manifesto had avoided a language of crusade to placate Catholic allies, other part of his imagery, less visible from Austria or Spain, presented him as a champion of the reformation. His army marched under banners proclaiming its cause to be 'God and the protestant religion'; prayers for the success of the venture spoke of the protection of the true, reformed, faith; and sermons preached on campaign seem to have interpreted the expedition as a defeat for a popish Antichrist.[11] These themes continued once William was king. In the sole ceremonial innovation of the coronation, a bible played a new role. It was carried in the procession along with the crown, orb, and sceptre; it was used in the swearing of the oath; and it was ritually presented to the monarchs after they had been crowned as the 'rule of their whole life and government'.[12] Since Elizabeth I's embrace of a Bible in her accession celebrations in 1558, the holy book had been a symbol of the Protestant cause in royal iconography, so bringing it to greater ritual prominence at William's coronation underlined the claims he was making about his God-appointed role.

Print propaganda also emphasised the point. In sermons and pamphlets which Williamite presses churned out energetically from the very first weeks of the reign, the new king was presented as providential saviour of true religion. He had broken the power of Rome, and would now institute a renewal of piety and morality among his people. Some of this rhetoric verged on the apocalyptic. There were predictions that the new king would initiate the last days, by finally defeating the forces of evil in the cosmos. In the coronation sermon, the ever-reliable Gilbert Burnet had suggested the world had, with William's accession, reached a point where 'we may expect to see the city of God, the new Jerusalem, quickly come down from earth to heaven'.[13] And towards the end of 1689, Burnet's suggestion, a few months earlier, that the prince of Orange should land at Torbay on 5 November, rather than the day before, paid dividends. The coincidence of date with Gunpowder Day meant the annual celebration of the failure of Guy Fawkes' anti-Protestant and anti-monarchical plot could now be adapted into a combined thanksgiving for deliverances in 1605 and 1688. In preaching, prayers, and popular pyrotechnics, William's arrival was lauded as a reassertion of God's protection of a Protestant people, once again under the leadership of a good Protestant Stuart.[14]

Thus, William picked up on powerful conventions of English monarchy. Yet he wanted support for his struggle with Louis as well as recognition of his position as an English king. And here, Stuart traditions were far less helpful. The sort of prolonged warfare which looked likely in 1689 would require close collaboration with Parliament and considerable public support, and William's Stuart forebears had been only very patchily successful in securing this sort of consent. The very claims to royal authority which the new king was trying to exploit had led too many of his predecessors into conflict with subjects. The English had had a strong sense of their rights, and had wanted their representatives in the legislature to be consulted in the formation of government policy, so strong assertions of the prerogative had been unpopular. Even those monarchs who had not lost their thrones to rebellion, as Charles I and James II had done, had frequently fought with Parliament, and the whole seventeenth century had been marked by constitutional tensions in England. William was determined to avoid this morass. Turning to draw on Orange-Nassau, rather than Stuart, strategies, the king resolved on far greater compromise, negotiation, and cooperation than had been seen among rulers since Elizabeth. This went beyond the tactical decision not to go to Ireland in 1689. It became a systematic approach to government.

It was not that William enjoyed surrendering authority. His offices within the United Provinces had had frustrating limitations in power, and he clearly coveted the greater prerogatives English monarchy bestowed. When it was politically safe to defend kingly power, he did so. We have seen him water down the proposals that led to the Declaration of Rights when he was in a dominant position in February 1689. And even when upholding royal authority was less possible, William would moan about restrictions on his power. Over the first year of his reign, the king was trying to persuade Parliament to resource his military plans against France. He could not therefore afford to alienate its members by throwing his weight around; and, as we are about to see, he bowed to pressure on his regular revenue, religious policy, and constitutional powers. Yet during this period, the king told George Savile, the marquis of Halifax, who had become a confidant, how he felt about his position: he was not happy. William saw himself as abused by politicians and he suspected republican sentiment was on the rise in England. Parliament, he complained, used him like a dog; and there was, he was sure, a design for a new commonwealth like the one that had ruled after the execution of Charles I. He also said he felt like 'a king in a play'. It seemed to him that he was acting out a role without it being real; and he felt he was being forced to read out lines penned by others.[15]

This resentment was of a piece with a general irritation at the expectations that others placed upon William now he was king of England, and a low opinion of the leaders of English public life. Halifax noted his monarch calling numerous politicians either 'mad' or 'blockheads'; and Huygens reported mutterings in court circles that the monarch was hurting himself by his reluctance to give individual audiences.[16] The king's first summer in the round of English social events did not go well. William visibly did not like large gatherings for entertainment, and as visibly, he did not like the particular people who pressed in on him. Instead of seeking out company in London, the new king surrounded himself with a very narrow circle of those he trusted. At the centre of this group was Bentinck, the boyhood companion who had accompanied the prince of Orange over to London. Bentinck was now ennobled with a high English title, the duke of Portland; and was he appointed Groom of the Stole – the official post at court which brought its holder intimate contact with the monarch, and which Portland fashioned into a close and confidential personal assistantship.[17] The Groom's apartments traditionally interlinked with the king's. This facilitated rapid and private contact with a small band of advisors, of the sort that William had favoured all his adult life, but it cut the great figures of England off from their monarch: Huygens was recording some of the first mutterings of public disquiet at this.

Yet, despite all this haughty separation, William was determined to apply the lessons of Dutch politics. He sought a partnership with Parliament, avoiding rows with them to secure the higher aim of war supplies, even when they seemed to him to be behaving unreasonably, and however much distaste he had for most of the Lords and MPs as individuals. For example, at the start of the reign, Parliament refused to grant William lifetime revenues from customs and excise. As these had been awarded to both Charles II and James II, the king could easily have viewed this as an insult, and privately he did so. Yet in public he remained calm, patiently urging a financial settlement in successive speeches to his legislature. Similarly, the king moved to forestall any hostile investigations into his spending by allowing the Commons sight of his accounts. In an early speech to Parliament, he had offered MPs his financial records, 'that you may be satisfied how the money has been laid out'.[18] Again, William avoided conflict over the Declaration of Rights. The legal position of this document had been questionable, since it had originally been compiled by an irregular convention and had not received formal royal assent. Consequently, Parliament worked to transform it into a binding statute over its sessions in 1689, and at this point the king wondered if he could try to block it and so preserve more of the Crown's traditional prerogatives. However, as he admitted to Halifax, this would only stir counterproductive tension with the legislature, so 'the condition of his affairs overruled his inclinations' and he made no move.[19]

Perhaps the masterstroke of collaboration was the declaration of war with France. This had been William's aim in intervening in English politics; and once he had royal power, he could have moved on his own authority to mobilise the nation. As king, he was commander in chief of the armed forces, and had full control over England's foreign policy. Yet, knowing such technical powers was pointless without the financial backing for the military that only Parliament could give, William did not immediately deploy his prerogative to fight Louis. Instead, in an extraordinary invitation to the legislature to advise him on international relations, the king persuaded, or perhaps trapped, his MPs into urging him to war. In his speech to the convention on 18 February 1689, William laid out the situation in Europe and in Ireland. He stated that allies such as the Netherlands would be in great 'hazard' if not offered English help quickly, and that the Irish crisis had become extremely dangerous. But then, instead of using these aggressions as his justification of a declaration of hostilities, the monarch asked his parliamentarians what to do. He told legislators he 'must leave it to you to ... judge what forms ... may be most proper to bring those things to pass, for the good of the nation' which he was 'confident are in all your minds', and which he, for his part, would always be ready to promote.[20] At one level this was an appeal that the convention resolve its status quickly, and convert itself into a Parliament which could approve funds for a war, but it also appeared to admit legislators into the formation of foreign policy, and reversed the usual pattern at the start of wars. Decisions to enter into conflict were standardly made at court, and then communicated to Parliament once royal policy was set.

Given the facts about the situation in Europe of which the king had reminded them, MPs (and it was the Commons who would have to propose financial expedients to pay for the war) had little choice how to respond. They went into committee to consider the state of the continent and noted a litany of threatening actions by Louis since 1672.[21] On the back of this, they addressed William, telling him that that would support him fully 'when your Majesty shall think fit to enter war against the French king'.[22] Parliament may have had only one thing it could say in circumstances where France had invaded England's Irish territories and where, as the Commons itself had noted, Louis posed a pressing danger to the English nation's interests across the globe; but – as with his elevation to the throne – William had produced at least the illusion of free deliberation. On later occasions, every time he asked the Commons for the tax revenues that he needed to fight the French, he reminded MPs that he had entered into the conflict 'with your advice'.[23]

Another essential dimension of working with Parliament, and another area where Dutch experience was helpful, was dealing with the Whig and Tory parties that split the legislature. William had had to deal with partisan factions in the Netherlands; but now he faced a deep polarisation in English politics. The Whigs and Tories – the opposed alignments which had been born in the exclusion crisis – had survived as the fundamental, if not rigidly organised, groupings in England: though the causes of division had shifted over a decade. Of course, the original argument about whether James was fit to be king had been settled by the catastrophic experience of his reign, and by the revolution. Yet Whigs and Tories remained at odds over religion – a dispute we will come to shortly – and over exactly what had been resolved by the events of 1688–9. Whigs maintained that James's deposition demonstrated that people had the right to remove tyrants. Tories disagreed. Those who did not become Jacobites accepted William as ruler, but they denied he had got there as a result of legitimate popular rebellion. He was king by conquest; or because James's flight meant the old monarch had abdicated and a vacant throne had thus required filling; or because God had installed William by providence; or because people had to obey a de facto ruler who had come to power by any means, for the sake of order. Tories thus desperately grasped at any argument that would accept the revolution, but that would, at the same time, avoid endorsing subjects' right to revolt. In this way, the parties remained divided ideologically. Whigs accused Tories of not fully endorsing what had happened in the 1688–9 revolution, because they did not accept the legality of resistance to James. Tories thought the Whigs dangerous anarchists and democrats, whose willingness to rebel against authority would undermine all monarchical government.

Perhaps more fundamentally, Whigs and Tories hated each other because of the history of the 1680s. They had, after all, spent the entire decade trying to extirpate one another. At the end of the exclusion crisis, from 1681, Charles II had allied with the Tories to remove the Whigs from all positions of national and local power, and had executed a number of leading Whigs for treason. This Tory-royal pact had lasted until some months into James II's reign, after which the Whigs got their revenge. The Catholic monarch, who became resentful that the Tories would not support his advance of his religion, turned to the Whigs. From that point, tables were turned. An anti-Tory witch hunt, led by the court, but with some Whig cheerleading, chased people from their posts and prosecuted them for actions in the earlier Tory reaction. Sections of a Whig party that had been born in opposition to James proved surprisingly willing to cooperate with that king, so long as he did down their rivals. As a result of this recent history, the two sides loathed each other with a deep visceral passion. Both had had experience of the other party trying to end their political careers, and in some cases, to inflict far worse sanctions.

William thus faced an English nation riven by party rivalry. His approach to dealing with this was, as with so much else, compromise. He wanted to be, as he told Halifax, a 'trimmer' between the two groups, balancing their power in government, and being captured by neither side.[24] The Whigs had hoped the new king would rule in their interests (those who had not come to collaborate with the court after 1685 had been prominent in the plot to bring the prince of Orange to England, and had thought they had an agreement with him to advance their interests), but the incoming monarch disappointed their hopes for dominance. William kept lines of communication open with the Tories; he appealed for an end to partisan bickering; and he ensured that both parties had a role in his first administration. Appointing ministers at the start of his reign, the king balanced a Whig Secretary of State, Charles Talbot, the earl of Shrewsbury, with a Tory one, Daniel Finch, the earl of Nottingham; and the other great offices of state were distributed across the political spectrum. In fact, William moved fairly steadily towards the Tories through 1689. Irritated by the Whigs' shrill demands for a monopoly of power, and by their disruptive attempts at legal action against their enemies, the king increasingly sought counsel from Nottingham, his leading Tory minister.[25] By early 1690, the king was coming round to the earl's view that there should be a general election to try to reverse the Whig majority in the Parliament that had first come together as the revolutionary convention. This elicited Whig fury. A letter, incandescent to the degree that it becomes hilarious, was sent by the arch-Whig Thomas Wharton to the king. This accused William of having admitted traitors to his ministry by including Tories, and went as far as the preposterous suggestion that Wharton's enemies might poison the ruler now he had given them close personal access. The letter was dated 25 December (English dating). This makes one wonder if Christmas alcohol may have played some role in the ranting, especially as Wharton had already been prosecuted for drunken behaviour, earlier in his career; but whatever the excuses for the tone of the message, its style of Whig bullying was counterproductive.[26] William knew the Whigs had nowhere else to go, politically, but to support him; and he was increasingly disgusted by their hysteria. Consequently, and ignoring their howls, he concentrated on placating the Tories. Without this, the king feared the Tories might drift back to Jacobite loyalty, so he called the controversial election early in 1690 to weaken the Whigs. In the campaign for this, the monarch remained largely above the fray (he tried to avoid utterly alienating either side), and the result was no Tory landslide, but it did rebalance the parties in the Commons in a way which pleased William.

State politics however was only one part of the king's strategy to calm the heat of party hatreds. As was mentioned above, Whigs and Tories were divided on religion, as well as justifications of the revolution and personal rivalries, and the monarch's approach had to cope with this. While Tories were champions of the established Church of England and supported the principle that everyone should belong to it by law, Whigs lobbied for greater freedom for those Protestants who dissented from the details of its doctrine, ceremonies, or government by bishops. William was to soothe these tensions in 1689, but to understand how he did, we need to continue our analysis of his own faith. The picture of the king's personal beliefs that emerges will be more subtle than the simple desire to be a Protestant warrior that may have appeared so far.

When we looked at the prince's upbringing, we noted a commitment to the Calvinism, style of worship, and particular structures of the Dutch Reformed Church. We also saw that William presented himself as an international champion of Protestantism. Yet these traits were not the whole story. As his theological bantering with Burnet on Brixham beach suggested, and as his eventual acceptance of his wife's Anglicanism confirmed, he did not insist on imposing his beliefs on others – even in his most intimate circles. More evidence for this tolerance came throughout his career. He restrained his Calvinist allies in the Netherlands from penalising other strands of Protestantism in the provinces. He was willing to ally with Catholic powers in his struggle with Louis; and he accepted followers of the Roman Church in his armies and other places of trust. During James II's reign in England, he signalled that he approved of a basic toleration of Protestant dissent and of Catholicism in England, even as he condemned the king's attempts to promote such toleration without consulting Parliament. On becoming king of Scotland, William had to be reassured that a phrase in the coronation oath which bound him to root out heretics would not result in any actual persecution before he agreed to swear to it; and we will soon see him promoting a wide toleration in England. William was therefore happy to live with quite a range of religious views in the nations he led, and there are hints that this was a sign of a set of deeper theological convictions – though he never himself systematically spelled them out.

If we examine who the prince of Orange's closest religious allies were once he was in England, a pattern emerges. He promoted Burnet to the vacant bishopric of Salisbury soon after becoming king, but he also advanced the careers of a number of men with whom Burnet had worked closely on scholarly, spiritual, and political writings in the 1670s and 1680s. Collectively, this group – which included a new archbishop of Canterbury, John Tillotson – were known as 'latitudinarians'. Exactly what that means has been debated by scholars, but it is only one feature of the group's beliefs that is important here.[27] In numerous sermons, prefaces, and other works these clerics stressed that the central feature of true Christianity was charity. Christ had set an example of love and service to others, and it was more important for his adherents to follow him in this than to uphold any particular details of doctrine.[28] This position had a number of consequences. It directed concern from theology to behaviour, and crucially, it included an insistence that it was damningly sinful to persecute anyone for their faith. Using coercive force to change people's beliefs was cruel, and cruelty was the opposite of charity. In fact, the latitudinarians saw persecution as the infallible mark of the Antichrist. It was the identifying characteristic of that perversion of the church, led by Satan, that the Bible's book of Revelation had described as the eternal foe of the godly. Thus, for the latitudinarians, Roman Catholicism was at least a limb of the Antichrist, as Protestants had always charged – but, for them, popery was Antichristian because it persecuted dissidents, not because of its precise teachings or its practices of worship. The beliefs and rituals of the Roman communion might be in error, but they did not, themselves, pervert it out of Christianity. Only its merciless attacks on others had done that. The latitudinarians also warned that it was as easy for a Protestant church to become Antichristian through violent intolerance as it had been for their catholic rivals to fall into this reprobation.

It seems probable that William's patronage of the latitudinarians was an indication of his own ecclesiological position. Burnet noted that his master 'always thought that conscience was God's province, and it ought not to be imposed on'; and this impression is strengthened by the works which had earlier been dedicated to the prince by close allies in the Netherlands, and which had argued that peace and concord between the faithful were more important than supporting one side in religious disputes.[29] If such 'latitudinarian' tolerance was indeed at the heart of William's thinking on church matters, it can explain his religious policy across multiple theatres. Yes, he was driven by his sense of his role as a providential defender of Protestantism. Yet the threat he thought that movement faced was persecution, not the raw mistakes of Catholic theology.

Thus, in Europe, William believed his role was to save Protestants from cruel spiritual tyranny, of the sort that was unfolding in Louis XIV's France. But if any Catholics would help him in this task, he would not denounce them on points of doctrine or worship. In the Netherlands, he was personally attached to the Dutch Reformed Church; and he wished it to have a privileged role in national life. Yet he disapproved of its punishing others for divergences from its views because that would make it as evil as Louis.[30] Once he arrived in

Britain, William hoped for a broad Protestantism which would end any persecution both by tolerating an internal diversity and by allowing a basic freedom of Catholics to worship. This explains appeals from his circle for supporters not to harm adherents of the Roman faith in the Stuart realms, and it suggests why he was happy to belong to two rather different Protestant churches in England and Scotland (though the political strengths of different ecclesiastical positions in the two nations perhaps also meant he had little choice).[31] As we saw, in the northern kingdom the revolution was accompanied by the abolition of episcopacy, and a rigorous anti-ceremonialism in a reformed state church. England, meanwhile, retained her bishops and her moderately ritualised prayer-book worship. This meant that William was in the bizarre position of being the most prominent member of two churches which rejected each other's principles. He could, however, live with this (and indeed he continued his personal membership of the Dutch Reformed Church, so in truth he belonged to three different communions), if all his churches stood against a persecuting popery.

The new king's ecclesiology also drove royal appeals for tolerance of a variety of denominations in his Stuart realms. In Scotland his entreaties largely failed. William's absence, his lack of finesse in understanding Scots politics, and the dour bigotry of his opponents meant he could not secure the encompassing comprehension he had hoped for, and there was to be no quarter for those who preferred the prerevolution church. In England, however, he had more luck. Legislation against Catholicism remained on the statute book, but, under William, it was principally used to exclude its adherents from public office. As this involved no physical coercion or persecution of basic religious practice, such civil disabilities fit with William's latitudinarian principles.[32] William also made progress in settling the position of England's Protestant dissenters. As this had been a core cause of conflict between Whigs and Tories, this helped calm partisan conflict, and brings us back from the king's own faith to the knotty problem of party division.

In a way, William's resolution of English religious tensions was surprising because his first intervention in England's ecclesiastical politics would be inept in the extreme. On 16 March 1689, he made a speech to Parliament, which seemed to suggest that all Protestants should have their civil disabilities removed, particularly that they should be allowed to hold public office, even if they refused to conform to the Church of England.[33] This again fitted an antipersecutorial stance – but it enraged the Tories. In the aftermath of the revolution, some in that party had been willing to explore a limited toleration of dissenting worship; and some were even looking at a compromise on the rituals people had to accept to join the establishment, in hopes that this would allow many nonconformists to come back to that communion. Now, however, Tories were horrified that members of the state church might lose their distinguishing privileges. Tory members of Parliament met at Westminster, in what their opponents might think the appropriately named Devil's Tavern, and vowed to block any significant concessions. In the face of this, William, as had become habitual, backtracked. He dropped his demands that dissenters be allowed to take public offices; he channelled discussion of any change in church rituals into the church's own institutions, where clerics could control the process, and where it limped off to die; and, as we shall explore more in the next chapter, he surrendered ecclesiastical policy to his wife, who had proved a loyal member of the church, and was therefore more trusted by the Tories. However, the king still insisted on a basic liberty of Protestant worship outside the church. It was, to a large extent, a result of his pressure that a 'toleration' act passed Parliament in April 1689.[34] This was not quite the iconic charter of religious freedom that it came to be painted as in the later eighteenth century, but its clauses prevented Protestant dissenters being persecuted so long as they satisfied conditions on their worship outside the church. In this settlement, William's latitudinarianism, and his political pragmatism, had found what was perhaps the least alienating solution to tensions between Protestants in England. Both Whigs and Tories had been disappointed and riled in the legislative process, but the former had secured a good degree of religious liberty, and the latter had preserved unique advantages for members of the official church.

With neither party too badly estranged from the court on religious or secular grounds, and the king showing a willingness to work with Parliament, William avoided the rupture with political elites which had so often marked earlier decades in the Stuart realms, especially in times of war. Instead of carping about the king's motives for, or his competence in, the conflict, legislators got on with the business of starting to pay for the military – albeit launching some investigations into waste or corruption, as they did in the case of the commissary John Shales, who was partly responsible for the problems supplying Schomberg's army in Ireland. Even in the first year of the war, the sums granted were remarkable and this allowed a rapid expansion of England's armed forces. As early as May 1689, the Westminster Parliament was paying for ten thousand troops that had been sent to Flanders to defend the Netherlands. In September, Schonberg had been able to leave for Ulster with twelve regiments of men, and his expedition had been made possible by a navy that was undergoing urgent enhancement.[35]

Such resourcing meant William's English realm was ready for battle. The situation on the continent was also moving in the king's direction. To a considerable degree, this was because Louis XIV continued his counterproductive campaign to alienate almost everyone else in Europe. His invasion of the Rhineland in the autumn of 1688 had been brutal. The bombardment of Koblenz, together with the burning of much agricultural land as part of a deliberate scorched-earth policy, shocked a whole continent. For weeks, the *London Gazette* was full of reports from foreign correspondents detailing the devastation.[36] William used such material in his propaganda across all his countries: the disgust this engendered ensured that the urban elites of the Netherlands, among other key groups, remained committed to his aggressive approach to France. In Holland, this compensated for a major blow to the prince in Dutch politics. Just as Orange-Nassau forces were advancing on London after landing at Torbay,

Gaspar Fagel died in the Hague. As we saw, Fagel had managed William's relations with his leading province, Holland, and with the states-general; and had also run a network of spies and agents that stretched across the republic and beyond to all of Europe. He had therefore been vital to the prince of Orange's control in the Netherlands, and in other circumstances, Fagel's death could have been catastrophic. Yet with the Dutch elites united behind William's policies, the damage was contained. Although the city of Amsterdam used Fagel's death as an opportunity to make trouble, the old Grand Pensionary was replaced by another Orange-Nassau loyalist, Anthonie Heinsius. Heinsius was charming and skilful, and soon proved as capable in advancing the stadhouder's agenda as his predecessor. He became close to the prince as Fagel had been – he proved another of that very small handful of people who gained William's full trust.

Louis's Rhineland invasion also consolidated the international alliance William had been trying to build against the French ever since 1672. The prince of Orange had been a competent diplomat, but in the rapidly shifting geopolitical balance of Europe in the second half of the seventeenth century, where all states had had to constantly recalibrate their interests as France replaced the Habsburgs as the continent's leading power, basic competence in international relations was about as much as could be hoped for. William's earlier attempts to cement allies in place against Louis had often ended in disappointment. Other rulers had seemed to sign up for a crusade against the French, but had later drifted away from their commitments. From 1688, however, Louis's reckless miscalculation locked other states in with William. To start, the occupation of the Rhineland convinced most German leaders that France was a pressing threat to their sphere, and they began to collaborate more closely with the prince of Orange. Brandenburg, under its new elector, Frederick III, offered cover during the Dutch invasion of England. He lent his armies to defend the borders of the Netherlands whilst the expedition unfolded, and that meant the provinces felt could safely send their best troops across the Channel. Similarly, the Holy Roman Emperor, Leopold I of Austria, came to see the traditional role of his office, defending all Germany, in terms of protecting the Germans against France. Over the previous decade, he had had to repulse a Turkish incursion into the empire, but now progress against the Ottomans freed his hands, and French aggression made itself his priority. Leopold declared war on Louis on 3 April 1689 (continental dating); he concluded an offensive alliance with the Netherlands a month later (the core of what became known as the 'Grand Alliance'); and he formally united with England in a treaty of 9 September (continental dating – 30 August in London). Meanwhile Bavaria moved towards William's camp; and the bewildering number of other German princes and cities came to range from a wary neutrality – which was sometimes the result of French bribes – to active help for the anti-French cause.

Beyond the Holy Roman Empire, further international support arrived. Spain joined the Grand Alliance in June 1689. It did so because of its traditional Habsburg sympathies with Austria, but also out of fears for its territories in the Netherlands south of the Dutch republic, which looked likely to be the prime battleground as Europe mobilised itself against Louis. Meanwhile, Victor Emmanuel of Savoy considered his options, leaned towards the anti-French forces, and formally joined them in 1691. Similarly, Christian V of Denmark had been an ally of Louis, but he had found that the French king supported him little in his ongoing struggle with Sweden for predominance in the Baltic (he had been, perhaps, foolish to expect Louis to do much that was not in France's own direct interests); and in August 1689, Christian signed a treaty of military assistance with William's England. This explains what those Danish troops were doing helping the anti-Jacobite forces cross the Boyne. France's hostility to its rivals, and her neglect of her supposed friends, had thus constructed the committed pact to contain her that had eluded William since 1672.

Such an impressive continental alliance against the French allowed William to tackle Irish defiance. He could now do so, without worrying too much that he was diverting resources which would be needed for the protection of the Dutch, of the buffer zone in the Spanish Netherlands, or of his German allies. With money and broad political support from the Parliament in Westminster, and the states-general in The Hague, he was ready, by the early months of 1690, to stage the personal intervention he had yearned to make the year before. The road to the Boyne had had many tributaries – now they could coalesce into a concrete military campaign.

The start of the expedition was delayed somewhat by continued wrangling over the king's revenue in England. William was eventually granted the proceeds of excise for life, and customs for four years, pending a later review. There was also a need to make arrangements for government in London whilst William was away. For this, Mary was given the executive power she had been denied at the revolution settlement – but she was to be closely advised by a regency council of leading aristocrats and politicians. William had also hoped to make a trip to Scotland in the early months of 1690. This had to be abandoned, due to pressure of other business, but this too had prevented any early embarkation to deal with the Irish threat. It was therefore not until 4 June (British dating) that William was ready to set out on the second great amphibious operation of his career.

The journey to the Boyne was partly an exercise in military logistics. As importantly, however, it served as a royal progress through William's realms that allowed his subjects to see him, and for him to bond symbolically with them. For all the pragmatic calculation in the new king's rule, he was again going to draw on English traditions of royal display, and on the magnificent self-presentation of his Orange-Nassau forbears as princes of Orange. William was always more of a showman than his highly private personality, and his later image as a humourless Dutchman, would suggest. The first stage of the trip was to Chester, whence the ship to Ireland would sail. William took four days over this. He left London to cheers from large crowds, and then passed through the country houses of a series of political allies, both for lunches and overnight stays, on his way north. These visits enhanced the status of supporters within localities, and allowed contact with more regional elites, as guests joined their monarch for meals and receptions. As Julie Farguson has noted, those who met William in this way found him more charming and convivial than his withdrawal from London society suggested.[37] William also engaged in civic ceremony. He entered Chester with strong echoes of the sort of magnificent ritual which had been invented by the late medieval dukes of Burgundy for their 'joyous entries' into cities, and which had become de rigueur for royal leaders across Europe in the renaissance. Accompanied by noblemen, the king met Chester's mayor and aldermen outside the town, then went through the gates in a grand procession, accompanied by the applause of spectators. He then went to the cathedral, to be met inside by 'a fine showing of the nobility and gentry', and attended divine service including a sermon from the bishop, before leaving to stay one more night in a leading subject's house. This time it was the seat of William Clegg, Gayton Hall, which was conveniently located on the Dee for naval embarkation. Only after this rigmarole did the king board the royal yacht and sail across the Irish Sea.[38]

On arriving in Ireland, at Carrickfergus just north of Belfast, another dimension of the prince's charisma took over in the presentation of the expedition. William, as on all earlier occasions when taking command, was keen to be seen in the thick of the military effort, and to be urging a forward approach to the campaign. Over the winter and spring, the commander in Ireland, Schomberg, had refused to advance, fearing that a lack of supplies and of fighting-fit men would lead to disaster. William, however, swept aside this caution, ordering a march towards the enemy five days after arriving in the country. As Stephen Baxter pointed out, the comparison with Schomberg is rather unfair, since the king had sailed with the very resources his subordinate had been demanding for months; but there can be little doubt that William's boldness galvanised his forces, as did his sacrifices of his own comfort for them.[39] As always, he camped among his men. He spent his days on horseback. He worked long hours reviewing his troops, moving from unit to unit to meet officers well down the chain of command. He also took the initiative in reconnoitring the territory ahead, often in the company of his brother-in-law, prince George of Denmark. This cemented William's place in a wider royal family with international connections and it probably helped to attach the Danish troops in the army to the cause. All these activities made William highly visible to his soldiers; and they allowed him to display some considerable personal courage, since they took him right to, and often beyond, the front line. The fearlessness, or recklessness, of this approach would be underlined on the eve of the actual battle at the Boyne. Examining possible crossing points of the river, William became obvious to James's troops on the far side, and they fired their six pounders at him. The Jacobites scored a grazing hit on the king's right shoulder: he lost part of his coat and shirt, and about a spoonful of blood. However, William showed no great reaction to this injury beyond rising in his stirrups for a moment, and he continued his tour of inspection after the application of a plaster. This bravery continued the next day. In the thick of the fighting, the king crossed the Boyne almost immediately behind his guards. In a heroic action, these crack soldiers had waded the stream and secured the far bank in the face of a Jacobite defence so fierce that it had claimed the life of Schomberg. Once again, William's drive to show his masculinity through military vigour had inspired his forces and played a considerable role in their triumph.

Reviewing this account of William's victory in Ireland, it is hard not to be struck by the variety of character traits that had contributed to it, and to wonder how many other figures could have pulled it off. It had taken battlefield boldness. It had drawn on kingly authority, and on traditional presentations of this. It had required political and diplomatic skills that were perhaps best learned in an open and contested government such as that of the Netherlands. It had needed religious conviction, but not bigoted attachment to any narrow confessional strand. It had involved collaboration with his wife; and had resulted from talented alliance-building over diverse ranges of opinion, both within his own realms, and across Europe. Above all, it had exploited the king's hybrid heritages. In origin, William's success was both royal and republican; Stuart and Orange-Nassau; English and Dutch. This unique combination would continue to benefit the king through to his next great military triumph, at Namur in 1695. It was though, a difficult mix to sustain. The next two chapters will explore these contradictions playing out in the triumphs and disasters of William's wartime rule.

Notes

1 Jane Garrett, *The triumphs of providence: the assassination plot, 1696* (Cambridge, 1980), chs.1-4 give a good chronological coverage of Jacobite plots in the early 1690s. There is a large scholarship on Jacobitism beyond these direct threats – one of the best works is still Paul Monod, *Jacobitism and the English people* (Cambridge, 1988).
2 For a good summary of the revised view see Tim Harris, *Revolution: the great crisis of the British monarchy, 1685–1720* (London, 2006), chs.4, 9.
3 *Acts of the parliament of Scotland* (Edinburgh, 1822), vol 9, 9–10.
4 For coverage of the Scottish revolution see Ian B. Cowan, 'Church and state reformed? The revolution of 1688-9 in Scotland', in Jonathan Israel ed, *The Anglo-Dutch moment: essays on the Glorious Revolution and its world impact* (Cambridge, 1991), pp.163–84; Harris, *Revolution*, ch.9; Alastair Raffe, *Scotland in revolution, 1685–1690* (Edinburgh, 2018).
5 *His Majesties most gracious speech to both houses of parliament* [29 March 1690] (London, 1690), p.6.
6 P.W.J. Riley, *King William and the Scottish politicians* (Edinburgh, 1979), ch.2 gives the most detailed account of the consolidation of the Club, and William's wider problems with Scottish magnates.
7 John Miller, *James II: a study in kingship* (London, 1989), ch.15.
8 John Dalrymple, *Memoirs of Great Britain and Ireland from the last parliament of Charles II* (3 vols, London, 1790), appendix to part II, book IV, 167–81.

9 Julie Farguson, *Visualising protestant monarchy: ceremony, art, and politics after the Glorious Revolution,1689–1714* (Woodbridge, 2021), pp.70–96.
10 Farguson, *Visualising protestant monarchy*, pp.63–4.
11 John Whittel, *An exact diary of the late expedition* (London, 1689), pp.23–4; *A praier for the present expedition* ([The Hague], 1688); 'The expedition of the prince of Orange for England', in *A complete collection of papers, in twelve parts: relating to the great revolution* (London, 1689), part 3, pp.1–8 at p.3; Gilbert Burnet, *A sermon preached at the chappel of St James before the prince of Orange, 23 December, 1688* (London, 1689).
12 Farguson, *Visualising protestant monarchy*, pp.67–70; Lois G. Schwoerer, 'The coronation of William and Mary, 11 April 1689', in Lois G. Schwoerer ed., *The revolution of 1688/9 changing perspectives* (Cambridge, 1992), pp.107–30.
13 Gilbert Burnet, *A sermon preached at the coronation of William III and Mary II* (London, 1689), p.20.
14 For the adaptation, see David Cressy, *Bonfires and bells: national memory and the protestant calendar in Elizabethan and Stuart England* (London, 1989), p.31. With the preaching, Gilbert Burnet, as so often, led the way: Gilbert Burnet, *A sermon preached before the house of peers ... on 5 November, being the gunpowder treason day, as likewise the day of his majesties landing in England* (London, 1689).
15 H.C. Foxcroft ed, *The life and letters of Sir George Savile* (2 vols, London, 1898), II, 203–47.
16 Foxcroft, *Life and letters of Sir George Savile*, II, 222, 224; Rudolf Dekker ed, *The diary of Constantjin Huygens Jr: secretary to stadholder-king William of Orange* (Amsterdam, 2015), p.92.
17 David Onnekink, *The Anglo-Dutch favourite: the career of Hans Willem Bentinck, first earl of Portland (1649–1709)* (Aldershot, 2007), chs.3–4.
18 *His majesties most gracious speech to both houses of parliament on Saturday the 19th day of October, 1689* (London, 1689).
19 Foxcroft, *Life and letters of Sir George Savile*, II, 217.
20 William III, *His majesties most gracious speech to the Lords and commons, assembled at Westminster the eighteenth day of February 1688/9* (London, 1689).
21 *An address agreed upon the committee for the French war and read in the house of commons, April 19th, 1689* (London, 1689).
22 *The address of the honourable the house of commons presented to his majesty, Thursday the 25th day of April, 1689* (London, 1689).
23 William III, *His majesties most gracious speech to both houses of parliament on Saturday the 19th day of October, 1689* (London, 1689).
24 Foxcroft, *Life and letters of Sir George Savile*, II, 206–7.
25 Henry Horwitz, *Revolution politicks: the career of Daniel Finch, second earl of Nottingham, 1647–1730* (Cambridge, 1968), ch.6.
26 John Dalrymple, *Memoires of Great Britain and Ireland* (London, 1790), appendix to part II, book IV, 187–200.
27 For the debate see: Tony Claydon, 'Latitudinarianism and apocalyptic history in the worldview of Gilbert Burnet', *Historical Journal*, 51:3 (2008), 577–97.
28 For a key example of a latitudinarian arguing this way, see Simon Patrick, *A sermon preached in the chappel of St James before his highness the prince of Orange, 20 January 1688* (London, 1689).
29 Gilbert Burnet, *Bishop Burnet's history of his own time: volume two* (London, 1724), p.12. For examples of the earlier Dutch works, see Isbrandus van Os, *Vrede-vlagh, afwaeyende op Toren Zions* (Dordrecht, 1674) [The title translates as 'Peace flag flying from the tower of Zion']; *De weg tot vreede onder alle protestanten* (np. 1688) [title translates as 'The road to peace among all protestants'].

30 For William's ecclesiastical policy in the Netherlands, see Frits Broeyer, 'William III and the Reformed Church of the Netherlands', in Esther Mijers and David Onnekink eds, *Redefining William III: the impact of the king-stadholder in international context* (Aldershot, 2007), pp.109–24.
31 Burnet condemned attacks on Catholics in his first sermon on arriving in London in 1688: Burnet, *Sermon preached in the chappel of St James*, pp.27–30.
32 Jonathan Israel, 'William III and toleration', in Ole Peter Grell, Jonathan Israel, and Nicholas Tyakce eds, *From persecution to toleration: the Glorious Revolution and religion in England* (Oxford, 1991), pp.129–70.
33 William III, *His majesties most gracious speech to both houses of parliament, on Saturday, the 16th of March, 1689* (London, 1689).
34 Israel, 'William III and toleration', stresses the role of William in pressing for the 1689 'toleration' act.
35 John Childs, *The British army of William III, 1689–1702* (Manchester, 1987), p.34.
36 See in particular, *London Gazette*, nos. 2422–2437, 24 January to 21 March 1689.
37 Farguson, *Visualising protestant monarchy*, pp.106–11.
38 For details of the journey, see Farguson, *Visualising protestant monarchy*, pp.107–11.
39 Stephen Baxter, *William III* (London, 1966), p.264.

6 The end of a siege, 1695
Success in European war

Poets would soon laud it as William's greatest victory. Since the high summer of 1695, troops of the Grand Alliance had been attempting to capture the citadel of Namur. Namur was one of a string of fortresses in the Southern Netherlands, which Dutch strategists had identified as the 'Barrier'. This was a set of defences which, if held in friendly hands, could protect the provinces from French advance. In July, alliance troops had battered their way into the town, but the citadel behind was still controlled by Louis's troops, and his field army was beginning to disrupt supplies to the besieging forces. Running out of time, since disease had entered William's camp, the stadhouder-king ordered a final assault in the last week of August (continental dating). A vast artillery bombardment was followed by waves of ground assaults which cost thousands of lives on both sides. By the first days of September, the French had been forced back to their final defensible positions, and their commander concluded the situation was hopeless. Surrender came; from this point the French king became serious about seeking an end to a war he could not win.

In England, the triumph was celebrated not only in verse (poets had had few military successes to crow about since the days of Oliver Cromwell), but also in published accounts of the siege, and in a day of thanksgiving that ordered the population to their churches to express their gratitude to God for the military success. Preaching and panegyric praised William as the saviour of Europe from French tyranny, and as a stalwart protestant hero.[1] The rejoicing was perhaps greater because this victory came after years of indifferent military performance by the Grand Alliance in Flanders, the region that had become the main battlefield in the war. At the start of the conflict, Namur had been in the hands of William's Spanish allies. It had had to be recaptured in 1695 only because it had fallen to the French in 1692, and this had been only one of a series of reversals which had threatened military disaster in the early decade. The run of defeats had started with the battle of Fleurus in 1690s. All that could be said in William's defence of that debacle, which forced allied forces to retreat to Brussels and to abandon large parts of Flanders, was that he was not present. He was still campaigning in Ireland after the battle of the Boyne. In 1691, when the king first returned to the continent to lead his troops in

DOI: 10.4324/9781003267621-7

person, he had seen Mons capitulate to Louis. The French king had turned up himself to watch the fortress taken: this was perhaps the closest the two monarchs and rivals ever came to meeting. The French success at Mons had blown a hole in the Barrier, and the Grand Alliance had been fortunate to avoid a wholesale incursion by the enemy. In 1692, France's capture of Namur had been followed by the bloody stalemate at the battle of Steenkerk. This engagement had not been a catastrophe – it prevented further advance by Louis's troops – but the performance of the alliance's forces had been nothing to crow about, and the clash was read, unfairly, as a damaging defeat by many politicians in England.[2] The year 1693 had witnessed further losses with Huy and Charleroi falling to the enemy; and Liege and Brussels had only been saved because France's victory at Landen had come at a such a high cost that Louis's commanders paused their forward march to recover. Fighting in 1694 was delayed by abortive peace negotiations and then never amounted to much, consisting mostly of directionless manoeuvring between the two sides, though the alliance did recapture Huy in the closing weeks of operations. The 1695 taking of Namur thus represented a welcome reversal in the pattern of the war. It is only a little exaggeration to say it rescued William's military reputation.

As with the Boyne, the explanation for the victory was multifaceted, and demonstrated William's continuing mastery of a range of military, ideological, and political tools. Historians, especially in recent decades, have shied away from emphasising individual qualities in shaping history – perhaps being wary of lapsing into an older 'great men' model of change. Instead, they have stressed more structural factors in accounting for the course of events: political, social, economic, and cultural. Of course, this biography does not discount such underlying structures, but it wants to argue that William's unique combination of skills was important too, and that much of his success came from his ability to adapt to the wider environment in which he found himself. So, both levels of explanation for Namur are vital: we should perhaps start with one of the key personal factors – the monarch's inspirational leadership of his troops – while the list of early 1690s battles is fresh in our minds.

The stadhouder-king's individual courage and his commitment to campaigning played vital roles in ensuring his cause stayed alive through the difficult years up to 1695. As always, William spent most of the summer months with his men. He only returned to his hunting lodges in Gelderland, and his palaces in England, when colder weather began to preclude action.[3] As always, too, he put himself at the heart of action and so in considerable danger. At Landen, he had stayed with his army to defend one bank of a river, despite the appearance of a much larger French force. He was shot twice in the engagement, though the bullets ripped through his wig and his sash rather than doing more serious harm. During the initial assault on Namur, William led an attack on the outer defences, and endured ninety minutes of direct fire from the town which mowed down many of the men around him. Such leadership does much to explain why the alliance's armies did not dissolve in the face of a French advance that looked as if it would continue year after year. William's soldiers seem to have respected and loved him for his energy, his boldness, and his willingness to share peril with them. To put this in gendered terms, they admired a man who demonstrated all the most admirable qualities of full masculinity. As Stephen Baxter pointed out, the retreat at Landen was chaotic and in the dark, and there would have been a temptation for many members of William's army to desert. But the vast majority of the troops found their way back to their colours, determined to fight for the prince for the rest of the season – just as they would in the battles of the following years.[4]

So, personal courage was a crucial, and perhaps underappreciated, reason for William's ultimate triumph at Namur. Another area of individual success, to which we must give due weight, was his diplomacy on the European continent. Both within the Netherlands and within the Grand Alliance against Louis, the stadhouder-king found techniques to manage a challenging set of circumstances, and to deal with a gamut of other players, few of whose motivations aligned exactly with his own.

In an open and decentralised system of Dutch politics, the prince of Orange had never hoped to be absolutely dominant. Once he was king of England, his problems controlling his homeland grew, since he now had to spend so much of his time either on the battlefield or back in the Stuart realms securing the flow of resources for the war from Britain and Ireland. Some parties in the Netherlands tried to take advantage of his absence. In particular, the ever-troublesome city of Amsterdam came to pursue a quasi-autonomous foreign policy behind William's back. Its leaders explored possibilities for a peace with France, which would restore the vigorous trade that made them rich.[5] Yet despite the challenges, William's established reliance on allies, and his usual policy of avoiding too many internal disputes in Dutch politics, held the line. Grand Pensionary Heinsius remained an effective operator for the stadhouder-king's cause; William spent at least some time in The Hague before and after his campaigns in the Spanish Netherlands to maintain and repair relations with Dutch leaders; and Amsterdam's duplicity was tolerated and ignored in the knowledge that no acceptable peace terms were likely to emerge from France until it was absolutely convinced it could not win the war.

William also benefitted from an afterglow of his successful invasion of England in the Netherlands of the early 1690s. The Dutch were grateful and relieved that the 1688–9 revolution had brought them a substantial new ally. They were also proud that one of their sons had become such a prominent player on the European stage.[6] William's elevation to the English throne, and his coronation, had therefore been enthusiastically celebrated in the provinces (the historian Jonathan Israel has noted a virtual silencing of any criticism in the usually rumbustious Dutch press), and these sentiments were repeated when William first returned to his homeland in 1691.[7] His crossing from London, in mid-January, which turned out to be far too early in the year, was nearly disastrous. The king's ship got lost in fog and ice, as did the open rowing boat into which he had disembarked when he thought he was near the Dutch coast. He landed on a nearly deserted part of the shore, almost speechless with cold. The welcome, however, was warm. Locals cheered him on his journey to The Hague, and the leaders of the Dutch republic crowded around him when he arrived. A week later, he was treated to a ceremonial entry to the city, passing under 'very costly' triumphal arches which were 'imbellished with gold, and rich carving, and phantasies of curiosities in painting'; and he enjoyed a spectacular, if mist obscured, firework display in his honour.[8] Alongside William's political pragmatism, the magnificent charisma of the Orange-Nassaus was continuing to work its magic in the provinces. The Netherlands remained solidly behind the war effort.

After these celebrations, William's first order of business was to chair a congress of the allies. This met in February 1691 to discuss the state of the war and the strategy for the coming campaign. It resulted in agreement to put together a field army of two hundred and twenty thousand men. The congress illustrated another of the stadhouder-king's talents that would allow his victory at Namur: his ability to keep his disparate coalition of states and rulers together and committed to the war against France. The meeting in 1691 was grand (several sovereign princes from Germany attended, alongside high-power representatives from Spain and Austria), but it built on an initiative William had taken right at the start of the war. To give all sides a feeling of ownership of the military effort, the prince of Orange had convened a standing committee on the effort against the French. Coordinated by Heinsius, and assembling regularly in The Hague, this included envoys from the allied powers who discussed the priorities, tactics, and supply of their military efforts. The arrangement prevented any party feeling they were being ignored, and it made it far harder for any one of them to negotiate privately with France. Outside this body, William was active in the ceaseless cajoling and rewarding that proved necessary to keep all the other rulers on board. Fortunately, he was as tireless in diplomatic correspondence as in leading troops, and he had a good sense of what might win people over. He was not above bribes. For example, during the early 1690s, he kept Brunswick in the war by paying well over the odds for the troops that state supplied; he offered the Garter to George of Hanover to try to nudge him out of neutrality; and he persuaded Spain to appoint Max Emmanuel Wittelsbach its governor in Brussels in order to keep that prince's realm of Bavaria on his side.

The stadhouder-king also forged a working relationship with the Emperor Leopold. This was easier said than done. Austria had interests beyond simply defeating France; but William knew a basic understanding between him and the monarch in Vienna was essential to the working of the Grand Alliance. Thus, although William encouraged the emperor to make peace with the Turks to concentrate on the war in Flanders, he accepted that his Habsburg ally must look east as well as west for its security. He also understood that Habsburg pride meant Leopold must take the lead in managing relations with German princes. He thus deferred to the policies being adopted by the Austrians within the Holy Roman Empire, even when he might have preferred a different approach. For instance, Leopold arranged for the kidnap and imprisonment of the trouble-making minister Hans Adam von Schöning, who had been influencing George IV of Saxony towards friendship with Louis. William acquiesced in this extraordinary expedient, though he had been trying to win Schöning over with presents and conversations.[9] The stadhouder-king thus did a lot of the diplomatic heavy lifting to cement the anti-French cause: this is recognised (if somewhat exaggerated) in a pictorial celebration of the 1691 congress, printed in England (see Figure 6). In this image, which was set above an explanatory and idolising poem, 'Britain's monarch in the centre sits' (as the verse has it), while the Dutch states-general and the emperor pay court to the enthroned figure. In the somewhat cartoonish woodcut, William is drawn rather larger than anyone else in the frame. This was ironic for a person who was so physically slight; but it did, perhaps, reflect his significance within the process of coalition-building.[10]

From all we have just said, it is clear that the king of the Stuart realms had to spend a great deal of his energy and time outside those kingdoms in the early 1690s. Yet despite this, his most important task in these years was probably managing Britain and Ireland. It was their contributions of troops and money that tipped the balance of resources in the European war, giving the Grand Alliance the chance to outdo France; and William, as their ruler, had direct responsibility for their fiscal and military mobilisation. Although England, Scotland, and Ireland were all limited monarchies, with influential – and frequently troublesome – parliaments that needed to consent to the logistics of raising funds and men, their monarch was able to use his usual mix of skills to achieve the greatest mass organisation for foreign war that they had ever seen.

Our account should probably start in Ireland, since the last chapter left William victorious at the Boyne, but not yet in total control of the kingdom. Final dominance took longer to achieve than he had hoped. After the stadhouder-king's triumph, James went back to France, and William was able to occupy Dublin, but Jacobite forces held on in the west of the country, many muttering that the exiled ruler had once again preferred flight to leadership. William advanced to attack his enemies in 1690, but heavy rain foiled an effective siege of Limerick (although he again showed a reckless courage in the face of military danger, pitching his tent within the artillery range of the town's defenders, and appearing to be unconcerned as shells burst round him).[11] Despite this lack of care for his own safety, William was aware of political realities, and concluded that if Limerick could not be taken, he needed to be back in London. The king therefore withdrew his army to eastern Ireland, and left command of the next season's campaigning with Godert de Ginkel. Ginkel, an experienced Dutch general, proved rather more successful than his master in mopping up resistance. In 1691, he crossed the Shannon at Athlone (he would soon be made earl of the place in commemoration) and he gained a decisive victory, somewhat against the odds, at Aughrim in July.[12] This led to a second siege of Limerick, in which the Catholic defenders suffered steadily dwindling supplies. Nonetheless, it became clear that winkling the Jacobites out of the town was going to take

Figure 6 Frontispiece to *The royal assembly of Europe, consulting about the affairs of Christendom* (London, 1691), ink on paper. Houghton Library, Harvard University.

some time, and it was diverting forces from Flanders, so William's characteristic pragmatism again kicked in. Rather than going for a final glorious storming of Limerick, the king offered its garrison a deal. Those soldiers who wished to continue fighting for James were allowed to leave for France, where they formed an active Irish brigade in Louis's armies. Those who wished to disarm and return home, or to join William's forces, were permitted those courses of action. The Catholic civilian population, who had been under Jacobite protection, were promised exemption from land confiscation, and freedom to worship, if they swore an oath of allegiance to the new king in London. This Treaty of Limerick would soon become, and has long remained, controversial: we will explore this in the next chapter. For now, though, it ended a draining conflict, and allowed William to redirect resources to the defence of the Spanish Netherlands.

Ireland was also, at least to a degree, pacified by William's consultation with its Parliament. The legislature in Dublin had not been called since 1667, but the Dutch king summoned it far more regularly than his uncles had done: both in hopes that it would grant him funds and to try to forge relations with the Protestant landowning classes that controlled the kingdom now Jacobitism had been defeated. The Irish Parliament – which represented those elites – caused problems for William, but it did permit him to demonstrate his characteristic style of negotiation and compromise. For example, the session in 1692 exploded in anger (partly because Irish Protestants were horrified by the lenient terms their Catholic enemies had been granted at Limerick) and had to be dissolved with nothing achieved. However, the next meeting, in 1695, went far better because William sent a new and conciliatory lord lieutenant, Henry Capel, to Dublin. Capel offered posts to the leaders of the 1692 opposition in return for helping him manage the Irish Lords and Commons. They became the 'undertakers'. These were politicians who lubricated politics in Dublin on William's behalf, and ensured the government was voted at least enough funds to run and to defend Ireland itself, and so to ensure the kingdom did not become a drain or distraction for the king.[13]

Scotland too was just about kept onside by William's attempts to work with its elites. As we have mentioned, the king had less success ruling his northern kingdom than anywhere else, and we shall expand on his failings here soon. While we are trying to explain the victory at Namur, however, we should note that, for all the challenges it posed, Scotland largely paid its way in the early 1690s and did not rebel in any wholesale manner after the initial Jacobite rising in 1689. As in Ireland, part of the reason for this loyalty was that William respected the nation's Parliament. He called it frequently, and he stood back from methods that had earlier been used to try to manage the nation's representatives. In the first year of the new reign, there had been loud calls from many Scots to abolish the Lords of the Articles. The Lords had been a subcommittee of the legislature, stuffed with supporters of the monarch, which had control of the legislative agenda, so that it was difficult to bring forward measures of which the court disapproved. William had wished to retain this body as it gave him a lever of influence over an assembly that sometimes seemed ungovernable. Yet when he saw the anger the Lords of the Articles stirred, he acquiesced. Scrapping the subcommittee left the king reliant on a series of local aristocrats and politicians, whom he hoped would cobble together majorities in the Scots Parliament. Nobody ever really managed that feat in the fractious politics of the 1690s, but the approach at least meant there was no systematic estrangement from the Scots elites. William's aforementioned surrender on religious policy, and his acceptance of the 'claim of right', also provided foundations for a basic compromise on which government in Edinburgh could rest.

Collaboration with the legislatures in Ireland and Scotland (which mirrored William's earlier dealings with the representative assemblies in the Netherlands) thus provided some security for the regime. Yet it was the king's handling of the Parliament in Westminster, and his wooing of the wider English public, that truly explains his victory at Namur. Scots and Irish troops served in Flanders, but it was England, with her greater population and economic resource, that had to be mobilised to dent French pride. English troops, English taxes, and English credit were essential to turn the war in Flanders against Louis, so William's ability to persuade his English subjects to make the necessary sacrifices was key to this stage of his career.

The king's success here had many pillars, but as with the basic establishment of his regime in 1689, his wife was crucial. This era has been remembered as the age of 'William and Mary', and for once, popular labelling captures important truths. After the Boyne, Mary continued to provide a symbol of continuity and legitimacy as the daughter of the previous Stuart monarch, but in the early 1690s her role expanded well beyond such tokens. At a most practical level, she could head the government in London in the summers when William was on the battlefield – first in Ireland, and then, every year from 1691, in Flanders. A series of regency acts promoted her to the executive power, as had occurred in 1690: these allowed her the full authority of a monarch, though the legislation also appointed advisory councils of leading politicians, which dealt with a lot of day-to-day business; and in practice Mary made decisions, wherever possible, in close epistolary consultation with the king. Recent assessments of her periods in charge, especially by the historian W.A. Speck, have been favourable.[14] Although she had to cope with faction, and arrogant personalities, in her councils, she managed some challenging crises, including a full-scale invasion scare in 1690 when the Royal Navy blundered at the battle of Beachy Head, and Louis was briefly in control of the Channel. Over the next few years, the queen and her administration proved adept at countering Jacobite plotting, punishing military incompetence and misconduct, and inspiring the loyalty of those sailors and militiamen charged with the defence of the kingdom. Most notably, Mary helped to coordinate the victory at the naval battle of La Hogue in 1692, which was a rare ray of light in a bleak run of defeats for the Grand Alliance's cause. As Julie Farguson has pointed out, Mary took on further martial duties as she engaged in moral-boosting reviews of troops both at the army's camp at Hounslow Heath, and nearer the heart of the capital in Hyde Park.[15]

According to contemporary assumptions about gender, Mary's roles in substituting for her husband while he was abroad had involved her in conventionally 'masculine' activities. She had had to show the sort of political leadership and military command usually thought best reserved for men. Fortunately for her, the occasional legitimacy of a female performing these male roles, at least within the context of queenship, had been established in popular imagination a hundred years earlier, by the example of Elizabeth. The last Tudor ruler had come to be seen as a brilliant monarch, who had defended the realm against dangerous foreign threat, and united her people around her, despite her sex. To exploit this memory, Mary was frequently compared to Elizabeth in panegyric. In fact, one of the musical odes composed for her birthdays, and performed at court in the celebrations, suggested that Mary had not only built upon, but had actually eclipsed, the last Tudor's achievements in female rule.[16] Similarly, the frontispiece and text of a 1693 history of Elizabeth's reign paired the sixteenth- and seventeenth-century queens as epitomes of wise government; whilst a series of accounts of the Stuart age, which were published soon after the 1688–9 revolution, presented Mary and her husband restoring an Elizabethan 'Golden Age' after the horrors of the seventeenth century.[17]

With the glittering example of great Tudor queen set in the public mind, Mary could step outside her conventional gender roles as government required; but her contribution was perhaps even more effective when – as part of a joint team with William – she conformed very closely to contemporary models of womanhood. As the historian Cynthia Herrup has pointed out, royal authority in the early modern era was ambiguously gendered. Ideal qualities of rule were stretched across a spectrum from masculine to feminine in a manner that made it difficult for an individual ruler, who had to construct their own gender in specific ways, to satisfy all the expectations upon them. For example, mercy was seen as a feminine virtue, but also a royal one. It was therefore challenging for male rulers to demonstrate this essential dimension of authority without undermining a kingly masculinity based around 'harder' qualities such as individual decisiveness.[18] However, this situation could be eased in the joint monarchy. William and Mary could, between them, perform gender-diverse power with neither party having to step too far outside their own male and female identities. William could project himself as a strong man of action – particularly in the depictions of his exploits on the battlefield which dominated pictorial presentations of the king in the early 1690s; whilst Mary could fulfil more 'feminine' demands of royal office – leading in areas where masculinity might be thought inappropriate.[19]

One such area was charity. The Bible promised that virtuous nations would be rewarded with queens who would be their 'nursing mothers'. This suggested that female rulers should protect and nourish their people (though it also promised kings would be 'nursing fathers': an image which underscores the gender ambiguity of perfect rule).[20] Mary attempted to live up to this image, sponsoring a number of initiatives for the welfare of the people. The one with the most lasting and visible legacy was Greenwich Hospital. After the 1692 battle of La Hogue, the queen ordered the conversion of an existing royal palace to serve as a treatment centre for wounded sailors, and she commissioned work on a new edifice to house needy veterans of the navy. Over the next few years, a magnificent set of buildings rose on the banks of the Thames, which outdid Charles II's similar provision for the army at Chelsea, and rivalled Louis XIV's home for disabled soldiers at Les Invalides. One could argue that Greenwich represented a significant shift in focus for royal architectural patronage in England. We shall see that William and Mary did spend money on refurbishing and expanding their own residences, but the couple's chief construction project was to be an institution for public welfare. Beyond this establishment, the queen was praised for her generous support to those in need who applied to her for aid. In particular, her concern for impoverished clergy and for persecuted foreign Protestants was noted. She organised relief for people fleeing the Catholic regimes of France, Savoy, and Central Europe; and she sketched out a scheme to augment poorer livings in the Church of England, which would later be implemented by her successor as Queen Anne's Bounty.[21]

Royal entertaining was not inherently gendered (kings had traditionally been expected to be generous hosts, as an annual round of feasting at court through the early modern period attested) but it became so under William and Mary, because the queen took a lead whilst her husband concentrated on the war. Mary's work to maintain a social round that would still centre on the royal household and so bind elites to the monarchy contrasted with the king's sacrifice of this easier life of culture to be with his troops: panegyric explicitly divided royal work between the two figures. In poetry, and prose, the queen was assigned the role of maintaining the nation's love, while William took the more masculine role of fighting for England, sword in hand and suffering considerable hardship.[22] Mary's activities in the social sphere included attendance at theatre, patronage of poetry and music, and organising court balls to celebrate royal birthdays. These were all areas in which her taciturn and reserved husband would take no lead: indeed Julie Farguson, the most recent historian of royal presentation in late Stuart England, has suggested the king went along only highly reluctantly with Mary's initiatives such as organising concerts at court, or having the royal couple dine in public.[23] Closely allied with Mary's work to keep the royal household at the centre of social life was her role in influencing elite fashions. The queen's own passion for collecting Delftware sparked a craze for such porcelain in the upper classes, while her interest in horticulture did much to introduce formal continental garden designs to England.[24]

Another area often, though not exclusively, associated with femininity was piety. Queens were supposed to be examples of diligent worship of God and of moral behaviour; and more was perhaps expected of them than kings in these areas because gender assumptions held that women would not be so involved in politics, military command, and diplomacy – functions of royalty which could compromise ideal Christian behaviour. Mary, whose memoirs seem to reveal a woman deeply concerned about how God judged her, put much energy into activities aimed at promoting the faith and holiness of the nation.[25] Thus, she made a highly visible spectacle of her attendance at public worship. She promoted sermons at court: both employing some of the most popular clergymen of the day as royal chaplains who would address her as part of divine service and advertising her presence at these preachings by ordering systematic publication of the pulpit performances she had heard.[26] She also sponsored the contemporary campaign for a 'reformation of manners'. This was partly a spontaneous popular movement to improve English adherence to God's moral law. It concentrated on action against prostitution, Sunday trading, drunkenness, and profane swearing, and it encouraged ordinary people to report their neighbours to the authorities if they indulged in such illegalities. Yet while the campaign found traction at ground level, it also received patronage from above. In 1691, Mary wrote a widely publicised letter to the magistrates of Middlesex urging them to enforce statutes against various forms of immorality; and she issued a royal proclamation against 'vicious, debauched, and profane persons' which demanded the same action across the whole nation.[27]

There was one final area delegated to Mary within the performance of the joint monarchy: governance of the church. As we have already seen, William's support for the national ecclesiastical establishment was doubted by some, especially given his earlier loyalty to the rather different styles of the Dutch reformed Christianity. Fears about his commitment deepened after he had accepted the abolition of an Anglican-style kirk in Scotland; after he had called for dissenters to be allowed public office in March 1689; and when he deprived nonjuring clergy of their posts for not swearing adherence to his regime. In contrast to all this, Mary had a far firmer record of loyalty to Anglicanism. In the years before the revolution, she had resisted both her father's attempts to convert her to Catholicism and her husband's pressure to conform to the practices of Protestants in the Netherlands. Her prominent attendance at divine service in the English church after 1689 signalled this spiritual allegiance. Trusting Mary's deeper understanding of Anglican worship, and aware of the optics of having a true believer lead the faith, William surrendered the rulers' role as ecclesiastical governors to his wife. This was again to assign the queen an authoritative role that might clash with gender assumptions; but Elizabeth again provided a soothing precedent for a woman leading the church, and the Stuart queen's concern for the religious establishment could be presented as an outgrowth of her perfectly feminine piety and charity. It was therefore Mary who nominated the bishops who would replace those who could not swear loyalty to the new regime; it was Mary who worked closely with those she had appointed to chart a new direction for the church after the toleration act of 1689; and it was Mary who proposed a series of institutional reforms to improve the quality of the clergy just before she died in 1694.[28] Throughout this biography, we have seen William surrendering the initiative to others when they were better able to advance his cause: his award of ecclesiastical policy in England to his wife was one of the most important of these strategic withdrawals.

The joint monarchy was therefore far more than a shallow publicity stunt to veneer William's rule with a film of Stuart legitimacy, and we will see what a blow Mary's passing was to her husband in the next chapter. But the king also made his own success in England. He continued to apply lessons learned in the Netherlands to his Stuart realms, and benefitted from the unique combination of skills that he alone, perhaps, could call upon given his own personal history.

Public relations was a particular case in point. In the early 1690s, the king, and his supporters, continued propaganda themes that had served his cause well in the United Provinces, and during the Glorious Revolution, and which retained resonance in the war years. Crucially, as he had since 1672, William posed as a providential guarantor of Protestantism; and of national liberties from the threat of an expansionist and persecuting France. An extensive print campaign, ranging from proclamations, to pamphlets, to published pulpit oratory, outlined the danger Louis posed as a potential 'universal monarch' of the whole European continent; and lovingly described the horrors of the French's king's persecuting rule. It lauded William as the hero sent by God to oppose this Satanic tyrant and urged all good English people to back their ruler enthusiastically in his military efforts.[29] Typical of such propaganda was a 1690 pamphlet *The most Christian Turk*. This lambasted Louis as a man who was doing more damage to Christendom than its overt enemies in the Muslim Ottoman empire had ever achieved. France's monarch had slaughtered tens of thousands of fellow Christians in his wars; he had broken the religion's duties of unity, charity, and honesty; and he had abrogated treaties solemnly sworn before God. In this context, William's war could be seen as a crusade for the true faith, and his rule a part of the divine plan for human history. Sometimes such material made very explicit appeals for people to support the king's war effort with their lives or their cash because the monarch was the champion of all that was good and true. A clergyman, Richard Lucas, preaching at the assizes in Horsham, outlined the horrors that Louis's rule was bringing across Europe (faith destroyed, farmland and town burned, daughter ravished), and then asserted that these were the conditions from which his countrymen could redeem themselves by paying taxes to William's government.[30]

Appropriately for the image of a heaven-sent champion, there was a strong moral element in this material. England would, many authors asserted, be strengthened in her anti-French enterprise because her king's example and policy would lead her into new depths of faith, and a turn towards Christian virtue. Such repentance and religious renewal would earn heaven's blessing on the English military cause; and it would purge out the sin and wickedness that Catholic France had deliberately spread in England to weaken the nation for several decades. This argument gelled with Mary's support for court virtue and the reformation of manners movement, but it had a wider purchase which encompassed the king. Many of the messages came together in a remarkable series of public fasts. On an initiative from Gilbert Burnet (who retained his position as a chief spokesman for the regime, for all that William disliked this bishop personally), the whole nation was stopped from normal business one day a month every summer in the early 1690s and was required to perform religious exercises. On these fast days, the entire population was supposed to attend church services, where specially composed prayers and vigorous preaching reminded them what was at stake in the current circumstances. William was, the occasions stressed, leading England in God's true mission. He and his soldiers fought the forces of the French Antichrist directly on the battlefield, but everyone else must get behind him according to their ability. Support could be spiritual as well as material. A moral, pious, and fully reformed nation would be protected by the deity, who would see a people fully worthy of his crusade. Of course, it is hard to monitor the success of any propaganda campaign (who knows exactly why people rally round causes, even today?); but a strong argument can be made that this presentation of William played the major role in sustaining his rule and the war effort among his subjects at large. Flattering the English as a true Protestant nation, as a people united behind a godly king, and as a country that had set its face against a wicked foreign foe, ran with the grain of over a hundred years' self-identity in the Stuart realm.[31]

This image of the king was cemented by a personal and royal glamour which also carried over from his career before 1688. As he had in the Netherlands, William (though personally introverted, and perhaps happier to spend time in battlefield trenches) sustained a magnificence around his person which maintained a full royal style. Some of this was associated with architectural projects. William and Mary disliked the traditional royal palaces of St James and Whitehall in central London – partly because the king's asthma made living in the smoke of the capital unbearable; partly because the couple had been used to living in their rural retreats, such as Het Loo, when in the Netherlands. Accordingly, they resolved to develop two residences out in the countryside, to the west and upwind of London. The first was Kensington (a house which they purchased from the earl of Nottingham), the second was Hampton Court (a site that had been in royal hands since Henry VIII had confiscated it from its original owner, Thomas Wolsey, in the sixteenth century). Work at Kensington was relatively modest, but Christopher Wren, the leading architect of the day, who had already been commissioned by the church to design a new St Paul's Cathedral after the Great Fire of 1666, was asked to submit proposals for a major redevelopment at Hampton Court. Wren's initial suggestion was rejected – almost certainly on grounds of cost, and nervousness about charges of extravagance. As a result, William never got a house that might fully rival Louis's new palace at Versailles. Wren's first pitch for the new construction would have demolished all of the old buildings on the site except the Tudor Great Hall and replaced everything else with four large quadrangles in the contemporary baroque style.[32] Although nothing so comprehensive was attempted, what was being built in the early 1690s was impressive, and would – at the very least – have established the king as significant patron of builders and craftsmen: full analysis of the new works at the palace should wait until it was completed in 1701.

The king also maintained a high royal style through ceremonial. It is true that he left public religious observance largely to his wife, and that he abandoned a key royal ritual, which had been used by his predecessors to stress the divine status of monarchy. This had been 'Touching for the King's Evil': an occasion on which earlier rulers had claimed to be able to cure the disease scrofula by laying hands on sufferers. These therapeutic sessions had brought many ordinary people into palaces to see their ruler; and scrofula had proved a good choice of disease on which to found the pretence, since its glandular swellings can go into temporary remission, which could be associated with recent royal attention. Yet despite the potential propaganda advantages of the Touching ceremony, William seems to have doubted he had miraculous abilities. He may have felt the tradition was too close to Catholic healing superstitions, or that his own accession to the throne was too unorthodox for any extraordinary powers to have passed on to him.[33] Yet, notwithstanding this editing of the established round of royal appearances, William participated frequently in other forms of ceremony. His journeys to the continent were staged as royal progresses; he continued traditional practices associated with Order of the Garter; and in particular, he attended Parliament in full state. For reasons we shall soon explore, the Lords and Commons sat far more continuously in the 1690s than they ever had before. Their sessions therefore provided good opportunities for the king to present himself formally to his leading subjects, and William exploited these. He gave frequent speeches on the opening and closing of sessions, as well as on other ad hoc occasions; and he attended in person to give royal assent to the burgeoning number of statutes which a virtually standing legislature began to generate. These visits involved both grand processions, and the donning of impressive costumes of office. They were widely reported in the official government newspaper, as well as being witnessed directly by inhabitants of the capital. William's ceremonial life was thus not so much a curtailing of royal ritual, as a redirection of it into channels perhaps more suitable for a monarch who had been chosen by the nation rather than by God through heredity.[34]

Royal magnificence, providential Protestantism, and the gendered complementarity of the joint monarchy may do much to explain why the general populace of England held with their foreign king and his war. It is always impossible for historians to know exactly why ordinary people take the political stances they did – but a ruler presenting himself as a traditional king, claiming to defend the nation against popery, and supported by a popular wife who modelled herself on Elizabeth seems to fit what we know of late Stuart popular assumptions about ideal government; and there does seem to have been a widespread celebration of William and Mary at the level of mass material culture. The monarchs' images were widely available – and were consumed – in cheap pictorial prints; in woodcuts that adorned ephemeral broadsides and ballads; and on ceramics such as the charger which appears on the cover of this volume.

Yet, whilst the people as a whole might have been persuaded by the propaganda we have been examining, the elites above them – especially those serving or represented in Parliament – may have been trickier to win over. There were two main reasons for this. First, the parliamentary classes (if we can give this label to groups comprising the nobility, the substantial landed gentry, and urban leaders) had a legacy of suspicion of Crown power. Perceived attacks on their rights and privileges by Charles I, by James II, and perhaps by all Stuart kings before 1688 had bred a fear of court power. This had often been expressed in the legislature's opposition to government personnel or policy; and had resulted in a series of constitutional crises, including the mid-century civil war, and the revolution that had brought William to power. Second, this elite had been sundered into two great parties in the exclusion crisis. As we have seen, the fissure between Tories and Whigs was deep, and had produced an extremely polarised political system. Taken with the prevailing anti-court sentiment, party hostilities posed a poisonous challenge for William. He might want the parliamentary classes to unite with him, and with each other, to fight his war. Yet the prevailing mistrust made this unlikely. The king's easing of these tensions enough to prevent rupture must be central to any account of his triumph at Namur. His techniques were once again borrowed from Dutch politics; their success was, perhaps, his single most impressive political achievement.

In calming party sentiment, William continued try to work with a wide variety of opinion – an approach he had come to realise was the only way to succeed in the Netherlands, and which he had used in his first year as king of England. This represented a break with the policies of Charles II and James II. As we outlined in the last chapter, William's uncles had tried to bolster their own position through wholehearted alliance with one faction against the other. Charles had rested his last four years of rule on an alliance with the Tories; James had started with the same tactic but had then violently switched to the Whigs. Such a strategy had allowed the monarchs to harness partisan sentiment for their cause, yet it had come with a disastrous cost. As the Crown identified with one of the factions, and granted it a monopoly of power, the out-of-favour grouping was driven to desperation. Facing an all-out assault from both their opponents and the court, they had resorted to treasonous plotting against the regime. Thus, the Whigs had been involved in conspiracy against Charles II after their failure in the exclusion crisis, and some had tried to overthrow James II as soon as he came to power by aiding the Monmouth rebellion. Soon afterwards, the Tories had abandoned their loyalty to the Stuart dynasty when James abandoned them, and some had played a key role in the machinations which resulted in the Dutch invasion. After 1688, William broke this cycle of treason by altering the Crown's strategy. Perhaps realising disloyalty had been bred by hopelessness and fear – and being used to working with different factions in the Dutch provinces – the new king avoided either party feeling it had been completely proscribed. This explained that mixed administration which the king appointed for the year 1689 – but attempts at inclusion survived even after William's turn to the Tories later that year. Although the court now leant towards the earl of Nottingham's party, the monarch tried to reassure Whigs they had not been anathematised; and this same political style continued though the reign.

William's most basic technique to address the divisiveness of party was to prevent either side trying to destroy the other. This sort of partisan earth-scorching had been allowed under Charles II and James II. When the court had been in alliance with Whigs or Tories in the 1680s, it had collaborated in party action to prosecute enemies (sometimes to the point of execution, as suffered by Whig leaders during the 'Tory reaction' at the end of Charles's reign); and it had helped to chase rivals out of all local as well as national office. Given William's purges in the Netherlands after the *rampjaar*, it might seem surprising that he rejected this approach in London – but we have seen he learned the dangers of pushing people too far at later points in Dutch politics; and once he was in England, he refused to allow royal power to become an instrument of party vindictiveness. One of the reasons he soured on the Whigs in 1689 was their intolerance. He was appalled at their disruptive campaign to exclude Tories from the administration; and by their opposition to an act of indemnity which would pardon people for their political stances during and since the exclusion crisis. Similarly, the king rebuffed Whig attempts to impose unacceptable oaths of office on Tories. As we saw, many Tories were only prepared to accept William as king on de facto grounds: the proposed oaths would have demanded they recognise the king's full *de jure* legitimacy, but William insisted that forcing Tories to do this would alienate them. He therefore blocked the Whigs' initiative, even though it seemed to bolster his claim to the throne.[35] Again, both parties were disappointed in the king's partisanship beyond Westminster. Although William would switch between the parties in national administration, he never let his ministers destroy their rivals at local level. Men such as justices of the peace, sheriffs, and county lord lieutenants (the Crown-appointed pillars of regional and community administration) tended to stay in place even when their opponents held sway in national counsels.

And that party sway was never total. As a second tactic to avoid anyone renouncing his regime, the king avoided monopolistic governments. In the early 1690s, William tacked between teams of Whig and Tory ministers; but he did so gradually, leaving some members of the outgoing group in place, even as the other side grew in power. So, we have seen the king turned to the Tories in 1689–90, frustrated at their opponents' concentration on revenge, rather than uniting the nation in the face of Louis XIV. Yet the turn was only partial. Although Tories were promoted to leading posts, some Whigs remained. For example, Richard Hampden retained his important role as Chancellor of the Exchequer; and even the choleric Thomas Wharton held on as Comptroller of the Household. The new administration was therefore Tory-leaning, rather than unequivocally Tory. As an administration, it was reasonably competent: it mobilised England's resources fairly effectively for the war. Yet it was plagued by instances of corruption, and the lack of striking victories in the conflict with Louis in the early 1690s sapped morale. By 1693, the government was losing support in the Commons; and William, ever flexible, responded with a shift back to the Whigs. Yet again, this shift was gradual and moderate. The Tory earl of Nottingham was sacked as Secretary of State in November of that year, but he was not replaced by a Whig, the earl of Shrewsbury, for nearly six months. The commissions controlling customs and excise were not remodelled in favour of the Whigs until summer 1694; and the Tory duke of Leeds did not cease to operate as Lord President of the Privy Council until 1695. In much popular comment, the Whigs of the new government were seen as ruthlessly self-promoting. But their ambition had faced a slow and uphill struggle, and they failed to poison William's mind against their rivals.

Perhaps the most vivid example of William's reluctance to damn any politician absolutely was his relationship with Robert Spencer, the earl of Sunderland. No figure in late seventeenth century English politics deserved damnation more. Ambitious and unprincipled, the earl alienated virtually all right-thinking opinion during a colourful career. He had been an operator at the morally murky court of Charles II, worming his way into the circles of the king's French mistress, the duchess of Portsmouth. As a Secretary of State when the exclusion crisis had begun, he first supported the Whig aim to bar James from the throne, but then abandoned the cause when it was defeated, and snuck back into government as it became a Tory monopoly. Sunderland was retained by the Catholic king when he ascended to the throne in 1685. Yet he rapidly betrayed his former Tory allies, throwing in his lot with a group of Catholic courtiers who urged bold use of the royal prerogative to erode the legal privileges of Protestants. Trying to gain favour with the monarch, he claimed to have converted to the Roman Church, and became the architect of many of the policies of James's reign. In fact, if William's strictures against 'evil counsellors' in his manifesto for his 1688 invasion had been aimed at real people rather than bogeymen, Sunderland would have been very much in the frame. This arch-operator was dismissed by James as the Dutch invaded for his failures to stem opposition to the court, and he entered William's reign disgraced, friendless, and – briefly – in exile. Despite all this, however, the new monarch recognised a man with finely tuned political instincts, and someone who had negotiated the rancour between parties successfully until the catastrophe of the revolution. From 1691, William increasingly sought advice from Sunderland: to the widespread horror of everyone else in English politics. The earl was behind the king's swing to the Whigs in 1693, advising that only that party had the coherence and determination to manage the war and the House of Commons.[36] That the king could deal with such a man tells us a great deal about him. Almost nobody could assume every bridge with the court had been burned. There was a way back to favour if one could make oneself useful – finding a way to be useful was the clear path to power.

Throughout all these processes, William retained lines of communication with those not in his government – albeit sometimes via intermediaries such as

Sunderland. As a good example, the prominent lawyer John Somers was a pretty hard-line Whig, who came to be seen as the highly partisan leader of the Whig ministry after 1693. Yet he had continued to work with, and be consulted by, the king right through the earl of Nottingham's Tory regime. Somers had been the solicitor-, and then the attorney-, general; so, he had talked with the king regularly – on legal affairs at least.[37] William thus retained links to all sides; and was also keen to reassure those losing influence that they were not in total disgrace. When sacking Nottingham he told the earl he had always valued his 'fidelity' and that he was not being removed for personal failings.[38] The king's retention of many allies of dismissed ministers similarly soothed fears of outright purge. The whole approach softened the attraction of outright, or violent, resistance when a party lost control of government; and it offered new routes to power. William had proved that people would be advanced if they looked as if they could gain majorities for the war in Parliament, and if they appeared loyal and competent administrators of the conflict. In these circumstances, convincing the monarch one had these qualities became key to the political game; and the old tendency to conspiracy and rebellion at moments of low fortune came to seem pointless. If there were imaginable means of recovery without such dangerous expedients, it was surely better to pursue them than engage in treason. The Jacobites might still threaten risings (we shall see more of this in the next chapter), but the ending of partisan plotting after 1689 was a remarkable feature of the post-revolutionary age.

William thus found ways to contain party division in England. He also handled Parliament adeptly (at least by the disastrous standards of earlier Stuart kings). Versed in sharing power with representative and legislative assemblies in the Netherlands, the new monarch found ways to work with a body that had – at repeated points in the seventeenth century – led opposition to the Crown. Although Parliament had not always been united (one could not expect a gathering of six hundred representatives in the Commons, and tens of aristocrats in the Lords, to agree on everything), majorities in the two houses had frequently expressed discontent at royal policy. Particularly in the 1620s, 1640s, and 1670s, such parliamentary rancour had extended as far as action against unpopular ministers, refusals to grant the Crown tax revenue, attempts to alter the succession, and – famously in 1642 – organising outright rebellion. The Lords and Commons seem to have given voice to a strong contrarian spirit in the English political nation. Parliamentarians had been highly suspicious of the perceived extravagance, corruption, ambition, and authoritarianism of their rulers. William himself had exploited this 'country' (or anti-court) sentiment in his 1688 manifesto for the invasion. His picture of a royal government perverted by evil counsellors, and flexing its powers beyond all legality, gelled with the prejudices of many English people. Yet the tactic proved troublesome once William was king. He had encouraged the belief that governments were vicious; this mistrust now turned back on William himself, as Parliament expressed disquiet about his executive and its actions.

There were three main areas of dispute: finance; civil liberties; and the Crown's influence over Parliament itself. On finance, Parliament was willing to vote funds for the war – indeed we shall soon see that it granted money on an unprecedented scale. Yet it became increasingly concerned about how the money awarded was spent. In particular, the House of Commons, which had always had special responsibility for fiscal affairs, began close investigation of budgets. It scrutinised the 'estimates' (or the government's programme of planned spending) line by line; and it audited detailed accounts of past expenditure. This second process was led by a subcommittee, the commission of public accounts. Members of this group (men like Sir Thomas Clarges and Robert Harley) became something of an unofficial parliamentary opposition to William's administrations, and they began producing annual reports which excoriated the extensive waste, corruption, and misallocation they claimed to have found. In the area of civil liberties, tensions centred on the rights of those suspected of aiding Jacobites. William suspended habeas corpus early in his reign, so that he could detain potential enemies without trial. However, a good block of Parliament objected to this, seeing it as an example of un-English arbitrary power. Similarly, a series of treason bills were introduced, which were designed to tighten the processes that must be used against those accused of disloyalty to the king. This was unwelcome to William, as it hampered his ability to deal swiftly and certainly with traitors who were trying to overthrow him. The final dispute centred on the king's influence in Parliament. As the 1690s wore on, many MPs became concerned that the court was eroding their own independence – first by buying members off with profitable jobs in the government; and second by extending the life of each Parliament so that corrupted members stayed in place. In response, and very much against the king's wishes, bills were introduced to eject 'placemen' (those MPs who were paid salaries or pensions by the court); and to limit the length of each Parliament to three years. This, the measure's sponsors hoped, would mean representatives facing their electorates regularly, and so being beholden to their voters, not the central regime.[39]

At first glance, these disputes look like sort of tensions that had dominated the 1620s and 1670s, and that had fed into the crises of the civil war, the exclusion era, and the 1688–9 revolution. Parliament was once again raising fears of an extravagant and self-interested court. Yet the similarities were more superficial than they appear: this was to a large extent the result of William's approach to dealing with his legislature, and the nature of his regime. To start, the prince of Orange's installation as monarch in London had meant that English politics in the 1690s came to lack the controlling narrative of earlier eras of tensions. In the decades before, a lot of suspicion of the court had crystalised around fears that a popish conspiracy was operating there. Catholics, it had been feared, had found an entry point through the series of non-Protestant wives the Stuart kings had taken; and were operating around the monarch to undermine morality, to encourage absolutism, and to betray England's role upholding the true faith in Europe. This had been at the core of suspicions of courtiers and arbitrary power in the 1620s, it had fed the anger that had led to the civil war, and it explained attempts to exclude James from the throne in the late 1670s, once his conversion to Rome was revealed.[40] But, under William, this source of unease could gain no real traction. William was a Protestant himself; he had married a Protestant; he had been a champion of international Protestantism in his earlier career; he now posed as champion of godly Protestant virtue in England; and his crusade against Louis XIV countered Protestantism's leading enemy. The ideological core of earlier opposition was therefore missing. And it was not only William's faith that soothed. He also showed a deference to Parliament that had perhaps not been seen since the days of Elizabeth. Where his Stuart predecessors had dissolved the body in anger when disputes arose – or had attempted rule without the advice of their Lords and Commons – the Dutch king met his legislators for several months every single year, and never dismissed them before they had enjoyed a substantial session of debate. It is true that William's desperate need for war finance meant he could not afford to ignore Parliament. Yet even if his actions were driven by necessity, they calmed fear that this king would close his ears to the nation's representatives: this monarch had a keen sense of the theatre of reassurance. His frequents visits to Westminster, and his frequent speeches there, created an impression of royal respect for the legislature.

Parliamentarians were therefore persuaded they were unlikely to be swept away by a popish plot at court; and many of the criticisms of the executive were couched alongside acknowledgment that – whatever might be going wrong – the basic quality of this court was far better than what had come before.[41] And William had specific techniques in dealing with Westminster, which eased tensions in the main areas of dispute. Take finance. In the Netherlands, William had been used to the provincial states and the states-general keeping close tabs on state spending. He was thus unlikely to object if the Commons played the same role: in fact, there were advantages in allowing it to do so. A Parliament given access to the details of finance would be less suspicious of the government's actions; whilst parliamentarians committed to uncovering extravagance and corruption would be fine instruments for revealing any waste. William, just like the court's critics, wanted money that had been voted for the war to be spent efficiently in the cause of defeating Louis. It therefore made sense for the king to collaborate with such investigators in ensuring cash went where it was supposed to. Indeed, the king did more than collaborate. He played a very large part in establishing the system of Commons audit of royal accounts that emerged in the 1690s. We have already seen that William offered MPs sight of his financial dealings very early in his reign, but this was part of a wider strategy of encouraging scrutiny. The king's offer came before the House had thought to ask for this access to the financial records (which had hitherto been thought a king's private business): indeed, MPs did not initially respond to the king's initiative, not having thought how to deal with the novel process of audit. Eventually, William himself had to suggest they set up a committee with special powers to work through the numbers.[42] Only after this hint did Parliament come up with the system it used to scrutinise the court. William was thus far more the architect of the commission of public accounts than its target, and when the committee produced its first report, the king thanked its members for their care, for all that it had produced a rigorous condemnation of his administration.[43]

William's political strategies thus reduced conflict over money. They also, eventually, solved the issues around civil liberties and the independence of the Commons. In the early part of the 1690s, these played out as classic disputes between Crown and legislature, of which Charles I or Charles II would have been proud. William disliked measures to regulate treason trials; to prevent him employing MPs in his service; or to control how long he could retain a helpful Parliament. He consequently manoeuvred to have the proposed bills defeated: sometimes he went as far as using the royal veto on legislation that had been approved by both houses. This ramped up discontent, till some parliamentarians were muttering the darkest things about the court. By the mid-1690s, there were open threats to cut off the supply of taxes if the king did not change course, and resentment led one MP to complain that when he had voted to make William monarch he 'had thought to have seen better times than these'.[44] But, just as things were getting to the point of constitutional crisis, and just at the sort of stage where William's predecessors would have ensured one would have ensued through their intransigence, this new style of Dutch king backed down. Knowing from the Netherlands that rulers could never have all they wanted, and realising that lesser objectives sometimes had to be sacrificed to greater ones, William decided to salvage good relations with Parliament. He knew his war would not survive a breach with the legislature, and so resolved to avoid that, rather than insist on his powers. The tipping point here was William's veto of a place bill (aimed at those MPs who had jobs with the government) early in 1694. This elicited an explosion of anger in the Commons, and an address to the king asking who had advised him to his outrageous action. William's reply to this address was noncommittal on the specifics, but he did promise to follow Parliament's advice in future, and from this point he accepted large parts of his critics' platform.[45] Later in the year he approved a triennial bill. This forced him to hold parliamentary elections at least every three years. In 1695, he acquiesced in a treason bill which insisted that no one be convicted of the offence without the evidence of at least two reliable witnesses.

There was one further area in which William's regime tried to accommodate views in Parliament. It was perhaps not absolutely central to his strategy, but it is important to cover – both because it shaped the development of England's overseas empire in a crucial period and because it represents a considerable stain on the king's long-term reputation. The issue centred on two trading organisations which had been granted monopolies of commercial activity in parts of the world by the Crown earlier in the Stuart age. The Royal Africa Company operated on the west coast of Africa and across the Atlantic to the Americas; the East India Company was active in the Indian Ocean. Through the reigns of Charles II and James II these two bodies had advanced England's global power, but they had been controversial, with many people objecting to their monopolies. Some protested on political grounds. The companies had been very close to the Stuart court and had supported its policies before William's arrival in London. Some, however, were simply rival merchant interests who wanted to trade freely without worrying about the companies' exclusive rights. With the 1689 revolution, these opponents saw their opportunity to attack symbols of the fallen regime: lawsuits in the courts, and petitions and attempted legislation in Parliament, took aim at the established privileges of the two institutions.

William's attitude to the campaign against the companies broadly fitted his approach of putting support for the war, and pleasing legislators, above defending the Crown's traditional influence (in this case its prerogative to grant monopolies). After 1689, the Royal Africa Company suffered considerable erosions of its protected status, allowing other traders access to transatlantic activities. The East India Company fared better, partly because it suggested giving loans to finance William's war. It largely staved off attacks until 1695, though the case put by its rivals was eventually recognised when they were allowed to form an alternative body – the New East India Company. As a result of these changes, discontent at government was dissipated and English imperial activity expanded; but the policies were some of the darkest pursued by William in his whole career. A second reason the East India Company survived was considerable use of bribes to politicians close to the king.[46] Far more disturbingly, the ending of the Royal African monopoly greatly increased volumes in the Atlantic slave trade. With restrictions gone, a growing market for enslaved labour in the Caribbean was satisfied by a free-for-all in human misery – among both Europeans and local Africans capturing souls for trading abroad. The Royal Africa Company had been founded to exploit this shameful and tragic commerce, but its effective demise made the situation even worse.[47]

Taken all together, William's approach to the rest of the political nation revealed that he was a new and very different sort of king. He cooperated with Whigs and Tories, but he prevented them driving their enemies into hostility to the Crown itself. He tussled with Parliament, but was determined to try to work with it, and he knew when he had been defeated in struggles with his Lords and MPs. Unlike his Stuart predecessors, he had an objective beyond bolstering his own power (his European mission to stop Louis was his highest priority), and he was prepared to sacrifice that power for the greater cause. This new set of political strategies brought greater horrors for those caught up the expanded slave trade; but from William's perspective it worked because it resulted in a sustained and unprecedented supply of wartime finance. The king now faced a Parliament that, despite disagreements, trusted that the king trusted it. He ruled a nation in which grievances were addressed and often settled. He dealt with politicians who had to gain power by serving the king well, rather than destroying enemies at court. As a result, the English people collaborated with the executive in paying for, and organising, the war effort.

The early 1690s saw a massive expansion of what historians have come to call, clumsily, the fiscal-military state. William's reign may, in fact, have been the most significant stage in the development of the administrative and martial machinery that would allow Britain to emerge as the prime global power in the eighteenth century.[48] It was certainly essential to his victory at Namur.

Raw figures tell a lot of the story. In James II's days the English state had spent around two million pounds a year. Yet by the mid-1690s, this had more than doubled. James had had an annual tax income of under two million pounds. William's, by contrast, was around three and a half million. James's army had been around thirty-five thousand soldiers at its peak. William's land force would top out at over one hundred thousand, and his navy would grow to twice the size of his Stuart predecessor's. Not all new spending was on fighting men and their equipment. The central civil service grew from around five thousand bureaucrats to nearly ten thousand. Administrators had been drafted into the Admiralty and the Army Office to manage supply to the fighting men, and into departments such as customs and the excise to collect finance. Parliament had consented to all this. It had done so partly because its members had agreed that France must be contained, but also because their new roles signing off each budget item, and scrutinising how cash has been dispersed, reduced fears that what they approved would be perverted.

The involvement of the legislature also guaranteed a major innovation in finance that revolutionised the possibilities for state action. Because it became clear the Crown could use Parliament to tap the nation's resources, creditors had more confidence to lend to the Crown. Their collateral when giving money was no longer just the wealth and current cash flow of the monarch (which had proved illusory at points in the seventeenth century). Rather, borrowing was now backed by the entire economy of England, which Parliament could access – and was clearly prepared to access – through taxation. With this greater expectation that their money would be repaid, creditors were prepared to lend more money, for longer periods of time, and at far lower interest rates than they had done for earlier regimes. A boom in customs and excise revenue in the 1680s had allowed James II to rule with no debt outstanding: yet by the end of William's war, in 1697, he had borrowed over sixteen million pounds, a good deal of it in the form of long-term bonds, to be recouped over decades. Much of this money had been raised through the Bank of England. This had been founded in 1694 to channel punters' money to the newly secure forms in investment.[49]

Historians have long debated how far these new techniques for raising funds were copied from the Netherlands. The Dutch had long enjoyed a secure public credit, backed by a willingness to tax the people heavily, which was managed by a central institution, the Bank of Amsterdam, to direct lending to the state. William himself showed familiarity with the basic principles (an experience obviously picked up in his homeland) when he, using his private wealth, became one of the largest early subscribers to the Bank of England.

Yet copying the Netherlands had only been part of the story. Much of the initiative in inventing new taxes, and raising public credit, had come from English projectors and politicians responding to local conditions; and it was clear that the importation of William himself was more significant than any Dutch methods or financial know-how. Deploying political tactics that prevented rupture with his parliamentarians, the king established the basic consent and trust on which such mass mobilisation of resources had to be founded.

Namur, then, was captured by an inspirational commander, leading the international forces of an alliance that he had done much to forge and maintain. But it was also won by a man who had mobilised the money and men of multiple realms: the Netherlands, Ireland, Scotland, and – perhaps most impressively in terms of the scale of change – England. In this story, the key factor had been the stadhouder-king's willingness to work with others. Over and over again he had compromised, negotiated, and let subordinates operate for him in spheres where they were more capable. So, he had bargained constantly with representative assemblies in The Hague: in Dutch cites and provincial capitals; in Dublin; in Edinburgh; and in Westminster. He had listened to the concerns of these bodies; he had brought them into the process of government; he had showed them ritual and real respect; and he had surrendered to them when their opposition was becoming dangerous. Behind all this, he had campaigned for support among wider populations. Both the traditional pomp of rule and vigorous preaching and print campaigns had presented William as a providentially appointed authority, but one whose focus was on the protection and welfare of the people. Where the stadhouder-king's direct exercise of power might have alienated potential supporters, or where it would have been based on too little expertise, he delegated. Mary, Heinsius, the undertakers in the Irish Parliament, the Scots elites, and party leaders in England were each essential to the successful working of his regime. All of this was a world away from the style and approach of earlier Stuart kings in England, Scotland, and Ireland. It was even some distance from the autocratic tendencies of William's forebears among the Orange-Nassaus, and his own youthful arrogance in the aftermath of his *rampjaar* coup. Namur, and the logistical transformations on which that triumph rested, had depended on a ruler who learned from political missteps, and one who recognised the future lay in national mobilisations based on consent.

Notes

1 For a selection of this material, see *An exact journal of the siege of Namur* (London, 1695); *An exact account of the siege of Namur* (London, 1695); Thomas Knaggs, *A sermon preached at All Hallows Newcastle upon Tyne, on 22nd September, 1695, being the day of thanksgiving* (London, 1695); *A poem on the taking of Namur by his majesty* (London, 1695); Thomas Yalden, *On the conquest of Namur* (1695); *A form of prayer and thanksgiving to almighty God* (London, 1695).
2 Henry Horwitz ed, *The parliamentary diary of Narcissus Luttrell, 1691–1693* (Oxford, 1972), pp.251–7.

3 Julian Hoppit, *A land of liberty? England 1689–1727* (Oxford, 2000), pp.39–40 calculated that William spend nearly 40 per cent of his time as king out of England.
4 Stephen B. Baxter, *William III* (London, 1966), p.314.
5 Tensions with Amsterdam are covered in Jonathan Israel, *The Dutch republic: its rise, greatness and fall, 1477–1806* (Oxford, 1995), pp.854–6.
6 P.J.A.N. Rietbergen, 'A fateful alliance? William III and England in Dutch historiography, 1688–9 to 1988–9', in Jonathan Israel ed, *The Anglo-Dutch moment: essays in the Glorious Revolution and its world impact* (Cambridge, 1991), pp.463–80.
7 Jonathan Israel, *The Dutch republic: its rise, greatness and fall* (Oxford, 1995), p.856.
8 *An account of the magnificent public entry which his majesty of Great Britain made into the Hague on the 5th of February* (1691).
9 Baxter, *William III*, p. 296.
10 *The royal assembly of Europe, consulting about the affairs of Christendom, at the Hague in Holland* (1691).
11 Gilbert Burnet, *Bishop Burnet's history of his own time: volume two* (London, 1734), p.59.
12 Harman Murtagh, 'Ginckel, Godart van Reede, first earl of Athlone, *Oxford dictionary of natoinal biography*, https://www.oxforddnb.com (Accessed 25/04/23).
13 David Hayton, 'Constitutional experiments and political expediency', in Steven G. Ellis and Sarah Barber eds, *Conquest and union: fashioning a British state* (London, 1995), pp.276–305, at pp.300–1.
14 Mary's reputation was revived by W.A. Speck, 'William – and Mary?', in Lois G. Schwoerer ed, *The revolutions of 1688/9* (Cambridge, 1991), pp.131–46.
15 Narcissus Luttrell, *A brief historical relation of state affairs* (6 vols, Oxford, 1857), II, 80, 88.
16 Lyrics to Henry Purcell and Thomas Shadwell, *Now does the glorious day appear* [Birthday Ode for Queen Mary, 1689] (London, 1689).
17 Edmund Bohun, *The character of Queen Elizabeth* (London, 1693); for the histories, see Tony Claydon, *The revolution in time: chronology, modernity, and 1688–1689 in England* (Cambridge, 2020), pp. 225–33.
18 Cynthia Herrup, 'The king's two genders', *Journal of British Studies*, 45:3 (2006), 493–510.
19 For William's martial masculinity in this period, see Julie Farguson, *Visualising Protestant monarchy: ceremony, art, and politics after the Glorious Revolution (1689–1714)* (Woodbridge, 2021), p.133–9; and Owen Brittan, 'The print depiction of King William III's masculinity', *The seventeenth century*, 33:2 (2018), 273–90.
20 Isaiah 49:23.
21 Gilbert Burnet, *An essay on the memory of the late queen* (London, 1695).
22 Lois G. Schwoerer, 'Images of Queen Mary II', *Renaissance Quarterly*, 42:4 (1989), 717–28.
23 Farguson, *Visualising protestant monarchy*, pp.129–30.
24 Lois Schwoerer, 'The queen as regent and patron', in R. Maccubbin and M. Hamilton-Phillips eds, *Age of William III and Mary* (Williamsburg VA, 1988); John Dixon Hunt 'The Anglo-Dutch garden', in Dale Hoak and Mordechai Feingold eds, *The world of William and Mary* (Stanford, 1996), pp.188–200. For contemporary comment on the magnificence of Mary's porcelain collection, see Christopher Morris ed, *The illustrated journeys of Celia Fiennes* (London, 1982), pp.240–1.
25 R. Doebner ed, *Memoires of Mary, queen of England (1689–1693)* (London, 1886).
26 Tony Claydon, *William III and the godly revolution* (Cambridge, 1996), pp.95–8.
27 Mary II, *Her majesties gracious letter to the justices of the peace* (London, 1691); *By the king and queen, a proclamation against vicious, debauched, and profane persons* (London, 1691).

28 These eventually emerged as 'Injunctions given by the king's majesty to the archbishops of this realm', printed in Gerald Bray, *The anglican canons 1529–1947* (Woodbridge, 1988), pp.830–5. For the process, see Claydon, *William III and the godly revolution*, p.173.
29 For the balance of these narratives, see Tony Claydon, 'Protestantism, universal monarchy and Christendom in the William's war propaganda, 1689–1697', in David Onnekink and Esther Mijers eds, *Redefining William III: the impact of the king-stadholder in international context* (Aldershot, 2007), pp.125–42; Tony Claydon, *Europe and the making of England, 1660–1760* (Cambridge, 2007), pp.152–91.
30 Richard Lucas, *A sermon preached at the assizes held at Horsham in the county of Sussex. August 23d. 1691* (London, 1691), pp. 18–19.
31 Claydon, *William III and the godly revolution*, pp.134–47.
32 Simon Thurley, 'The building of the King's Apartments', in *The King's apartments: Hampton Court Palace*, special issue of *Apollo Magazine*, 140:390 (1994), 10–21.
33 Stephen Brogan, *The royal touch in early modern England: politics, medicine and sin* (Woodbridge, 2015), pp.184–5.
34 For example, the report in the *London Gazette*, 2816 (3–7 November 1692).
35 There is more on William's disappointing the Whigs in Mark Goldie, 'Revolutionary justice and Whig retribution in 1689', in Brian William Cowan and Scott Sowerby eds, *The state trials and the politics of justice in later Stuart England* (Martlesham, 2021), pp.179–203.
36 W.A. Speck, 'Spencer, Robert, second early of Sunderland', *Oxford dictionary of national biography*, https://www.oxforddnb.com (Accessed 25/04/23); J.P. Kenyon, *Robert Spencer, earl of Sunderland* (London, 1958), p.251.
37 W.L. Sachse, *Lord Somers: a political portrait* (1975); 'John, baron Somers', *Oxford dictionary of national biography*, https://www.oxforddnb.com (Accessed 25/04/23).
38 Henry Horwitz, *Revolution politicks: the career of Daniel Finch, second earl of Nottingham* (Cambridge, 1968), p.146.
39 Perhaps one of the clearest accounts of the campaigns, if the interpretation of motivation and organisation is outdated, is Dennis Rubini, *Court and country, 1688–1702* (London, 1967).
40 From some of the earliest debates in the convention, the influence of papists at court was identified as the cause of England's disastrous history in the seventeenth century, see Anchitell Grey, *Debates in the house of commons from 1667 to 1694, collected by A. Gray* (10 vols, London, 1769), X, 26–9.
41 Claydon, *William III and the godly revolution*, pp.210–15.
42 Claydon, *William III and the godly revolution*, pp.206–7.
43 Letter from Henry Sidney to earl of Suffolk, 29 June 1691, *Calendar of State Papers Domestic, 1690–1*, p.428.
44 Grey, *Debates of the house of commons*, X, 376.
45 *Journals of the House of Commons Vol 11, 1693–97*, p.74.
46 Henry Horwitz, 'The East India trade, the politicians, and the constitution, 1689–1702', *Journal of British Studies*, 17:2 (1978), 1–18.
47 William Pettigrew, 'Free to enslave: politics and the escalation of Britain's trans-Atlantic slave trade, 1688–1714', *William and Mary Quarterly*, 64:1 (2007), 3–38.
48 A strong case for the 1690s being the vital stage in the development of the state was put by John Brewer, *The sinews of power: war, money, and the English state* (London, 1989), though other works stress the 1650s as more significant.
49 There is a good summary of the fiscal and financial developments in Anne L. Murphy, 'The financial revolution and its consequences', in Roderick Flood, Jane Humphries, and Paul A. Johnson eds, *The Cambridge economic history of modern Britain, vol 1* (Cambridge, CUP, 2014), pp.32–43.

7 The loss of the army, 1698
Challenges and defeats for William after the Glorious Revolution

He had to be persuaded out of it. After the House of Commons had voted to reduce the English army to only seven thousand men in the autumn of 1698, William talked about abdication, or at least retiring to the Netherlands and leaving his British and Irish subjects to their own devices.[1] He had wanted to command a much larger force, because he viewed France as a continuing threat, despite the peace of Ryswick in September 1697 that had ended the war with Louis. Parliament had snubbed this royal desire, and this left the king feeling betrayed and ignored. His legislature had rejected his analysis of the European situation; it had suggested he could not be trusted at the head of any effective military force; and it had seemed to repudiate the whole thrust of his career since 1672 – that he must lead resistance to a France which was intent on imposing itself on all other nations. To add insult to all this injury, legislators had insisted that the Dutch Guard be sent back to the Netherlands, despite the king's personal appeals for them to stay, and his evident affection for 'A Regiment who had faithfully attended his Person from his Cradle'.[2] This was, perhaps, William's greatest political defeat. In his anger and depression he declared himself 'unkindly used' and he doubted his future as king of England.[3] Fortunately, he retained supporters who talked him round. John Somers, still the king's chief minister (though his Whig government had itself been shaken by the Commons revolt), convinced him the situation might be salvaged. Abdication, Somers doubtless pointed out, would leave William with no sway over the Stuart realms, and this was surely worse than his current state of merely reduced influence.[4] The king therefore reconsidered, but it had been a close-run thing. Explaining how William had reached such a desperate pass, especially so soon after his triumph at Namur, will balance our appreciation of his rule in the 1690s. For all the skill and success that had led to military victories, the king had made mistakes, and not all circumstances had been favourable to him.

The immediate reason for William's defeat had been that peace of 1697. England had ceased its war with France, so the need for a large military force had evaporated: at least in the minds of many of the king's subjects. Given the domestic political cost of the treaty, and William's obvious conviction that

DOI: 10.4324/9781003267621-8

Louis was still a danger, we might ask why he had agreed to a settlement. Exhaustion is the best answer. The stadhouder-king's military mobilisation of the Netherlands, of the Stuart realms, and of his allies across Europe had been impressive, but it had not been without huge monetary and human cost. The economies of the Dutch, the British, and the Irish were all heavily dependent on international trade; and this had been disrupted by the threat of French action on the seas, and by an agreed boycott of commerce with France. Taxes had been raised successfully across all William's territories, but their impact had been considerable, particularly as they bore heavily on an agricultural sector that was also suffering a string of poor harvests in the depths of Europe's 'Little Ice Age'. When the tragedy of bloodshed on the battlefield was added to all this financial loss, a weariness with war inevitable – especially as the two sides had fought each other to a standstill. Despite some advances by the French in the early 1690s, and by the Grand Alliance in the mid 1690s, the front in Flanders had not really moved much, and it soon became likely that any final settlement would be close to the status quo antebellum. The combatants appeared to acknowledge this from remarkably early in the conflict. A series of contacts began to explore possibilities for peace as soon as 1692, and the campaigning seasons of both 1694 and 1696 had been restrained because of active negotiations.[5] By the winter of 1696–7, Louis and William seemed ready to deal on who would control which parts of Flanders, though other issues - such as France's occupation of the city of Orange, her hosting of the Jacobite court, and Austria's reluctance to settle with some war objectives unachieved – delayed a final settlement till the following autumn. When peace came, it was widely welcomed on both sides. This had been England's longest running conflict since Elizabeth I's war with Spain, a hundred years before.[6]

Peace might therefore have seemed sensible and desirable in 1697, but it transformed William's political position. To start, it undermined the ideological justification for his rule. Much of his propaganda had focussed on his military exploits: much of it was now rendered obsolete. Without war, there could be no inspiring courage on the battlefield, and no dramatic presentation of ideal elite masculinity. Without war, the glamour of leading an international alliance faded away. In the Stuart realms, those who had been loyal to William for fear of a return of the Catholic and absolutist James II, now had less reason to rally round, since the treaty with France included a promise by Louis not to support the restoration of the exiled king. Underpinning many of these shifts was a loss of providential legitimation. William had countered questions about how he had come to the throne in 1688–9 with claims that he was the God-appointed protector of true religion. He was, his regime had asserted, the head of a holy crusade against a persecuting France that was expanding into Protestant territories in Europe and that was trying to hoist a papist ruler back onto the Stuart thrones. William was also, it had been claimed, the head of a pious and virtuous court that had led a godly rearmament in England and so had brought God's blessing on the armed struggle. Without war, many of these claims to be the champion of the reformation collapsed. Doubts about

William's right to rule might resurface, and some may have reflected more deeply that this was a monarch appointed by the nation, who should respect the will and welfare of the people as expressed in Parliament, rather than acting as if he had a mandate from heaven.

Peace thus hampered a propaganda which had been centred on a divine mission. But it also restructured the substance of political debate in ways that made William's Protestantism less relevant to the concerns of the day. As we saw, the controlling narrative of Stuart debate had been the fear of popery at court. This had eased William on to the throne, and had then secured him there, since his rule seemed the best guarantee against Catholic influence. But with the end of the conflict, another set of concerns emerged, against which the king had no strong defence. At the most prosaic level, there was anxiety about the cost of post-war government. Taxes were, many felt, crippling; and the level of national debt was terrifying. Much of the public, and a clear majority of MPs, therefore felt state expenditure must be radically reduced, and disbanding an expensive army was the swiftest way to do this. Yet cost was only part of the concern. In the pamphlets that fed widespread discontent with the military, there was a subtle analysis of what was presented as a new kind of danger to English liberty, posed by a new kind of rule. Since this did not centre on a threat of popish corruption at court, William's careful cultivation of himself as the antidote to such corruption became useless.

Before we look at the detailed content of this opposition case, it is also worth noting another dimension of its threat. The press campaign against the army represented an emerging kind of politics, in which direct appeals were made to a reading public. Party disagreements had fed the ferment of published opinion, and from 1695, pamphlet polemic had been further encouraged by the lapse of prepublication censorship (to some extent because there was not enough consensus between Whigs and Tories about which views should be censored, and who the censor should be).[7] An already vigorous press was thus freed from the need to have its content approved by officials before printing, and the result was a culture of open debate. As we have suggested, this was not necessarily a disaster for William. He had proved himself adept at pitching himself to readers: in the Netherlands, in his manifesto for the 1688 invasion, and in his subsequent propaganda promoting his rule and his war. Yet the developments in print also allowed sustained pressure by those opposed to the court. A series of pamphlets, intellectually coherent and coordinated with each other, fed directly into parliamentary action. William had fallen victim to the first effective mobilisation of public opinion in the post-censorship age.[8]

The arguments of the anti-army writers rested on a view of long-term historical processes. In the old feudal world, they suggested, England's power structures had been in a 'Gothick' balance. Medieval kings had had their prerogatives, but their effective authority had been limited by the independence of aristocrats who had raised and commanded most of the country's armed forces; and by a freeholding class who had been recruited as troops, but had served, broadly, voluntarily. Over time, however, this balance had eroded. Since the renaissance – and as society had become more luxurious, commercial, and sophisticated – fewer freeholders had been willing to take time out from their economic lives to serve in armies; and aristocrats had tended to cluster at court, dependant on the king, rather than managing their estates and leading their communities. As a result, the checks on the executive had weakened. A military structure, which had relied on the monarch gaining consent from the people, was replaced by professional and standing forces. Such armies would not resist ambition for greater authority by the court. Soldiers were paid by that court, and they had no interests outside their own military livelihood to defend. These processes had been working themselves out across Europe for a couple of centuries, and they explained the increasing prevalence on the continent of absolutist regimes, backed by powerful armies.[9] England had at first resisted the trend. Elizabeth, a benevolent queen, had been reluctant to impose the burdens of an army on her people; and then the early Stuarts had been so politically incompetent that they had raised rebellion against their schemes of absolutism before they got a chance to strengthen their state. Under Cromwell, however, the danger of a military dictatorship had stood starkly revealed. And in the following decades, the expansions of armies under Charles II, under James II, and now, under William, showed that the continental disease was crossing the Channel. English freedom was being lost because the capacity of Englishmen to resist the coercive power of their government was endangered. An urgent disbandment of the army was the only solution.[10]

William's supporters had counterarguments, and themselves went to print to put them. In particular, the king's chief minister, Somers, pointed out that there was no way to reverse the deep social changes on which the anti-army critique rested; and that it was not realistic to return to feudal structures when England's international rivals had modern militaries. Instead, he argued, a professional standing army could be made safe if its funding relied on parliamentary approval (this was effectively the position in the 1690s – the Commons had voted all the money for the war). In this way, Somers suggested, the spokesmen for the people, and the defenders of their liberties, would be in charge.[11] But his opponents had an answer for this. Armies, they said, cast such a wide penumbra of influence that too many ordinary folk, and too many of their representatives, would fall under that shadow. Having much to lose if the army were restricted, MPs would be unwilling to vote down its power. Armies, after all, were huge customers for people's goods, in the form of food, horses, armaments, uniforms, buildings, and so on. Armies also employed vast numbers of people: not only as troops, but as bureaucrats engaged in logistical support, or as tax collectors gathering the funds to pay the soldiers' wages. Again, armies ran at a financial deficit: in the 1690s tens of thousands had lent money to finance William's forces, and these creditors would now be nervous of criticising the system if it might endanger repayment. Attacks on the military thus widened into a wholesale criticism of the fiscal-military state that had grown up since 1689. It now, some hinted, posed a greater threat to the liberties of Englishmen than the foreign foes all these fiscal and military structures had been raised to resist.[12]

It is perhaps already obvious what a catastrophe for William the emergence of this set of arguments was. He had built a reputation opposing an expansionist France, a persecuting popery, and a line of Stuart rulers who had made too free a use of royal prerogative. But this new rhetoric identified none of these forces as the real problem. The danger to English liberties was no longer a corrupt and ambitious court, fired by Catholicism, and driven to excesses by theories of French-style monarchical absolutism. It was, instead, the whole state system that posed the threat. The driving force was not the faith or political ideology of particular rulers, but the deep cultural, economic, and social change that had tipped the balance towards the executive and away from ordinary subjects. Illustrating how little old religious concerns mattered in this new analysis, one of the leading writers against the army explicitly said they should have no weight. Complaining that state power was driving all to subservience, either John Toland or Walter Moyle (for they cowrote the pamphlet) pointed out that with tyranny 'Protestant and Popish are both alike, and if I must be a Slave, it is very indifferent to me who is my Master.'[13] Worse than this bypassing of William's established image, was the fact that he could be seen as the cause of what had gone wrong. It had only been in the 1690s, on his watch, and in pursuit of his war with France, that the state had expanded so rapidly, polemicists suggested. Most of the pamphleteers were polite about the king when they wrote about him explicitly. They reassured readers they were sure William himself would not use the executive's new influence for evil purpose. But they were attacking a major institution – the army – which William had built and wished to retain; other elements of their analysis pointed to things that had developed most rapidly under the king's rule; and some dated the dramatic deepening of the problem to 1689.[14] William lost the standing army debate to a large degree because it occurred in a new rhetorical universe, and one in which he was ill-equipped to engage.

In some important ways, William had been a victim of his own triumph. The shifts in the framing of political argument had been the result of things he had achieved or encouraged. He had, for instance, been relaxed about a vigorous press, perhaps believing he could intervene effectively in print debate. Similarly, the decline in concern about court popery had resulted, to a large extent, from the unimpeachable Protestantism of his household and policies. Again, the new anxiety about the state had largely arisen because he had had unprecedented success in mobilising and organising the nation's resources for war. All this, however, was scant comfort to the king in his despair at losing a large army; and not all the sentiment against William was a flip side of his achievements. Resentments had been building before the treaty of Ryswick, and not just as consequences of that peace. To understand this, we will have to go back to resurvey the whole period since 1689, looking this time, less at the king's skills and advantages, and more at his weaknesses and mistakes.

Part of William's problem in the 1690s was that he had had no great successes in his other realms to balance growing discontent in England. The Netherlands had remained committed to the war against Louis; but the provinces did feel the strain of the military effort, and the fact that William was usually absent from The Hague began to foster a republican sense that the Dutch could run their affairs without close supervision from the house of Orange-Nassau. The celebrations of 1691 proved to be the pinnacle of popular enthusiasm for the stadhouder – it soon declined; and as we shall see, the Dutch did not see a need to replace William in his offices when he died in 1702.[15] Scotland and Ireland had not provided a serious threat to the king's rule after the battle of the Boyne, and working through their parliaments had allowed William to avoid outright rupture with their elites. However, this basic achievement had perhaps encouraged a neglect of the non-English kingdoms on the monarch's part, which soured relations with London, and magnified internal tensions in both countries. William never did go to Scotland, and he never returned to Ireland after 1690. This left him ruling through proxies who failed to demonstrate the skills of accommodation and cooperation that the king showed in Westminster, and his absence meant he was insensitive to the popular moods, and ignorant of the details of problems, in Dublin and Edinburgh. In the eyes of many of his subjects outside England, William knew rather little about their concerns, and cared even less. If we examine his approach to his northern and western kingdoms in a bit more detail, it is hard not to conclude these people were right.

The historian Allan McInnes has pointed to political and confessional grounds for the common modern perception that William's rule had been a 'disaster for Scotland'.[16] The nation's Catholic community – which lost its champion when James VII (as he was there) fled from Westminster – has had obvious reasons to think ill of the Dutch ruler; and supporters of Scottish independence tend to denounce everything that happened in the years before union with England in 1707. Nonetheless, it is undeniable that William's rule of his northern realm was unhappy. The fundamental problem with his not being in Edinburgh was that he had to appoint a team of ministers to run the country for him – and in a highly factionalised polity, there were not enough rewards of office to win over enough of the elite to ensure stability. If one group gained power, all their factional rivals united against them. As a result, the opposition found it could cause endless misery for the ministry in a Parliament that had become far more influential since the abolition of the Lords of the Articles (considered in the last chapter). The situation bred ceaseless, and perhaps maliciously overheated, political turmoil. This was particularly true in the aftermath of two famous missteps of government in the years before 1697, mistakes which stoked deep resentment at William's rule.[17]

The first catastrophe was the Glencoe massacre. The background here was that Jacobite rising that William had suffered in Scotland in the immediate aftermath of his elevation to the throne. The forces of the loyal government in Edinburgh may have crushed Dundee's immediate rebellion against the new regime, but the Highlands, from which he had recruited most of his troops, remained discontented. These tensions, disastrously, fed into established clan rivalries. Whilst some alignments upheld William's rule (notably the Campbells who controlled much of south-western Scotland), others still felt the pull of allegiance to James. Resistance thus rumbled on till a truce of July 1691, which gave anyone still in arms for the exiled king a period until the start of 1692 to swear support for new government, or to face extirpating consequences. Many Jacobite clans scrambled to comply. But the MacDonalds of Glencoe missed the deadline by a few days. In response, William's Scottish Secretary of State, William Dalrymple (who wanted to eliminate a group of potential troublemakers, and to prove his loyalty after a career which had included service to James), manoeuvred to have the monarch in London condemn those who had been late. Pursuing this policy, Dalrymple made use of clan enmities. Following the Secretary's lead, soldiers of the earl of Argyll, the head of the Campbells, slaughtered over thirty MacDonalds in the Glencoe valley, despite the troops having been their victims' guests for several days beforehand. Although the numbers involved were modest by the standards of seventeenth century conflict, the massacre became, and has remained, a symbol of treachery and brutality.[18] A Victorian monument now marks the site of the slaughter, just off the A82 highway; and even in 1692 politicians in Edinburgh exploded in anger. Some of this wrath was generated by genuine horror of what had occurred; some of it was synthetic, fired by hopes among factional opponents of using the incident against Dalrymple. The king eventually had to set up an enquiry, which reported in 1695.[19] When it did so, it led both to the dismissal of the Secretary of State, and uncomfortable questioning of William's role in the whole affair.

By the time the Glencoe commission finished its work, a second Scottish debacle was brewing. The context here was perceived weaknesses in the economy. Scotland had not been as prosperous as many other European states in the early modern period, and contemporary analysis insisted this was due to limits on its trade, and its failure to develop an overseas empire. Scottish commentators warned that English navigation acts frustrated mercantile activity by barring Scottish ships from carrying goods to and from England's colonies, and that the Scots were missing opportunities because they had not managed to establish significant trading bases outside Europe. In 1695, a group of merchants attempted to solve these problems. They secured a charter from the Edinburgh Parliament, which incorporated them as a company to manage Scotland's long distance commercial activities (in particular, a scheme to set up a trading post at Darien in Central America). This allowed them to raise funds from the Scottish public as they promised investors a share in any future profits from the enterprise. The initiative was initially successful: very large sums flowed in. Yet the scheme rapidly ran into trouble. The London East India Company protested at supposed breaches of their trading privileges; and William himself was concerned about the geopolitical implications. Darien was on the territory of his ally, Spain – and Spain was outraged at what it saw as the illegal settlement of its empire by foreigners. A trading post, New Edinburgh, was eventually founded on the isthmus of Panama. Yet incompetence, disease, Spanish hostility, and a total lack of support from England led to its surrender to Spain troops within eighteen months. Two thousand Scots died, and much of the nation's liquid capital, which had been attracted to the project the initial mood of reckless euphoria, was lost.[20]

The failure of the Darien scheme is usually interpreted as an important cause of the 1707 union between England and Scotland. William himself began to think a full incorporation of the two kingdoms, under one Parliament, was the only way to prevent maverick initiatives – and this logic would triumph under his successor, Anne. At the same time, significant tranches of Scottish opinion began to assess the possible advantages of gaining a united 'British' empire, exploiting English resources for Scottish benefit after a merger of the two realms.[21] It is true that this was all in the future when the king was considering abdication. The full folly of the Darien escapade had not fully emerged by 1698: the trading post was only established in that year, and it was not abandoned till 1700. However, William's failure to stop Scotland's imperial shenanigans was already obvious when the English House of Commons attacked his army; and so was the raw resentment of Scots that their king was so hostile to a project that they conceived as their national economic salvation. None of this can have helped the king's mood as he considered his future in the wake of the English vote to disband his forces.

Ireland was perhaps calmer once its own initial Jacobite rebellion had been quelled, but William's rule there was little source of comfort to him as he pondered his prospects at the end of 1698. He had established decent relations with the Dublin Parliament, and his delegated government was more stable than the ones in Edinburgh. But the price had been painful compromises with the Protestant elites who dominated the legislature. These compromises stored up anger in the majority Catholic population; and they had run counter to the king's preferred policies. The problems centred on the treaty of Limerick. As we saw in the last chapter, William had purchased a rapid end to the war in the west of Ireland by offering generous terms to those still in arms against him, and those under their protection. But the treaty had to be ratified by the Irish legislature, and the Protestants' fears of Catholics (who in truth had not always treated them well during the 1689–91 rebellion) blocked this. The government did not dare introduce a bill to embody the treaty in the 1692 Parliament, and when, later, it finally did try to get a statute passed, it had to sit by as lawmakers butchered the text. By the time all was confirmed, in 1697, significant parts of the original agreement – the famous 'lost clauses of Limerick' – had been expunged. The protections for Catholic property were weakened; the numbers of people who could benefit from William's promises had been slashed to only those still actively fighting when the war ended; and the prospect of freedom of Catholic worship had gone.[22] The last deletion was particularly heinous as it allowed the Dublin Parliament to begin passing the schedule of 'Penal Laws' against adherents of the Roman faith, which would remain grievances through the eighteenth century. In 1695, Catholics were forbidden to bear arms, or send their children abroad for education, or own houses worth more than five pounds in rental a year. In 1697, all Catholic bishops were exiled from the country, along with all monks, Jesuits, and friars. If we were right that horror of persecution was at the heart of William's religiosity, he cannot have welcomed these provisions; and he must have felt the disgrace and dishonour of being forced back on his promises to his Catholic subjects. Ireland, along with Scotland, fed the sense of failure the king felt as he lost his army in Westminster votes.

And even the situation in England had not been as reassuring for William in the war years as his triumphs in handling party and Parliament might suggest. Although he had got consent for his campaigns against Louis from the majority of the political nation, there had been complaint about his rule: some continued to reject it altogether. Through the 1690s, an underground Jacobite movement had plotted a return of the exiled king. It had planned a series of uprisings that were to be coordinated with French invasion attempts, so that foreign troops would land in a nation in turmoil. It is true these attempts had all been foiled, often infiltrated by Williamite agents; and they had suffered from Louis XIV's scepticism about the strength of English Jacobite forces. The French ruler did not think it worth sending help unless James's supporters could show they could rebel in numbers – but very few people in England would act for the cause without a guarantee of French protection. Sometimes, too, Jacobite conspiracy was counterproductive. The failure of a 1696 plot to assassinate William as he returned from a hunting trip had rallied opinion around the king, just at the point that war weariness had been making him and his government unpopular. More generally, the steady diet of treason in the news had consolidated the regime's political position. Notwithstanding all this, however, Jacobitism had been a concern. It had elicited a security crackdown that had alarmed those worried about English personal liberties (partly why there had been that campaign to regulate treason trials which formed part of the parliamentary tension with the court); and elements of a Jacobite propaganda campaign had skilfully exploited and stoked discontents with the government.[23]

Evading the regime's censorship had proved fairly easy for its opponents. Declarations by James, laying out his approach to a future restoration of his authority, had circulated widely in 1692 and 1693 (though, being attempts at successful politics by that hopeless king, they had undermined each other by varying wildly in approach).[24] Beyond these royal statements, and throughout William's reign, works by Jacobites had appeared regularly, sometimes setting the political agenda. Often this was because they disguised the ultimate motivation of their authors, and instead concentrated on lambasting the court without openly calling for the return of James. They therefore stirred up discontent, without reminding audiences of the disastrous years of the exiled monarch's actual reign. A prime example was the 1693 'hush money paper'.[25] Written by the Charlwood Lawton, an advocate of Stuart restoration, this suggested the king's ministers were bribing MPs, and led to loud calls for investigation when the Commons next met. Other themes in the Jacobite literature also caught the popular mood, at least at particular moments. There is a strong case that James's supporters pioneered the critique of the infrastructural power of the Williamite state, which we saw was central to attacks upon the army in the late 1690s; and surveying their other lines of argument from the start of the decade gives a good sense of the public relations challenge facing William all through his rule in England.[26]

Xenophobia was a promising line of attack. The English may have been relieved by William's arrival in 1688, but it had also been humiliating to have to be rescued from popery and arbitrary power by a foreign prince: a sentiment that the joint monarchy, with its prominent role for the English Mary, was designed to soothe. Moreover, William was not just foreign, he was Dutch. The Netherlands and England might have shared Protestantism as a faith, and they may have shared a sense of threat from France as a key feature of their politics, but they were also trading, imperial, and ideological rivals. Differences so severe that they had led to war three times in the recent period between the 1650s and early 1670s. Worse, the circumstances of the 1690s war stoked suspicion. England was being heavily taxed, but most of the military action that this money supported took place in Flanders. The English-financed troops were therefore primarily defending the United Provinces, rather than England herself, so it was too easy to see William as a Dutch infiltrator, syphoning off English resources to defend his homeland at little cost to that country. William's own itineraries, spending long periods of each summer out of England, among his Dutch soldiers and consulting Dutch politicians, encouraged this suspicion; and Jacobite authors did all they could to fan it. A fine example was the pamphlet *The people of England's grievances*, printed around 1693. Historians have debated who the author might have been, but tone of the attack on William's whole policy strongly suggests that a supporter of James was responsible. The work was a systematic savaging of Dutch influence in England. It blamed economic dislocation, arbitrary judicial action, military defeat, heavy taxation, and a catalogue of other ills on men from the Netherlands who had the king's ear. As the author summarised pithily 'Dutch counsels and Dutch measures of acting are the true source of all these mischiefs.'[27]

The notion of false councils opened another theme in Jacobite polemic. This was an attack on favourites. Here, again, William's own actions had not helped him. We have noted that he relied on the company and the advice of a small circle, and that he became very close only to a very limited number of individuals. One of these had been Hans Bentinck, his childhood friend from the Netherlands, and this relationship continued once William was in England. Bentinck was given an English title – the earl of Portland – and served as the king's Groom of the Stole. This was the court office that allowed the most intimate attendance on the monarch: traditionally, the Groom lived in apartments which intersected with those of the king, saw the monarch daily, was frequently a close advisor, and carried out errands that required the highest trust and confidentiality. Bentinck stepped easily into all these roles after the revolution. In fact, his appointment really just gave an official English recognition to functions he had performed for William in the Netherlands for some years. In return for these services, the king gave many rewards. Portland had a huge influence at the heart of government and soon started to pick up material benefits. In 1695, William gave him such extensive estates west of Offa's Dyke that a pamphlet came to dub him a 'Dutch prince of Wales'.[28] Wider press reaction to all this was hostile, and much of it fanned by Jacobites. As the historian David Onnekink has shown, authors developed an existing rhetoric which had lambasted favourites of the monarchs to accuse Portland of arrogance, greed, social ambition, and corruption; and they then added the spice of xenophobia.[29] If the Netherlands was trying to exploit England, Bentinck, it was alleged, was its chief agent.

The examples of criticism we have cited were from Jacobite sources, but they inspired similar complaints across a broad spectrum of opinion. Anti-Dutch sentiment, and concern at the king closeting himself with a small group of advisors, was expressed in the non-Jacobite press, and in wider society. Comment in Parliament on these issues was perhaps most damaging, because it could come dangerously close to questioning why MPs were voting funds for William's war. Starting remarkably early in the 1690s, debates in the Commons expressed anger about the number of Dutchmen among the king's advisors; the drain of cash from England to Flanders; the fact that English troops were commanded and frequently sent to their deaths by foreign generals; and the pensions and lands that had been granted to non-natives by William.[30] There were also complaints about corrupt advisors around the king. Such men, it was charged, were lining their own pockets, and were advocating policies which facilitated their plunder, rather than considering the national good.[31] Inevitably, Bentinck's role came under scrutiny as these two rhetorics combined. The backbencher Sir Thomas Clarges, who was a leader of anti-court sentiment, brought the issues together in an intervention on 9 December 1692 (English dating). He observed that England was paying for the war, rather than the Netherlands, even though the English had been drawn into the conflict by the Dutch provinces, and even though England had far less interest in the outcome of the battles in Flanders. 'These things', Clarges darkly observed, 'are occasioned by having one of the Dutch states in your council.'[32]

Another Jacobite accusation brings us back to issues of William's personal relationships, and perhaps our understanding of his masculinity. It again centred on Bentinck, and was the suggestion that William was homosexual. Playing on William's extraordinary closeness to his Groom of the Stole, and later, on his connection to the handsome courtier Arnold Joost van Keppel (who had worked his way up from the position of page in the king's household, and who came to displace the earl of Portland in the king's affections by 1697), Jacobites asserted that there was only one explanation for the hold these gentlemen had on the monarch. William was, they charged, sleeping with his favourites. For example, Robert Ferguson, in a pamphlet damning Dutch influence in England, spiced up his complaints about Bentinck's influence over the king with talk of 'privacies which I blush to mention'.[33] The author of an outrageous Jacobite pamphlet detailing supposed sexual misconduct at court presented William's supposed mistress, Elizabeth Villiers, declining to come to the royal bed – but instead suggesting Bentinck perform her services.[34] Similarly, verse satire had the king and his favourite as Italian lovers (homosexuality being seen as a vice imported from other countries, almost always, and almost everywhere). Authors expressed astonishment that 'a Low Country stallion, and a Protestant Prince should prove an Italian'; or that 'Billy with Benting does play the Italian'.[35]

Was this anything more than smear? It would be fascinating to know but – as with many other English monarchs accused of same sex attractions through the centuries (Edward II; James VI and I; Queen Anne) – the evidence is murky. Of course, the political motivation and potential bias of Jacobite charges are clear, but that does not mean they were spun from no facts at all. William's relations with Bentinck and Keppel were extraordinarily close. When the former was displaced by the latter in the king's favour, Bentinck wrote to his friend to warn him that he was doting so much on Keppel that it was giving rise to rumours of sodomitical practice. These were, Bentinck warned, starting to circulate well beyond the usual malicious suspects.[36] Similarly, Gilbert Burnet, summarising William's character some years after his death, praised his hero but admitted his two favourites had had a mysterious hold over him.[37] Even more circumstantially, the author of this present book has not been alone in finding Verrio's decoration of the ceiling of the Little Bedchamber at Hampton Court highly homoerotic. Yet absolute proof of homosexual activity on William's part slips endlessly through the historian's fingers. We could dismiss Bentinck's observation as the bitter and distorted reaction of a disappointed man; and Burnet did not speculate further on relations with Bentinck and Keppel. William's personal correspondence with his two favourites expressed affection, but nothing beyond what we might expect when people had become close friends and political allies; and as David Onnekink has pointed out, there had been no rumours of William's homosexuality in the Netherlands, or before the revolution gave Jacobites reason to sling mud.[38] The king did stay up late into the night with both of his possible lovers, but there is no way to ascertain what was happening when he did. Maybe there were trysts; maybe there were just lengthy consultations on war strategy and diplomatic dispatches with two trusted allies. In the end we may have to accept that history will never sate our curiosity; and that, at least in political terms, what was really going on may not matter. It was clear Bentinck and Keppel were hugely, perhaps damagingly, influential whether they were sleeping with the king or not. Accusations of homosexual lust were out in public, and they undermined William among those prepared to believe them, whatever their truth.

Far clearer in any account of the king's personal relations in the 1690s was his devastation at the death of his wife. Mary had fallen ill in late November 1694. By the middle of the next month she had not recovered, and she came to think she was suffering from measles. However, by Christmas, it became clear she had in fact contracted an aggressive case of smallpox, and that she had only a few days to live. She died at Kensington on the 28th (English dating).[39] Her loss threw her spouse into paroxysms of grief so severe that they generated adverse comments in the press – reflections which may have done as much to undermine the king's image of masculinity as the accusations of sodomy.[40] William holed himself in his chamber for weeks. He spoke to even fewer people than usual: though those admitted to his rooms did include Archbishop John Tenison, who had recently replaced John Tillotson in the church's chief clerical office (Tillotson had died only a few weeks earlier) and became a close spiritual advisor.[41] Given William's mental state, it was perhaps fortunate that he did not have to play any prominent role in the magnificent funeral that was planned and staged for his wife. This occurred in March 1695, after a long period of lying in state. It included a huge procession through the streets of London, before a service in Westminster Abbey, for which Henry Purcell's famous musical settings of the prayer-book funeral sentences had been composed. By tradition, the chief mourner for a queen had to be a woman. The duchess of Somerset therefore performed the duty on the day, saving William from a highly public and emotional outing which would probably have been unbearable for him.[42]

The king's reaction was, no doubt, genuine horror at the loss of someone with whom, after a cold and distant start, he had developed a close and effective partnership. Tenison also hinted that William recognised at last that he had not always treated his wife well, and may have seen her death as a punishment for this. Yet his deep mourning was also understandable in political terms. Mary's loss damaged William's rule: not least because it gave the Jacobites new lines of attack. Some writers took the opportunity to rehash objections to the revolution itself. For them, the queen's early death was divine chastisement for a woman who had illegally usurped the power of her father.[43] Similarly, some used the loss of a hereditary Stuart to insist all pretence of legitimacy in the regime had ceased. One called for fresh parliamentary elections, since the body sat at Westminster was clearly *her* Parliament.[44] These assaults were countered by celebrations of the life of Mary from the Williamite press; and in truth, they probably did little to shake anyone who had welcomed the Dutch invasion of 1688–9.[45] But the Jacobites' mischief-making pointed to a real problem. All the work the queen had done for the regime now had to be shifted on to the king alone. William staged an elaborate funeral for his wife, acknowledging the part she had played in his rule, and underlining the challenges he faced without her.

After 1694, William could no longer leave a loyal lieutenant in London during his summer campaigning seasons. At least while the war lasted, the court ceased to be any real kind of social or cultural leader. Work at Hampton

Court, planned as a glorious theatre of power for the new monarchy, paused when the queen died – this architectural grandeur had lost its chief advocate in government. Without his wife, William's natural introversion and hostility to public display tipped over into anti-popular crankiness. It is hard to imagine that Mary would have allowed the cancellation of public celebration (at least in the form of building triumphal arches in London) that occurred when William returned from signing the peace treaty in 1697.[46] It is true that the king attempted to take up the mantles of moral reform and piety from his queen – for example sponsoring the movement for the reformation of manners in speeches and proclamations – but the image of godliness was probably less convincing than when Mary had adopted these roles.[47] William's new self-presentations, when bolted on to his existing depiction as a martial general, created contradictions and gender ambiguities that a division of labour between a royal couple had avoided. And it did not take Jacobite pamphleteers to point out that the regime had taken a stark step away from hereditary tradition. Stuart loyalists – many of whom had been prepared to swallow the post-revolutionary regime because Mary had been part of it – now had far less reason to be enthusiastic. It is noticeable that William's great political defeat in England came after Mary's death, and really quite soon after.

The loss of the queen also weakened her husband's position in a further area where he was attracting serious criticism by the end of 1698: again, an arena in which Jacobites stirred discontent. This was William's governorship of the church. As we saw in the last chapter, Mary had helped hugely in ecclesiastical matters. She had played the lead role in an institution to which she had always belonged, and to which she had always shown great loyalty. Despite this, however, not all church members had been happy. Many fretted that the toleration act had gone too far (a rich and influential dissenting community rapidly emerged from the shadows of persecution in the 1690s). Some worried that the 'latitudinarian' bishops whom the king and queen had appointed were unsound on points of Anglican – even Christian – doctrine (the bishops' commitment to noncoercion of belief seemed to many to have opened them to questioning the church's traditional position on the full divinity of Christ). Others were shocked that large numbers of clergy, including bishops had been heroes of Anglican resistance to James II, had been removed for refusing loyalty to the new regime. Those ejected, or 'nonjuring', clerics included some leading Jacobite writers; and in the early 1690s, they had developed criticisms of William's religious role that became mainstream by the later years of the decade.

The key issue was how far the church should govern its own affairs. Nonjuring clerics had been deprived of their offices under the 'Erastian' principle that monarchs were heads of the Church of England, and that churches should ultimately obey their local lay rulers. Erastianism insisted clergy could not oppose princes, so there could be no place in ecclesiastical institutions for people who could not swear loyalty to the post-revolutionary government. To defend themselves against this principle, and to facilitate protest that their removal had been illegitimate, Nonjurors insisted the church must be independent of royalty. Opposing the Erastian position, they argued that clerics sometimes had to criticise rulers for their sins, or defend the community of the faithful from evil governments; and that to have the freedom to fulfil these duties, Christian ministers must never be beholden to whoever held worldly power. Departing from the old Anglican alliance with the Crown, these nonjuring writers insisted that the English must be an autonomous, and so self-governing, part of society.[48]

These were powerful arguments, and eventually proved attractive beyond the core of nonjuring authors. Those who worried about the novel visibility of dissent, or fretted about an erosion of doctrinal certainly – or, to be frank, those who were disappointed in their own clerical careers since 1689 – nursed resentment at William's approach to religious affairs. These people saw, in the nonjuring case, a way to reduce his influence. Rather than leave the king in control, disaffected priests began to think it better that the church should be directed by its own clergy: men who could be trusted to defend the establishment's true interests. Such sentiments found full expression just as the debate about William's standing army was coming to a head. In 1696, Francis Atterbury, the minister of the Bridewell and Bethlehem hospitals in London, and a superstar preacher, published his *Letter to a convocation man*. This popular and controversial work echoed nonjuring arguments. It insisted that much was going wrong with the contemporary church and demanded that the institution be allowed to tackle this through its own legislative body: convocation. Convocation was a sort of clerical parliament. It was a body elected by the clergy to shape religious law in England, but it was also a body that monarchs had called infrequently because of its tendency to cut across their preferred policy in ecclesiastical affairs. Following the notion that the church must govern itself, Atterbury now insisted convocation had a right to meet every time Parliament met.[49] As Parliament was in session for several months every winter under William, this was a call for a virtually standing body challenging the king's ecclesiastical rule. Given the ugly mood among the majority of Anglican priests, it would be a platform for endless stinging attacks on the king's position: this of course, was precisely why he had not summoned it since 1689.

Jacobite rhetoric had thus stirred wider discontent in yet another arena. Atterbury's pamphlet crystalised demands for the church to seize control of its own affairs, and sparked a wider 'convocation controversy' as writers close to the court penned answers to his work, which then generated reposts of their own. Worse, this dispute gelled with arguments over the standing army to create a wide-ranging opposition to William in Parliament. The front against the army had been led by dissident Whigs. These men, people like the authors of the anti-army pamphlets, had fallen out with the leadership of their party in the mid-1690s, disgusted at the compromises traditional critics of the court had made in order to gain high office and to form the Whig administrations of those later war years. Yet the bulk of the votes against the army had come from Tories. The Tory party was keen to do anything to embarrass the Whig ministers, and it had set itself up as the spokesman of a land-owning class that was paying for an expensive military through its taxes. In addition, however, Tories also saw themselves as defenders of the Anglican church. They therefore took up Atterbury's demands for ecclesiastical self-government, and so forged a throughgoing and broadly based critique of William's rule. Not only did they raise fears of dictatorship through a standing army, but they claimed that the king was overreaching himself by bullying a clergy who must retain an independent moral voice.

Tory discontent with William had further causes. As a party that had its origins in defending Stuart legitimacy, it would always be more susceptible to Jacobite critique than the Whigs, and – having greater sympathy with Mary than William – it would be more detached from the court by the death of the queen than other groups. And there was one more issue. Just as Tories felt a pull of loyalty to Mary, they felt a similar draw to her sister Anne (she was, of course, another direct descendant of the main Stuart line). Unfortunately, however, William fell out with his wife's sibling and allowed her to become the core of a Tory-leaning opposition to him. This was extremely unfortunate, because relations had started well. Anne had supported the revolution, and had participated in the early ceremonies that had cemented it (the offer of the Crown to William and Mary, and the coronation, in the early months of 1689). Her husband, prince George of Denmark, had similarly defected to Dutch forces during the 1688 invasion, and accompanied the king on his 1690 Irish campaign.[50] But things soon soured. This was largely as a result of tensions between the two Stuart princesses, and it perhaps illustrates Mary's influence over her husband. William was usually good at working with those he did not like – if he had to – but in the face of his wife's chagrin, he failed to bridge divisions here.

At the core of the problem was the two women's *amour propre*. Anne seems to have felt unrecognised and neglected by the monarchs. Mary seems to have felt Anne was making demands above her station. The queen was also suspicious of her sister's close relations with Sarah Churchill, the ambitious duchess of Marlborough, whom Mary feared (pretty accurately) was poisoning her royal friend's mind against her for her own advantage. Early tensions came to a head, and they politicised disastrously, when Anne asked for a substantial pension in 1689. The king and queen resisted this, but Tories in Parliament took it up as a cause, eventually securing the princess a sum close to what she had wanted. Mary, in particular, was furious at the outcome. Emotions ran high, and the queen barely spoke to her sister afterwards. In fact, their last face-to-face meeting was in the spring of 1692, nearly two and a half years before Mary died, and even that had only been prompted by the tragic loss of Anne's newborn son. From the pension controversy forward, Anne's 'Cockpit Circle' (named after the part of Whitehall she had originally been granted as apartments) functioned as a sort of rival and opposition court. It flirted with Jacobitism (sending letters to James in France that hinted, probably dishonestly, that Anne might support his restoration in due course); and it acted as a focus for anyone – especially

Tories – discontented with the post-revolutionary regime.[51] After the disasters of James II's reign, the Stuarts gained a reputation for family disunity, which was magnified by the bitterness between Mary and Anne. Under William, internal dynastic disharmony fed into party rivalries, and gave Jacobites another potential route to political influence.

Given this litany of troubles, William's thoughts of abdication at the end of 1698 were understandable. They came at a nadir of his career: Jacobite attacks had reached fruition in multiple areas. By 1698, the king stood condemned as a Dutch alien; as a homosexual; and as a ruler of narrow counsel, holed up with overrewarded favourites. His enemies had hinted he was using the state he had built up to overawe English freedoms; and that he had weakened the church by denying it means to defend itself. He had fallen out with his sister-in-law, and her household had become a potential entry point for James's interests. Beyond all this Jacobite success in England, William was losing support in the Netherlands, and had screwed up his rule of Scotland and Ireland. He had lost Mary, who had been able to deflect some of the attacks upon him; he had lost the army which he thought was essential to his political approach; and he had lost his sense of support from his people. Perhaps, with the end of the war, he had even lost his chief mission in life. Without a crusade against a persecuting hegemon, he may have been far less sure what God's purpose for him was on earth. Perhaps therefore the surprise of 1698 was less that he considered retiring, than that he was talked out of it. The narration of the last years of his life, which saw him regain control of political initiative, must therefore explain how he recovered from a truly dire situation.

Notes

1 William Coxe ed, *Private and original correspondence of Charles Talbot, duke of Shrewsbury* (London, 1821) p.572–3.
2 Abel Boyer, *The history of William the Third in three parts* (3 vols, London, 1702–1703), III, 373.
3 Boyer, *History*, III, 371.
4 Stuart Handley 'Somers, John, baron Somers', *Oxford dictionary of national biography*, https://www.oxforddnb.com (Accessed 25/04/23).
5 M.A. Thompson, 'Louis XIV and William III, 1689–1697', in R. Hatton and W.S. Bromley eds, *William III and Louis XIV: essays 1680–1720* (Toronto, 1968).
6 David Onnekink, *The Anglo-Dutch favourite: the career of Hans Willem Bentinck, 1st Earl of Portland, 1649–1709* (Aldershot, 2007), pp.197–202.
7 R. Astbury, 'The renewal of the licensing act in 1693 and its lapse in 1695, *The Library*, 5th series, 33 (1978), 296–322.
8 The classic study of the dispute is Lois Schwoerer, *No standing armies! The antiarmy ideology in seventeenth-century England* (Baltimore, 1974), ch.8.
9 The case was well summarised in the work that kicked off debate: [John Trenchard and Walter Moyle], *An argument shewing that a standing army is inconsistent with a free government* (London,1697).
10 See, for example, [Andrew Fletcher], *A discourse concerning militias and standing armies* (London, 1697); [John Trenchard], *A short history of standing armies* (London, 1698).

11 John Somers, *A letter balancing the necessity of keeping a land force* (London, 1697).
12 For a longer summary of these arguments, see Tony Claydon, *The revolution in time: chronology, modernity, and 1688–1689 in England* (Oxford, 2020), pp.193–8.
13 [Trenchard and Moyle], *An argument*, p.18.
14 For the sense of 1688–9 as a turning point in opposition rhetoric, see Claydon, *Revolution in time*, pp.198–203.
15 For a summary of the mood in the Netherlands, see Jonathan Israel, *The Dutch republic: its rise, greatness, and fall* (Oxford, 1995), pp.960–8.
16 Allan I. Macinnes, 'William III – "Disaster for Scotland"?', in Esther Mijers and David Onnekink eds, *Redefining William III: the impact of the king stadholder in international context* (Aldershot, 2007), pp. 201–6.
17 Still the best coverage of the opposition is P.W.J. Riley, *King William III and the Scottish politicians* (Edinburgh, 1979).
18 For accounts, see Douglas John Sadler, *Glencoe: the infamous massacre of 1692* (Stroud, Amberley, 2008); Paul Hopkins, *Glencoe and the end of the highland war* (Edinburgh, 1986).
19 For the report, see J. McCormick ed, *State papers and letters addressed to William Carstares* (Edinburgh, 1774), pp.236–54.
20 For a recent account, see Karin Bowie, 'The Darien scheme', *History Today*, 71:12 (2021), 28–39.
21 Various aspects of this are explored in John Robertson ed, *A union for empire: political thought and the British union of 1707* (Cambridge, 1995).
22 Wouter Troost, *William III and the treaty of Limerick, 1691–1697: a study in Irish policy* (Cambridge, 2016).
23 For the plots and reactions to plots, see Rachel Weil, *A plague of informers: conspiracy and political trust in William III's England* (New Haven, 2013).
24 James II, *His majesties most gracious declaration to all his loving subjects commanding their assistance against the prince of Orange* (St Germains, 1692); James II, *His majesties most gracious declaration to all his loving subjects … given 17 April 1693* (St Germains, 1693).
25 The 'hush money paper' was the nickname gained by [Charlwood Lawton], *A short state of our condition with relation to the present parliament* (London,1693) as it became widely discussed.
26 For the role of the Jacobites in ideological innovation in the early 1690s, see Claydon, *Revolution in time*, pp.180–90.
27 *The people of England's grievances offered to be enquired into* (London, [1693?]).
28 [Robert Price], *Gloria Cambriae: or the speech of a bold Briton in parliament against a Dutch prince of Wales* (London, 1702).
29 Onnekink, *The Anglo-Dutch favourite* – for the criticism see ch.7.
30 Claydon, *William III and the godly revolution*, p.124.
31 For example, see Anchitel Grey, *Debates of the house of commons from … 1667 to …1694* (10 vols, London, 1697), IX, 289 – William Garroway in grand committee on supply 2 November 1689; William Cobbett ed, *The parliamentary history of England* (36 vols, London, 1806–20), V, col. 794 – Sir Francis Winnington, debate on the land forces 5 December 1693; Charles Sedley, *The speech of Sir Charles Sedley in the house of commons* (London, 1691).
32 Henry Horwitz ed, *The parliamentary diary of Narcissus Luttrell, 1691–1693* (Oxford, 1972), p.304.
33 [Robert Ferguson], *A brief account of the some of the late incroachments and depredations of the Dutch* ([London],1695).

34 *A dialogue between K.W. and Benting* ([London],1695), p.7.
35 Verse is cited in William James Cameron ed, *Poems on affairs of state: Augustan satirical verse, 1660–1714. Vol. 5 1688–1697* (New Haven, 1971), pp.38, 221.
36 N. Japikse ed, *Correspondentie van Willemen van Hans Willem Bentinck* (The Hague, 1927), XXIII, 198–200.
37 Gilbert Burnet, *Bishop Burnet's history of his own time: volume two* (London, 1734), p.306.
38 Onnekink, *The Anglo-Dutch favourite*, p.189.
39 Tony Claydon and W.A. Speck, *William and Mary* (Oxford, 2007), p.144.
40 Owen Brittan, 'The print depiction of William III's masculinity', *The Seventeenth Century*, 33:2 (2018), 219–39, at 230–1.
41 William Marshall, 'Thomas Tenison', *Oxford dictionary of national biography*, https://www.oxforddnb.com (Accessed 25/04/23).
42 For a description of the funeral, see Francis Sandford and Samuel Stebbing, *A genealogical history of the kings and queens of England* (London, 1707), pp. 719–21.
43 See, for example, [Charles Leslie], *Remarks on some late sermons* (London, 1695), and the works summarised in Claydon and Speck, *William and Mary*, p.145.
44 [Robert Ferguson], *Whether the parliament be in law dissolved* (London, 1695).
45 See, for example, Gilbert Burnet, *An essay on the memory of the late queen* (London, 1695); Thomas Manningham, *A sermon preach'd at the parish church of St Andrew's Holborn ... on the most lamented death of our most gracious soveraign Queen Mary* (London, 1695); Edward Fowler, *A discourse of the great disingenuity and unreasonableness of repining at afflicting providences* (London, 1695).
46 Gilbert Burnet, *Bishop Burnet's history of his own time: volume two* (London, 1734), p.205.
47 *By the king: a proclamation for preventing and punishing immorality and prophaness, given 9 December 1699* (London, 1699); *Journals of the House of Lords Vol 16, 1696–1701*, p.175.
48 Mark Goldie, 'Non jurors, episcopacy, and the origins of the convocation controversy', in Eveline Cruickshanks ed, *Ideology and conspirarcy: aspects of Jacobitism, 1689–1759* (Edinburgh, 1982), pp.15–35.
49 [Francis Atterbury], *A letter to a convocation man concerning the rights, powers and privileges of that body* (London, 1697).
50 For George's role, see Julie Farguson, 'Dynastic politics, international protestantism, and royal rebellion: Prince George of Denmark and the Glorious Revolution', *English Historical Review*, 131:555 (2016), 540–69.
51 Edward Gregg, *Queen Anne* (London, 1980), ch.3.

8 A new hope, 1701
William's recovery at the last years of his reign

It was a final diplomatic and political triumph. On 7 September 1701 (continental dating), the Stuart realms, the Netherlands, and Austria signed the Treaty of The Hague, and so formed a Second Grand Alliance to constrain Louis XIV's aggression. Although there was to be no substantial fighting involving English or Dutch troops until 1702 – by which time William would be dead – his initiative in bringing the allies together would shape British foreign policy through to at least 1713; and it would set his realm on course to become the premier European power. In the War of the Spanish Succession, the name given to the conflict that would dominate the next decade and more, England would become the economic, financial, and military powerhouse of the anti-French cause; she would provide the outstanding military commander of day in the person of John Churchill, the duke of Marlborough; she would accelerate her expansion beyond her home continent; and she would merge with Scotland to form a new united polity of Great Britain. So, whilst a new super-state would only fully emerge in the reign of his William's sister-in-law, Anne, and under her competent leadership, it would be born very much in the king's image. The nation would become pre-eminent as it fought an enemy William had spent his life opposing; and it would do so at the head of a group of other nations which he had brought together.

How the king managed this, after the debacle of the standing army defeat, will be the subject of this last section of this book. Many of its themes will be familiar from what has come before. The explanation will rest on William's determination, on his pragmatism, on his flair for publicity, and on the missteps of his enemies. But the recovery from the failure to retain a standing army in England was still remarkable. In 1698, William's European allies had lost the cause that had held them together, and some were resentful that England had sought peace before all their anti-French objectives had been achieved. In Scotland and Ireland, and to some extent in the Netherlands, there had been complaint about the stadhouder-king, as people away from London felt that their ruler was neglecting them. In England, William had led a country which had largely demilitarised itself; one which was at dangerous odds with its monarch; and one in which the public mood was so opposed to

DOI: 10.4324/9781003267621-9

the effects of war that outside observers must have wondered if it could ever be persuaded to make any significant further effort in geopolitics. Perhaps worse than all of this, there had been no immediate improvement in the king's position after he had lost his English army. If anything, discontent had grown deeper on all fronts as the century had drawn to a close. The king's achievement in nudging everyone back to mobilise again against Louis was therefore astonishing; and to fully understand it, we shall have to start in the same pessimistic mood that dominated the preceding chapter.

There were no fresh catastrophes for William's government in Scotland after the Darien fiasco. Yet we have to remember the political effects of that disaster were working themselves out in the years from 1698 to 1701, and the basic structural problem of Scottish government remained. The duke of Queensbury served as chief minister in this period and had some success using patronage and compromise in holding an administration together. But factions continued to snipe and circle, and an opposition led by the duke of Hamilton whipped up anti-English sentiment to try to lever itself into power. The Scottish parliamentary sessions of 1700 and 1701 accordingly proved almost completely unmanageable. As a result, even William, whose disregard of Scottish affairs was notorious, recognised the state of affairs could not continue. In the last years of his reign, the king came to advocate the solution that was eventually imposed in 1707. Although he had always liked the abstract idea of a full union between England and Scotland, and had thrown it out as a possibility almost as soon as he had become monarch, for most of the 1690s he had tended to think the project would be so controversial that it would distract from his wider aims. By the end of the century, however, William had become convinced that an amalgamation of Britain's parliaments and ministries was the only route out of endless Scottish instability. He encouraged bills in the Westminster assembly to advance the idea. Legislation was defeated in the Commons in 1700, having originally passed the Lords, but the king's pressure created enough momentum that commissioners from the two kingdoms were discussing union by the end of 1702.[1]

Royal government in Ireland, meanwhile, suffered blows highly reminiscent of the Darien controversy. As with Scotland, English politics and English interests interfered with any smooth running of the country, and stoked resentments in a sister kingdom. One issue was the grants of land that William had made to his supporters at the end of his Irish war of 1689–91. The Westminster Commons, in anti-executive mood after the standing army disputes, investigated these gifts and decided they had been an illegitimate use of the prerogative, and a bill to reconfiscate the estates passed in 1700. This was a personal slight to the king (he had given the land to colleagues and favourites – including his close friend, and probably mistress, Elizabeth Villiers – and these people now had to disgorge his generosity); and it exacerbated disputes about Irish property, which had been endemic since the mass transfers from Catholics to Protestants earlier in the century. Worse came in trade policy. The English Parliament wanted to promote England's wool production, and – resentful that this was suffering competition from Ireland – passed the Irish woollens act of 1699. This measure banned Irish exports and so poleaxed one of the western kingdom's few developing industries. William accepted both pieces of legislation because, weakened by his tussle over the standing army, he could not afford to alienate his MPs in London; and because his Whig administration, which had been defeated over troop numbers, lacked the strength to stand against attacks on the court. However, the laws enraged Irish public opinion. The English had legislated in areas that affected Ireland deeply, but without any consultation with the people who would be impacted. In response, many came to agree with the sentiments of William Molyneux's famous tract, *The case of Ireland stated*.[2] This had been written as proposals for the woollens act were starting to circulate at Westminster, and it had argued for an end to Ireland's subordinate status. Molyneux insisted on the full ability of the Dublin Parliament to make policy for its own kingdom; and demanded that Irish ministers should enjoy the confidence of the Irish legislature, rather than being appointed from London. Amid the rancour, William's government in Dublin lost control of legislative sessions in the late 1690s. Many historians would see this souring of the mood as the first steps in the long march of Irish Protestant nationalism through the eighteenth century.[3]

It is true that there were no such dramatic setbacks for William in Dutch politics. The stadhouder cultivated support in regular, if not lengthy, visits; his able lieutenant, Heinsius, kept control of the vital assemblies in the province of Holland and at the states-general in The Hague; and public opinion seems to have broadly followed the William's insistence that France remained a potential problem, against which the Dutch must protect themselves. Yet not everything was rosy. The war had caused considerable economic strain in a trading nation (hardship with which William was identified, if for which he was rarely directly blamed); and the Netherlands' political system, with its decentralised power, continued to facilitate faction. Not everyone was in love with the prince of Orange. Some people felt that the prerogatives of an individual should be restrained in a republic; others probably calculated that their own influence would grow, if only William's could be diminished. In these last years of the prince's life, opposition was most clearly manifest in discussion of succession to the stadhouderships of the southern provinces. William was keen that his relative Johan Willem Frisco, who had taken over as chief executive of Friesland and Groningen in 1696, should inherit his own offices at provincial and federal levels when he died – but the campaign to get this handover recognised as an official policy never gained traction. Regents outside the north kept options open. Orangeism had been dominant in the republic since William had become king of England, but it had never triumphed utterly.[4]

The English situation also deteriorated after the army vote. The mood against any aggressive military policy, and against the Whig ministry that had supported William in his bellicose approach to France, darkened further in the years after 1698. The administration weakened, and then effectively collapsed, as its members resigned in the months following the defeat over troop numbers. The whole group who had managed William's war then found themselves vilified in the press and in Parliament. John Somers, who had been chief minister in the mid-1690s, narrowly escaped impeachment in 1701. He was joined in this judicial peril by his allies Admiral Edward Russell and Charles Montagu. By this stage, vigorous pamphleteering had painted the whole gang as corrupt and ambitious chancers and – worse for William – had reinterpreted their (and his) war as something shameful. The conflict with France was now described less as a necessary defence of the revolution, of Protestantism, and of the nation, than as a scheme to advance factional interests. Particularly in Charles Davenant's brilliant satire *The true picture of a modern Whig* (1700), the party which had been in power through the later war years stood accused of promoting conflict with France solely because it served its selfish purposes. Davenant charged that taxes and credit that had been raised for the military had been siphoned off into private hands; that the Whigs had opposed moves to peace to ensure a continuing flow of money they could embezzle; and that their shrieking about the danger from Louis was being used drown out sober analysis of the true geopolitical situation.[5] This was largely the rough and tumble of partisan rivalry, but it touched William because it questioned his whole anti-French stance since 1689. The full scale of all these problems was revealed in the general election which occurred in the early weeks of 1701. Exploiting resentment at the Whigs and their war, and also feeding on the attacks on William's governance of the church that we covered in the last chapter, a Tory-country alliance gained a majority in the Commons. This alignment was led by Robert Harley. Thus, the man who had headed the attacks on William's standing army, and who might be considered his most dangerous enemy, came to be the most powerful figure in Westminster.[6]

These troubles weakened William in the various countries he led, but they also damaged his whole international position. Though Louis's advances across the continent had been stalled by the 1697 Ryswick settlement, the French king was still a threat, and one situation offered him a chance of a devastating augmentation of power. For decades, the king of Spain, Carlos II, had been expected to die within a few months or years. He had stubbornly defied these predictions, but it was clear that his demise, when at long last it came, would cause an international crisis. Carlos had no heir, and numbers of other dynasts, including the one in Versailles, had claims on his inheritance. And Carlos's estate was vast. He not only ruled Spain, but also southern Italy, the Spanish Netherlands, the Philippines, and the best part of a continent in the American New World. If all this territory fell to France, any hope of containing Louis would be gone. Over half of the Habsburg contribution to the anti-French alliance of 1689–97 would have switched sides; French troops would sit on the borders of the Netherlands; and riches from a vastly augmented French empire would be stupendous. William was aware of this danger – indeed it must have been his continual nightmare – but in the late 1690s he was too weak to threaten the French to try to face it down. Instead, he entered into negotiations with Louis to ensure that France would get some rich prizes on Carlos's death, but that she would not snaffle all of Spain's dominions. These talks resulted in two compromise 'partition treaties': Louis himself had resource problems and was looking for a deal to avoid war. These agreements attempted to forestall conflict by dividing Carlos's lands. Under the terms of the first, in 1698, Spain's empire would go to the six-year-old elector of Bavaria, but France would be compensated with Naples and Sicily. Under the second, in 1700 – a new treaty needed because the Bavarian elector had inconveniently died – France again gained the Italian lands, but the rest of Spain's possessions went to the younger son of the Austrian emperor (in fact, the provisions were more complex than this, with numerous territory swops envisaged after the basic settlement – however, the details of all this are, frankly, impossible for anyone other than a diplomatic trainspotter to remember, and they do not have to detain us here).[7]

As realistic diplomacy, the partition treaties were probably astute. Neither the Stuart realms nor the Netherlands looked strong enough to sustain a new period of warfare to defy France in the immediate aftermath of the Ryswick treaties. Politically, though, they weakened William even further. They alienated his Habsburg allies, Spain and Austria, neither of whom had been consulted in the direct negotiations between William and Louis's agents, and one of whose territories were to be dismembered without its consent. They also caused resentment in England. There was anger that the treaties had been concluded without involvement from Parliament, and Harley's Tory-country alliance complained that they dangerously enhanced French power and French trading opportunities.[8] This lament was hypocritical in the extreme (Harley's group had been demanding peace, but now objected to policies designed to preserve it), but hypocrisy is, sadly, not always a bar to political advantage. The Tory-country block used attacks on the partition treaties to savage Whig enemies whom they claimed had been behind the deals (again dishonest, the Whig ministers had been as far out of the loop as everyone else): supposed misconduct over partition was the meat of the impeachments of 1701.

As if all these insults, failures, and obstructions had not been enough, William's health started to fail in the years after 1698. He had never been a very fit person, as has been recorded in earlier chapters, and he had sacrificed his bodily wellbeing in the hardships of military campaigns. Yet, by the king's late forties, long-term medical problems were causing serious concern. His susceptibility to asthma continued, as did his tendency to fall victim to passing infectious diseases (perhaps exacerbated by the psychological effects of losing his wife, and the viciousness of the personal attacks upon him in gossip and media). Now he also began to suffer from painful swellings in his legs. The resulting immobility must have been purgatory for someone whose performance of masculinity, and whose response to adversity, had always involved vigorous physical action. It also began to have political consequences. William was forced to spend much of the summer of 1701 in Het Loo, his rural retreat in Gelderland, where some of his physicians feared for his life, and where he was cut off from contact with politicians he needed to work with.[9] He was not able to return to London until November that year: this perhaps gave Harley, and other opponents, more room to build their own alliances against him.

The situation for William thus looked grim in many ways in the years from 1698 to 1701. But this chapter started with a diplomatic and political triumph, and we must begin to explain how that was achieved against so many odds. The account could start with the reflection that, in Louis XIV, William had always been fortunate in his chief enemy. Although the French king had been impressive in building his power through his long reign, he had also made a series of mistakes which had benefitted his Dutch rival, consolidating popular opinion and international alliances around the prince of Orange. As we saw, in 1672, Louis's invasion of the Netherlands had brought William to power domestically, and rallied support from Spain and Austria. In 1685, the French monarch's revocation of the Edict of Nantes had weakened James II's position by seeming to show the English, the Scots, and the protestant Irish what Catholic persecution could look like; and it had stiffened resolve against France in the United Provinces. Louis's invasion of the Palatinate in 1688 had confirmed to everyone else in Europe that France's ruler was dangerously ambitious, was often brutal, and must certainly be contained by a coalition which William would lead. And then, at the end of 1700, Louis again played into his old rival's hands. On 1 November (continental dating), Carlos II of Spain finally did die. He left a will which gifted his entire, undivided, empire to Philip of Anjou, a grandson of Louis in a cadet line (the heir of a younger son, so some distance from the French succession). The monarch in Versailles accepted this, even though it broke the terms of the partition treaty he had agreed with William. This allowed the Orange-Nassau to paint him as a terrifying potential hegemon of all Europe, and to appeal for aid in defeating him across the continent.[10]

There are certainly excuses for what Louis did. Spain had never accepted the division of its empire, and looked likely to fight to avoid it. This would mean France would have to take military action to secure the Italian lands the partition treaties granted, so it might have looked sensible to go to war to gain the whole empire, if conflict were inevitable anyway. Louis might also have hoped that the grant of Carlos's inheritance to someone who was unlikely to come to the French throne might calm international opinion. Spain would still have a separate monarch (albeit from the ruling dynasty in Versailles), and this ruler might well put the interests of his new realm above those of his family. It was therefore not inevitable that the new ruler in Madrid would aid France's dominion of Europe (in fact, this doubt would ultimately prove well founded – in the late 1710s, Bourbon kings of France and Spain came to war with each other). Unfortunately, however, people beyond the French court refused to see what Louis thought was reason. Austria began mobilising to prevent the augmentation of French power that Carlos's will represented; many in Spain itself were horrified at the prospect of a foreign French monarch; opinion in the United Provinces demanded that something be done to stop a French ally taking control of the Spanish Netherlands on their borders; and in the Stuart realms, William's warnings about France suddenly seemed more cogent.

In a closely related misstep, Louis broke promises made at the treaty of Ryswick, as well as over Spanish partition. We recall that in 1697 the French king had agreed to stop supporting James II's claims still to be king of England, Ireland, and Scotland. This had given the revolution settlement in the Stuart realms some security: a security it had badly needed because of problems with its succession. William had had no children with Mary; he had not married again; and despite numerous pregnancies, the next heir, the Princess Anne, had had only one child who had survived beyond a few months. And then in July 1700, this one child, William, duke of Gloucester, died. This had led to an act of settlement in 1701 (of which more later), which had named the heirs after Anne to be the descendants of the electress Sophia of Hanover, who was a granddaughter of James I, and, perhaps more importantly, was a Protestant. However, this line of future rulers was somewhat remote from the direct Stuart descent, and, having been raised in the Holy Roman Empire, they could well be seen as foreign, and so unsympathetic to the Stuart kingdoms. The situation gave succour to the Jacobite cause. The exiled dynasty might start to look a more patriotic choice than German interlopers: indeed some people, even some mainstream politicians, were to work for a Stuart restoration through Queen Anne's reign, which would they envisaged would take effect when her life ended.[11] Into this uncertainty, Louis pitched more confusion when James II died in exile in Paris in September 1701. Reneging on his Ryswick promises, the French king endorsed James's son (James Francis Edward, of the warming pan myth) as heir to the English, Irish, and Scottish thrones.

Taken together, Louis's actions drove people across Europe into closer support for William. Dutch and Austrian politicians denounced France as a potential universal monarch of the whole landmass, a man who would snuff out the independence of other nations, and who could not be relied upon to keep to agreements sworn before God. Most powers – except for France herself and a handful of her allies – began seeking a new international alliance to limit the threat and punish the impiety. Perhaps as importantly, Louis's foolish expedients began to reverse opinion in England. Many English people were war weary, but they began to accept that a new struggle might be needed. More conflict seemed a price that had to be paid to protect the liberties secured in 1688–9, to exclude the Catholic Stuarts from the throne, and to prevent Louis attaining international dominance. William thus began to secure the sort of political victories he had not seen in parliaments since the mid-1690s. For example, his pleas to the Lords and Commons to settle the succession after the death of the duke of Gloucester resulted in reasonably rapid action. Although the Hanoverian line was little known in England, and many were suspicious of it, the act of settlement passed reasonably smoothly, and the German dynasty's right to the throne was recognised in English law.[12]

William thus benefitted from an enemy who had frequently overplayed his hand, and whose judgement was perhaps weakening towards the end of his reign. But the king of England also had important roles in his own reversal of fortune. Old habits of compromise and pragmatism, and established skills of propaganda and presentation, allowed him to withstand the countercurrents of 1698–1701; and then, slowly, to reverse them.

Let us examine William's pragmatism first. It was, perhaps, in these years that refusing to pick fights with leaders of popular opinion – something which had marked William's career – paid the most spectacular dividends. Our account here can start with the defeat over the army in 1698. As we saw, the king's first, petulant, reaction to this was threaten a de facto abdication. However, he was talked round, and then his skills of compromise, and allowing strategy to flex tactics, kicked in. Speaking to Parliament at the start of 1699, he again warned them that reducing the army was a national security risk, but then said he would do it. He stated he would accept a force of only seven thousand men, the largest number his legislators would vote to finance; and said that he was doing so because the only thing worse than a shrunken military force would be a breach between Crown and Parliament. Such a rupture, he said, would be 'even more fatal' than the slashing of the size of the military.[13] The king thus explicitly acknowledged that he must respect the opinion of the nation's representatives, and he played what proved to be a longer game. By not wholly alienating MPs, he avoided the total breakdown of trust which had overthrown his grandfather, Charles I, and his uncle, James II. This meant that as the threat posed by Louis once again became apparent, William still had an audience for arguing that England must remobilise.

The king bowed to Parliament in other ways in these years. He was, as was to be expected, upset by the Irish resumptions bill of 1699. This was the measure that reconfiscated those lands in Ireland that the king had granted to his followers earlier in the decade. Yet the king acquiesced when Harley's majority in the Commons tacked it on to a finance bill. This meant that the more sympathetic House of Lords, some of whom were affected by the Irish clauses, could not remove the land provisions unless they were prepared to deny the court money by voting the whole measure down: the upper chamber had no right to amend a finance bill, they could only reject it outright. It was thus a combined finance and confiscation measure that came to the monarch's desk. Yet, notwithstanding its highly unpalatable nature, William agreed to enact it. He therefore signed away his own supporters' estates to avoid a constitutional and financial breach with MPs. Similarly, William accepted parts of the act of settlement which amounted to wholesale criticism of his influence in politics, and of his foreignness. This statute certainly named the house of Hanover, the king's preferred heirs, as successors to the English throne; but it also limited what these Germans could do once Anne's reign was over. According to the terms of the act, none of the new dynasty's office holders would be able to sit in the Commons (thus reviving the principles of the place bills of the early 1690s); Hanoverian monarchs could neither leave the English realm, nor use

English resources to wage a war to defend their foreign possessions, without parliamentary consent; and they could appoint no foreigner to the Privy Council.[14] Given that William had opposed the place measures when they had been thrust at him in the early 1690s; that he had spent time and resources outside the kingdom on his foreign wars; and that he had appointed Dutchmen such as Bentinck to his council, the act was a stinging rebuke to much of his rule in England. The king, nevertheless, swallowed hard, and agreed to these insulting measures in order to maintain relations with his Parliament.

It was perhaps at the personal level that William's pragmatism had its most dramatic illustration. Robert Harley had begun his political career as a passionate Whig, and as an enthusiastic Williamite. In the revolution, he and his family had helped raise the Welsh marches, their ancient area of influence, in favour of the prince of Orange's invasion. But the 1690s changed Harley. This once loyal figure was alienated from the executive by his service on the commission of public accounts, which had revealed shocking waste and corruption in government; and his disgust that leading members of his Whig alignment, people who had always joined with him in their suspicion of the royal court, had flocked to take profitable offices in the mid-decade.[15] By 1698, as we saw, Harley had become the leading critic of William's administration, heading a Tory-country alliance which savaged the standing army, demanded the sitting of the church's convocation, pushed through the reconfiscation of Irish land, and attempted the impeachment of the Whig ministers who had managed the king's war. One might imagine the king would never countenance such a person, and that he would do all he could to undermine Harley. Yet the king also needed someone who could secure a basic support for government in the legislature. Without this, England would slide into the sort of unmanageable parliamentary chaos that was afflicting Scotland and Ireland by the end of the decade. Harley, with his backing among a solid majority of MPs, could guarantee that basic support. And he was prepared to do so, as he retained strands of his enthusiasm for the 1689 settlement. William thus stooped to work with his nemesis. Although Harley had no direct role in the administration (he took a role as Speaker of the House of Commons), the king appointed key people from the Tory-country alliance to the great offices of state early in 1701, and he negotiated with Harley to secure votes for an adequate financial supply to the court and for the act of settlement. We have stressed that William only fully liked and trusted a tiny handful of people in his career. Yet he compensated by being prepared to work with a much wider group than that, including old enemies and people he detested. Harley was a dramatic example.

All this willingness to compromise blunted potential resentment. Unlike earlier Stuart kings, William avoided turning opposition into political crisis by bowing to his subjects' representatives in Parliament, even when those representatives pressed policies that horrified him. This meant there was still at least a chance the leaders of the political nation would listen when William was proved right about the threat Louis posed. In 1701, politicians who had been arguing for cuts to the government's budget voted to increase funds again when they reflected on the European situation. As leader of the ministry, Harley resisted further savage cuts to the court's resources; and, as an extreme example, the admittedly maverick member of his caucus, John Howe, seems to have experienced a whiplash conversion. Howe had introduced a motion to cut the civil list funds going to the king, which he won in the Commons on 5 May 1707 (English dating); but only four days later was arguing for a generous response to Dutch appeals for English money to help their remobilisation. The 'liberties of Europe were in danger from France', he declared.[16] The starkness of Howe's change of course was exceptional, and was commented upon at the time, but there was a wider willingness to support William's international approach. A House of Commons that had been elected only a few months before, on a mandate to rein in the court, voted nearly unanimously after Howe's speech to assist the king in his support for his European allies.

Pragmatic sensitivity thus did a lot to help William's cause, avoiding alienating people so completely that they would always work against him. But the monarch's flair for popular propaganda also played an important role. As in all his earlier years, the stadhouder-king cultivated public messages that won extensive support. As far as he could, William maintained his personal image as a virtuous champion of Protestantism, and he used skills first perfected in the Netherlands to mobilise public opinion in an English polity that was increasingly dominated by open and widespread discussion of national affairs. It was in this last period that the techniques he had been forced to learn and adopt in his early twenties paid some of their richest dividends in the Stuart realms.

A good deal of William's propaganda in the last years of his reign involved continued presentation of monarchical magnificence. The intriguing thing about his rule had always been his combination of media innovation within a new print-led public sphere with a far more traditional princely imagery: this hybrid approach remained a feature of his final years. So, the king continued his participation in public ceremonies, especially opening and closing Parliament; and he still went on progresses – at least to and from summer trips to the Netherlands. Both of these kinds of appearances ensured visibility to subjects, and William also carried on employing court gatherings to bind members of English elites to his person and his cause. Hunting – and the associated hosting of hunt dinners – remained as important to this as it always had been: though the king's problems with his health began to impinge on such energetic hospitality.[17] The presentation of the royal image through painting also continued to play a key role, as it had for English royalty from the days of Henry VIII. In fact, these last years of William's reign saw the production of probably the most impressive picture of his whole career – Godfrey Kneller's equestrian portrait of 1701 (see Figure 7). This canvas, originally over fifteen feet high and wide (it has been cut down subsequently), depicted the monarch in classical armour, wielding an imperial baton of command, and seated on a pale horse (perhaps therefore presenting him as God's champion from the book of Revelation). In the picture, various deities gaze upon William in awe and offer him both command of the seas, and the endless prosperity of

Figure 7 Godfrey Kneller, *Equestrian portrait of William III* (1701), oil on canvas. Royal Collection Trust © His Majesty King Charles III.

cornucopia. Meanwhile an inscription – in Latin, from Virgil – had him reigning over a pacified world with the virtues of his ancestors.[18] Iconographic analysis suggests the viewer is supposed to see the king as Aeneas here, and so comparable with the mythical founder of the glories of Rome.[19]

The portrait thus argued for a kind of semi-divine elevation of William above the ordinary world. Such claims were taken even further forward at Hampton Court. Work on this new palace had largely been suspended when Mary died, but it took off again after the end of the war with France, and especially following a fire a 1698 at Whitehall which largely destroyed that residence, and left William a grand house down. When finished, the wings that Wren had designed, a quadrangle around the new Fountain Court, were a substantial advertisement of monarchy. The Kneller portrait, described above, had been commissioned to hang in this new residence, and the architecture had been heavily influenced by what diplomats reported of Louis XIV's residences at Versailles, Fountainbleau, and Marly.[20] Visitors approached the new royal apartments by climbing an extraordinary staircase. This was enlivened by the Italian artist Antonio Verrio, whose huge scheme of wall and ceiling painting used a complex pictorial scheme to present William as martial hero, a bringer of fortune to his nation, and as the purger of the corruptions of earlier regimes.[21] Once at the top of the stairs, people would enter a guard chamber, embellished with a vast design, composed entirely of the weapons of war (pikes, swords, kettledrums, rifles, and so on, were hung in geometric patterns). This underlined the king's military success, as well as the magnificence of his wealth: expensive precision instruments of war were here deployed simply as a form of wallpaper. Beyond this room was an enfilade. This was a series of chambers, of gently decreasing size, but also of increasing privacy, which protected the ruler – who mostly remained, elusive, and unattainable – at the far end of the range. The enfilade was decked out with paintings of William's Stuart ancestors; with costly tapestries; with virtuoso wood carving by Grinling Gibbons, craftsman extraordinary; and with expensive mirrors and furniture. It would also have featured rich ceiling paintings by Verrio if he had been able to complete the work before William died (the two bedchambers at the end of the set of rooms give us some sense of what the whole might have looked like). All the spaces enjoyed views on to a Privy Garden. There an army of horticulturalists maintained a vast parterre of carefully pruned box hedges and exotic plants (including the inevitable orange trees); and hydraulic engineers looked after the fountains (a marvel themselves, requiring a header tank some miles away). Running through all this architectural bling were images of Hercules. The Greek demigod appeared on murals, tapestries, sconces, statutes, fire guards, and whatever else his muscle-bound (and yes, perhaps, homoerotic) body could be made to fit. Hercules had been what Julie Farguson calls the 'house symbol' of the house of Orange-Nassau, stressing their relationship to Henri IV of France, whose personal badge it had been; but his mythology also ensured he represented the ability to achieve victory over overwhelming odds.[22] Taken together, all this was a significant statement of wealth and power which was perhaps best captured in Leonard Knyff's drone-like view of Hampton Court from above, produced only a couple of years after completion (see Figure 8).

Such material boasting might seem to contradict the sense the king was a new kind of ruler, seeking consent and compromise with his subjects. But we have to remember that, from his earliest days in Dutch politics, William had combined up-to-the-minute techniques of political management with older presentations of personal magnificence; and that it would have been hard to break wholly with his own, or his subjects', sense of what monarchical power should look like. Moreover, there were strands of public service, and of causes far wider than personal aggrandisement, encoded into all this extravagant display. In these years, the Crown's public ceremony centred on meeting the representatives of the monarch's people in Parliament, and it did so perhaps more exclusively than it had earlier in the reign. Similarly, much of the iconography at Hampton Court could be read as advertising William's lifelong struggle against France: the country which had become recognised as the national, ideological, and religious enemy of the English people. So, the insistent martial imagery of the palace would have reminded audiences that the king's struggle had been a decades-long one against the persecuting and ambitious Louis XIV.

Figure 8 Leonard Knyff, *A view of Hampton Court Palace* (c.1703), oil on canvas. Royal Collection Trust © His Majesty King Charles III.

The corrupt regime which Verrio's murals had shown the new monarch expelling had been the Catholic and Francophile one of James II. Hercules was a symbol of irresistible individual strength – but was also a figure who had chosen to use that strength for virtue, and for the wellbeing of others, not for his own glory. For all his great magnificence therefore the resident of Hampton Court was the champion of his subject's faith, and their liberty from a foreign and absolutist enemy. It was an image that would stand William in good stead as Louis re-emerged as a threat to everything the English held dear.

And William did continue his mastery of new, public-facing, media in his last years. It is true that, for the late Stuart period, it can be difficult to establish the exact links between the court, and those who put the case for the Crown's preferred policies in the press. Evidence for direct payment or patronage of writers is very patchy, and, although the court certainly had people with contacts in the media, the Crown had no formal press office whose personal or records we might trace. Nevertheless, an effective publicity campaign pushed back against the anti-war sentiment of the Tory-country alliance and its writers. Some of this effort clearly came from the court, and – given William's effectiveness in using authors sympathetic to his position from at least the 1672 *rampjaar* – it is hard not to interpret the wider campaign as a quasi-official strategy to win the argument for a remobilisation against Louis XIV.

Part of the campaign came through William's regular communications with Parliament. Through 1701 he reminded his legislators – in speeches and in printed versions of those speeches – that the Dutch had asked for support in facing the French threat, and he thanked them when they voted funds that could be sent abroad to help allies.[23] Repeating the trick he has used at the start of the 1689–97 war, he asked for close cooperation on the international situation from the Lords and Commons, thus again implicating them in his mobilisation.[24] Another tactic was to translate and print some of the diplomatic exchanges that occurred between European powers, to educate and agitate the English public on the danger Louis posed. Key here was *The answer of the states general of the United Provinces* (London, 1701). This accused the French monarch of breaking the partition treaty that had been agreed to avoid the whole Spanish realm falling into his hands; and of refusing to take seriously Dutch proposals aimed avoiding the war that was likely once he had breached this trust. Quite a number of standalone pamphlets also appeared. Certainly, some of these were sponsored by Whigs and aimed to undermine Harley's Tory administration, but all tried to stiffen resolve behind William's desire to challenge Louis. Works attacked the current government for its lukewarm response to Versailles' action; they reminded everyone of France's insatiable ambition; and they urged Englishmen to send more bellicose representatives to Westminster at the next election.[25] All of this rattled Tory writers into a vigorous response, and so sparked a robust print exchange which became known as the 'paper war'. Several Tory works defended the House of Commons' measured approach to the European situation throughout 1701, though these were pulled on to Williamite-Whig territory by stressing generous funds had been voted for defence against France, and they acknowledged the wave of popular sentiment their opponents had managed to create.[26] One talked of an 'uproar and howling' out in the country, which Tory MPs were having to withstand.[27] As in 1672, and 1688, William was buoyed by a mass movement that he and his propagandists had fanned into existence.

One individual incident illustrates the sophisticated and multifaceted nature of the pro-war campaign. In the spring of 1701, and probably as a result of the monarch's lead on geopolitics, there was a palpable mood of concern in some parts of England. Many were clearly worried that the House of Commons was not doing all it could to block Louis's domination of Europe, so grand juries in Kent, Warwickshire, and Cheshire composed addresses urging prompter greater action to support the Dutch. The Kentish petition was presented to Parliament on 8 May (English dating). However, a majority of the Commons, suspecting that Whig agitators had been behind the protest, voted the document a 'scandalous, insolent, and seditious' work, and arrested the five knights of the shire who had come to deliver the paper.[28] The result was a press and political controversy, in which supporters of William's robust foreign policy accused the Tory-country group of ignoring both national sentiment and national security. Daniel Defoe – later a staple of English literature courses, but for the moment most remarkable for his unflinching print support for William – enhanced his emerging career as a pamphleteer by contributing to the paper row. His *Legion memorial*, appearing only days after the petitioners' arrest, claimed to speak for the English people. It threatened popular vengeance on MPs who abetted France by delaying aid to the Netherlands.[29] Defoe also penned a *History of the Kentish petition*. This protested at the injustice done to the petitioners, but also stressed the popularity of their cause. Defoe's pamphlet claimed the original address would have been signed by many thousands, but the Kentish justices refused to add more sheets of parchment to it to avoid it becoming too bulky; and it described the fêting the prisoners had enjoyed (banquets, receptions, bonfires) once they were released and made a triumphal progress from London back to Kent.[30] John Somers, the veteran Whig statesman, and long-time ally of the king, also got involved. His pamphlet was partly a lawyer's defence of the English people's right to petition, but – as perhaps was excusable for a man who had just been impeached – it included a long preface accusing the Tory majority of the Commons of being a treasonous party, bent on frustrating the united will of the monarch and his subjects.[31]

Interestingly, it was in this controversy that the political ideas of John Locke were first discussed at any length. Locke's *Two treatises of government* had been published immediately after the revolution, and was later taken, in the eighteenth and nineteenth centuries, to be the definitive statement of the principles of 1688–9. Its argument that people had the right to overthrow a tyranny came to be presented as the definitive, semi-official, apology for William's accession.[32] In fact, however, Locke had been little cited in the 1690s. It was only when discussion of the Kentish petition raised the issue of how far the people should influence their governors, that Locke's theories of popular sovereignty gained traction. This might seem an aside in a biography of William, but it speaks to the new political world – the emerging set of circumstances in which the king had to act. In the Stuart realms, public opinion had started to matter. There was a sense in which the people had become sovereign, just as Locke insisted they were, and that a ruler's job was to shape and lead their views, rather than simply ordering them about. The public's mood now affected politics; their representatives in Parliament decided if monarchs would have the resources to follow their priorities; and electors were taking closer interest in how their MPs behaved. In this respect, England had come to imitate the Netherlands – a country where politicians had long had to keep an eye on what a broad mass of people were thinking. A good deal of the shift had happened on the watch of a ruler from those provinces; and had been encouraged by his experience and skills in public relations.

William had therefore been lucky in the path to the signing of the Second Grand Alliance. His considerable political difficulties at the end of the 1690s had not proved fatal, and Louis had followed policies guaranteed to solidify European and English opinion around the strategy of the monarch in London. But William's own skills and experience had also been crucial. If he had not been a stalwart military leader and accomplished diplomat, the other powers of the continent might not have looked to him to bring together the great league of states that coalesced in the autumn of 1701. If he had not shown the capacity to work with others in his own territories, to compromise, and to galvanise the public in his lands, that alliance would have lacked the resources it needed to balance the French machine. Freely voted funds from the Netherlands and the Stuart realms were to be the sinews of the coming war; and even before conflict began, the likelihood that William could secure this finance and could mobilise mass armies reassured the Habsburg powers and others that it was worth joining a renewed effort against Versailles. Queen Anne and the duke of Marlborough may have received the plaudits of later historians for the defeat of Louis's ambitions; but they were figures standing on the shoulders of an underrated giant.

Notes

1 P.W.J. Riley, *King William and the Scottish politicians* (Edinburgh, 1979), p.160.
2 William Molyneux, *The case of Ireland's being bound by acts of parliament in England stated* (Dublin, 1698).
3 For the woollens act, see Patrick Kelly, 'The Irish woollen export prohibition act of 1699', *Irish Economic and Social history*, 7 (1980), 22–44.
4 Jonathan Israel, *The Dutch republic: its rise, greatness, and fall* (Oxford, 1995), pp.959–60.
5 [Charles Davenant], *The true picture of a modern Whig* (London, 1701) – the pamphlet was such a success that Davenant produced a sequel: [Charles Davenant], *Tom Double return'd out of the country* (London, 1702).
6 W.A. Speck, 'Harley, Robert, first earl of Oxford and Mortimer', *Oxford dictionary of national biography*, https://www.oxforddnb.com (Accessed 25/04/22).
7 There is a reasonably clear account of the partition treaties in Wout Troost, *William III, the stadholder-king* (Aldershot, 2005), pp.253–8.
8 For example, *Some reply to a letter pretended to be writ to a member of parliament in the country defending the partition treaty* (London, 1701).
9 Samuel Weller Singer ed, *The correspondence of Henry Hyde, earl of Clarendon* (2 vols, London, 1828), II, 410–13 and 419.
10 There is a clear account of Louis's reasoning in accepting the will in John A. Lynn, *The wars of Louis XIV, 1667–1714* (Harlow, 1999), pp.268–9.
11 Geoffrey Holmes, *British politics in the age of Anne* (revised edition, London, 1987), pp.279–80.
12 Henry Horwitz, *Parliament, policy, and politics in the reign of William III* (Manchester, 1977), ch.12.
13 William Cobbett ed, *A parliamentary history vol 5, 1688–1702* (London, 1809), col.1193.
14 12 and 13 William 3 c.2.
15 Speck, 'Harley, Robert'.
16 Henry Horwitz, *Parliament, policy, and politics*, p.289.
17 Julie Farguson, *Visualising protestant monarchy: ceremony, art and politics after the Glorious Revolution* (Woodbridge, 2021), p.163.
18 Farguson, *Visualising protestant monarchy*, pp.175–7; J.D. Steward, 'William III and Sir Godfrey Kneller', *Journal of the Warburg and Courtauld Institute*, 33 (1970), 330–6.
19 P.R. Rijkens, 'Nassau on horseback: meaning, form, and function of Nassau equestrian imagery in the Netherlands since the C16th' (PhD, University of Amsterdam, 2015).
20 Farguson, *Visualising protestant monarchy*, p.170.

21 Farguson, *Visualising protestant monarchy*, pp.172–3; Simon Thurley, *Hampton Court: a social and architectural history* (New Haven, 2003), p.212.
22 Stephen B. Baxter, 'William III as Hercules: the political implications of court culture, in Lois G. Schwoerer ed, *The revolution of 1688/9: changing perspectives* (Cambridge, 1991), pp.95–106; Farguson, *Visualising protestant monarchy*, pp.173–4.
23 *His majesties gracious speech to both houses of parliament on Thursday the 12th day of June, 1701* (London, 1701).
24 Cobbett, *Parliamentary history … vol 5*, col.1329.
25 From a large selection: *Observations and reasons offered for a war with France* (London, 1701); *The best choice of parliament men considered* (London, 1701); *The duke of Anjou's succession considered* (1701); *An essay on the present interest of England* (London, 1701); [Marchmont Nedham], *Christianissimus Christinandus: or reasons for a reduction of France* (London, 1701) – the last was a pamphlet from the 1670s, which had been reprinted every time there seemed to be a major threat from France over the next few decades.
26 For example, *The several proceedings and resolutions of the house of commons* (London, 1701); *A justification of the proceedings of the honourable house of commons* (London, 1701).
27 *A short defence of the last parliament* (London, 1701), p.2.
28 Cobbett, *Parliamentary history … vol 5*, col.1251.
29 [Daniel Defoe], *Mr S-----r: the enclosed memorial* (London, 1701).
30 [Daniel Defoe], *The history of the Kentish petition* (London, 1701), pp.1–2, 10–12.
31 [John Somers], *Jura populi anglicani: or the subject's right of petitioning set forth* (London, 1701).
32 The old interpretation of Locke was first challenged by Peter Laslett, 'The English revolution and Locke's *Two treatises of government*', *Cambridge Historical Journal*, 12:1 (1956), 40–55.

Conclusion
A stone in the floor: the legacies of William III

In the pavement of the floor of a chapel in Westminster Abbey, there is a commemorative stone. Little larger than a shoebox lid, it bears the simple inscription: William III. There is no elaboration of the king's career and virtues; no recognition of the role he had played in national, European, and global life. The monument is completely overshadowed by the surrounding tombs to women and men of far lower status and far less power; and it is dwarfed by the chapel itself, which a predecessor as king of England, Henry VII, had built as a permanent reminder of his rule (as well as a gift to the church to speed his soul through purgatory to heaven). As a strict Calvinist, and as a man dedicated to a cause beyond himself, William would not have wanted to copy Henry's extravagant gesture. He would not have assumed that patronage of church-building would have any influence on what happened to him in any afterlife; and William's architectural patronage had been impressive, but only a minority of it had sought self-glorification. Also, the last Stuart king might have thought his extremely modest grave was an appropriate match for that of his greatest political partner. His wife Mary's memorial is of identical size and style, and it sits right next to his own.

Yet, for all the understandable reasons that the memorial is small, it is still a surprisingly unprepossessing marker for a man who we have seen transformed England and had a substantial impact on a far wider world; and the tomb is much less of a statement than was once planned. The Privy Council discussed erecting an impressive celebration of a man who was thought to have saved England's liberty and Protestantism – but the project was abandoned in the early years of his sister-in-law Anne's reign.[1] The obscurity has, perhaps, deepened over the centuries. Apart from the recognition listed in the very first paragraph of this book, William is not a bestriding figure in popular culture. Some British people may have a vague sense that he was from the Netherlands; that he ruled in a joint monarchy with his spouse; and that he is important to some Irish Protestants. Some Netherlanders may know him as a member of their ruling dynasty, and as a local who became king of England. Yet awareness rarely goes deeper than that, if it even gets that far. In demotic memory, he is no William the Silent, Henry VIII, Elizabeth, Charles I, or Victoria; he is not

DOI: 10.4324/9781003267621-10

even a Henry V or Charles II – though his long-term impact was on a far greater scale than theirs. In Britain, William IV, the short reigning 'sailor king' of the early nineteenth century, has far more pubs named after him than William III.

This conclusion will spend most of its time speculating why someone who remodelled his world has sunk so far in common awareness. But it must start by charting William's personal story from his last great diplomatic triumph. A biographer should ensure a book's subject is safely dead before embarking on a summary of his reputation. After William had concluded the Second Grand Alliance in September 1701, he spent the rest of the year in preparations for the coming war. He stayed in the Netherlands until November: partly, as we saw on health grounds, but also so he could oversee the early mustering of Dutch forces and coordinate arrangements to prevent Louis's allies seizing control of the middle Rhine. He then crossed back to London, where he dissolved Parliament in hopes of strengthening the Whig party: the Whig alignment was more enthusiastic about resourcing the new conflict than its Tory rival, and the king wished to reconstitute his ministry in its favour. The election results were ideal for the Crown. The Whigs made substantial progress, but they did not enjoy the sort of overwhelming victory that might have made the king their prisoner, or which might have prevented William from following his usual approach of balancing the parties. With the two sides nearly equal in the House of Commons, the Whigs knew the monarch had options in forming a government, and had to stomach some Tories remaining in office. The winter also saw the consolidation of more European states around those who had signed the September treaty, and an apparent improvement in the king's medical condition (witnesses noted that they had not seen him look so well in ages when he opened his new Parliament).[2] The year 1702 therefore seemed to promise a fair wind for William's projects.

But then bodily disaster struck. Whilst trying out a new horse in Richmond Park, on 21 February (British dating), William suffered a nasty accident. The horse tripped on a molehill, throwing the rider, and breaking his collar bone. In subsequent folklore this incident was narrated as having led to William's death, and the mole became a hero to Jacobites. In later years, supporters of the exiled Stuarts would raise glasses to 'the little gentleman in black velvet' who was reputed to have killed their bogeyman. But, sadly for the cause of political wit, the mole was largely innocent. William's injury was serious, but not life-threatening. He was taken from the scene to Hampton Court, where some days of bed rest seemed to be leading to recovery. After about a week he was well enough to return to Kensington and start appearing in public: he hoped to be able to go to Westminster to meet his Parliament again soon. However, on 4 March (English dating), a new problem appeared. Walking up and down the gallery at his residence, William was overcome with weariness, and woke with a fever after a nap in a chair. Over the next days his condition ebbed and flowed, but by the 7th it was clear the illness was going to prove fatal. William died on the morning of 8 March, having met Bentinck one more time, and having clasped his old favourite's hand to his heart. The famous mole may therefore have weakened the king and so contributed to his end, but William was most immediately dispatched by the sort of infectious disease that had plagued much of his life.

Now we have recounted William's last months, we can turn to his posthumous reputation. In the immediate years after the stadhouder-king's death, he continued to bathe in the honour many Dutch people granted his family; and both within and beyond the Netherlands, he remained a hero to those who had worked with him in shielding Europe from France, or in securing a Protestant, tolerant, and parliamentary regime in the Stuart realms.[3] British writers such as Daniel Defoe, and Gilbert Burnet lionised William as the great, perhaps providential, champion of these causes.[4] The Whig party in Britain also retained a great nostalgia for this king for a considerable period after 1702. Despite being disappointed in William's nonpartisanship at the start of his reign, the Whigs, right through the Georgian era, kept looking back to the Glorious Revolution as the foundation of the free constitution they thought they defended; so, of course, the Dutch monarch was exalted by this reading of history. By the late eighteenth century, William's memory was expanded and adapted further as he became a symbol for political radicals. They celebrated the events of 1688–9, not on 5 November, as was decreed in the prayer book's instructions for an annual thanksgiving for the nation's deliverance, but on the day before. The 4th was, of course, William's birthday: radicals saw the king's defeat of absolutism as more significant than the disappointing political settlement that they believed had followed on its heels, so they were more inclined to give the Dutchman posthumous birthday parties than follow the official line of commemoration. Some of these traditions of celebration survived into the nineteenth century. Thomas Babington Macaulay's massively popular account of the late seventeenth century, published in the early decades of Victoria's reign, presented 1688–9 as the moment Britain rose above its rivals in liberty, prosperity, and general civilisation – and William's reputation was inevitably burnished by such a narrative.[5]

Yet, for all this lauding of our subject, Macaulay's work also illustrated a strange decline of the king into obscurity. William was prominently present in Macaulay's account of course – but he was not quite its hero. Instead, this historian tended to present a past driven by deep cultural processes, for all that he admitted the actions of some individuals could be significant. Macaulay saw the early modern age as one of steady enlightenment, to the point that, by the late Stuart decades, people were sufficiently confident of their own opinions, and sufficiently sophisticated in their understanding of politics and of the cosmos, that James II's brand of absolutism and superstitious Catholicism could not stand. The key moments in Macaulay's story were less William's preparations for his expedition to England, and its successful accomplishment, than English disillusionment with an old world. In particular, the account focussed on the Tories' eventual realisation that their support for the traditions of hereditary monarchy had led to disaster. In this story therefore the Dutch king had to at least share billing with wider shifts in belief and understanding – and it has been these more impersonal factors that have dominated interpretations in more recent times.

For example, in the high twentieth century, readings of the seventeenth century in Britain were heavily influenced by Marxism. Consequently, the instability of the era was read as the result of changes in the economic structures of society. Tensions were thought to be about wealth and income; rebellions were driven by classes that had been rising through the social ranks (or sometimes declining, there was much debate about this). William's revolution in England was shoehorned into this vision. It was, it was assumed, the victory of an entrepreneurial group which wanted old power structures weakened to accommodate its ascent (though quite how this fitted with the fact that it had been landed aristocrats who had actually invited Dutch forces into England was unclear).[6] As a result of this picture's focus on socioeconomic forces, William himself was rather painted out of it. It was true that there was a new burst of interest the king's career from the late 1980s, sparked by the tricentenary of his taking the Stuart thrones. This time, however, the prince of Orange was used as a symbolic microcosm of a different, but again much wider, account of his age. Convinced, as academics tended to be at this point in history, that Britain and Europe would have ever closer ties, historians now presented 1688–9 as an international event, in which the Stuart realms were subjected to a wave of Dutch influence and power. William played some role in this of course; but the emphasis was on less personal dimensions. Scholars examined the ability of the Netherlands as a state, and as a society, to effect the invasion; they looked at the motivations for supporting the prince of Orange among a broad Dutch public; and they recounted the Stuart realm's later imitation of key features Dutch culture, administration, religious policy, or finance.[7]

Quite why William has been obscured in this way is unclear. In the narrowly historiographic sphere, he has probably suffered from the turn away from narratives centred on 'great men'. With scholars wanting to tell the stories of whole societies, and concentrating on processes rather than personalities, there has been less interest in individuals, no matter how active or powerful. This cannot, however, be the whole story. Other figures, such as William the Silent or Elizabeth I, have fared better. These other leaders probably never exceeded William's achievements in defending their countries from foreign domination, from Catholicism, or from absolutism, but they are far more prominent in national memories and are the subjects of much greater academic attention. We shall thus have to seek explanations more focussed on specific characteristics and circumstances than scholarly trends: this is particularly true because William has disappeared so completely in culture beyond the academy. This biographer always has to remind contemporary British audiences that their country once had a Dutch ruler when asked what aspect of history he studies; and a 2004 poll of people in the Netherlands ranked our prince of Orange only at number seventy-two when it asked respondents who had been the greatest Dutchman of all time.[8]

William's personality obviously did not help commemoration. He was, as we have constantly stressed, an intensely private man who played cards very close to his chest. If it was difficult for his contemporaries to get to know him, it has been equally hard for later generations to warm to him. Not wanting outsiders to get too clear a sense of his inner thoughts or feelings, William left an impression of distance and indifference, and this had not made him attractive. Compounding his often-cold privacy was a focus on core objectives which verged on monomania. William prioritised his political and military goals over everything else in life. His interests in painting, hunting, gardening, and a small number of other pastimes were his few distractions; an almost crippling sense of duty kept him in the trenches during the military campaigning seasons, and at his desk doing paperwork and diplomacy in the winter months. All work and no play made William a dull boy. As a result, there are relatively few dramatic personal stories, or quotable quotes, to add colour to his biography; there were few flamboyant or funny moments in his life around which popular memory could form.

Specific political circumstances in both the Netherlands and the Stuart realms also submerged this figure. In the Dutch republic, suspicion of the Orange-Nassaus as ambitious dynasts always put a brake on unequivocal celebration of the one member of the family who did become a powerful king (albeit in another country). As we have seen, William did not get his wish that his relatives succeeded to his position at the heart of national affairs. As a result, in the eighteenth century, the provinces ran themselves with much the same structures that de Witt had maintained. Only Napoleonic upheavals soured sentiment to republican forms; only the early nineteenth century saw the establishment of an Orange monarchy which began to put down roots in Dutch society. And even then, monarchism was limited. The first Orange king, William I, who reigned from 1814 to 1840, enjoyed far-reaching power, but in 1848 the country adopted a liberal constitution that made government responsible to a representative Parliament. It was, fundamentally, the same constitution that governs the Netherlands today, in the democratic age. Strong attachments to a sovereignty in the people, rather than a ruling house, thus contained any glamour that the Orange rulers might generate from their history. Consequently, William III would enjoy only a mixed reputation. Suspicion of his role in ending True Freedom in 1672 has moderated gratitude for his salvation of the nation the same year.

In the Stuart realms, and England in particular, William's problem was his foreign origin. The English may have been grateful that they had been rescued from the popery and arbitrary power that they convinced themselves James II threatened; but it was embarrassing to have relied on salvation from abroad. Quite rapidly, celebration of the prince of Orange's providential role gave way to sullen resentment of what seemed like a Dutch conquest. We have seen that xenophobia was at the core of opposition to William in his lifetime, and it probably also played a role in the suppression of his memory after his death. His sister-in-law, Anne, certainly seemed to want to distance her reign from an era of foreign rule. Her first speech to Parliament stressed that royal actions would now be dictated by her heart, which she said was 'entirely English'.[9] Many saw this as a snide comment on William's continental priorities; and on a period of influence from abroad that should now be left behind. Responding to this mood, the English came to trumpet their own role in preserving their religion and liberty, rather than cheering one Dutchman's heroism. The Glorious Revolution therefore became a tale of England's native people rejecting tyranny. In the eighteenth century, Locke's political theory, with its stress on popular consent at the basis of authority, was repackaged as the true philosophy behind the change of monarchs in 1689. Macaulay's stress on the innate good sense of James's subjects, recognising the unacceptability of that king's rule, illustrated how the nineteenth century wished to see the events of that year.

There are therefore strong potential explanations for William's disappearance in reputation and memory in the centuries since 1702. But our analysis in this book perhaps points to another set of reasons his image has dimmed. Throughout, we have stressed that William used both traditional, and emerging, techniques in securing his position and in advancing his policies. In ways we will briefly recap in a moment, he could look both like a renaissance prince – magnificent and absolute; and like the pioneer of constitutional, limited, rule. He operated successfully in a world where old forms were still influential, but where new forces were rapidly reshaping political culture and where new approaches to leadership were needed. He can thus be tough to categorise. As a result, he has perhaps been hard to hold clearly in the popular mind. In English terms, he was neither a Henry VIII – exemplifying everyone's idea of personal power and display; nor an Elizabeth II – who, it is a fair bet, will retain a strong image for many decades ahead for embodying tireless and selfless service to her subjects.

We have seen the hybrid nature of William's career evident in many areas of his life. In his early career in the Netherlands, for example, he benefitted from the charisma of his noble family, and their quasi-monarchical role in the polity. He used their techniques of transmitting glamour through art, architecture, ceremony, and personal appearance. In this, he looked like most successful rulers in Europe since the fifteenth century. Yet it was perhaps his command of a different and novel world of public print culture that did more to advance his cause. Without the support of pamphlets, broadsides, published sermons, mass-produced cartoons, and commercial verse – and the open discussion these stimulated – it is hard to imagine the collapse of de Witt's regime, William's advance in 1672, or his smooth capture of the English throne.

Once the prince of Orange had seized power in the Netherlands, his priority was to contain what he saw as an aggressive France. Much of his effort looked like the personal battlefield leadership that had been at the core of medieval and renaissance kingship. Like England's Henry V, or the Habsburgs' Charles V, he had dedicated time to serving among his troops, inspiring them with his courage and willingness to share their hardships. However, the real roots of his success (for in truth his record in actual engagements with the enemy was patchy) lay in infrastructure and politics rather than his individual derring-do. In the end, Louis XIV was contained because the Dutch and the English were persuaded to accept a mass mobilisation of the resources of their nations, and because these nations were willing to use the most up-to-date methods of taxation, borrowing, administration, and logistical supply to their armies and navies. To make this work, William had had to deploy far more than the skills of a traditional war general. He had had to operate in a new world in which representative assemblies (the provincial states, the Dutch states-general, the parliaments of England, Scotland, and Ireland) had to grant the consent of their populations – particularly to fiscal exactions and schemes for raising credit; and where these assemblies demanded a role in the design of state infrastructure, at least in being able to audit spending. William therefore needed to be able to work with representative mechanisms. As we have seen, this required careful negotiation, alliance-building, and compromise. This was far more complex and subtle than simple courage and strategy in the face of opposed armies. Success in war also required continued deployment of widely broadcast propaganda to persuade a wide public of the virtues of the military cause: inspiring heroism witnessed first-hand by fellow soldiers was no longer enough.

There were similar ambiguities in other parts of William's career. Constitutionally, across his realms, he was attached to the traditional powers of his paternal and maternal families, and of the offices they had occupied. He worked to restore the prominence of the House of Orange-Nassau in the Dutch polity, and to secure the authority of his stadhouderships, of his admiral- and captain-generalships, and of his chairmanship of the Council of State. He cared about his position as sovereign of the principality of Orange, and had hoped to become sovereign lord of Gelderland. In his island realms, he used his position as a Stuart, both by descent and marriage, as his entry into British and Irish politics; and one motive for his expedition to England in 1688 was to save the Stuart monarchy from the threat of civil war, and the sort of overthrow that had occurred in 1649. He employed and defended the formal power of his offices. He used his stadhouderships to purge opponents from their posts; he resisted the erosion of the royal prerogative in England in the early months of 1689; and he deployed the royal veto against legislation he did not like in the early 1690s.

But for all this, William was no blind defender of autocratic power. He knew that his great project in European geopolitics, the taming of the French, would be best advanced by working with his fellow citizens and subjects, and that there was a real risk that his project would be derailed by internal strife over the limits of stadhouderial or monarchical power. After a shaky start, he learned to consult the Dutch regent class closely, and he cooperated with the provincial states and states-general: initially in person, then via agents such as Heisius when he had to spend more time away from The Hague. He therefore came to share power with representative assemblies. And in the Stuart realms, he also surrendered substantial parts of his personal influence as monarch to each kingdom's Parliament. In England he accepted the Declaration of Rights; he called his legislature every year for a substantive session and tolerated its investigations into his administration; and he surrendered over laws to curb his power, and over the standing army. In Scotland he accepted the abolition of the Lords of the Articles, the direction of Scottish affairs by local politicians, a religious settlement that had not been what he had wanted but was demanded by the Edinburgh Parliament, and the enquiry into Glencoe. In Ireland he called the Dublin legislature far more frequently than his predecessors had done, and stood by as it unpicked his settlement with Catholic and Jacobite forces at Limerick. In all these areas William's approach faced both ways. He looked back to a vision of monarchical rule that had been commonplace in the sixteenth century, and forwards to a world of parliamentary government that would emerge in the eighteenth and nineteenth centuries.

In religious affairs, William played a part in the great struggle that had unfolded across Europe for two hundred years after the reformation. Personally committed to Protestantism; aware that its future on the continent was in the balance; and convinced heaven had marked out a providential role for him in history; William opposed Louis XIV in large measure because he feared the French monarch was bent on extirpating his faith. He thus built an international alliance of Protestant rulers; and he acted to save reformed Christianity in the Netherlands, in England, and in Ireland from real and pressing threats. But William was not simply a confessional warrior, fighting the latest stage of the great crusade for Protestant truth that had begun in the early sixteenth century. As we have seen, his vision of Christian faith opened paths to less divisive and violent understanding of people's duties to God. His commitment to reformed theology was personal, rather than social. He accepted that others might have reached different conclusions about the divine, and he was prepared to collaborate with people who disagreed with him about religion, both in his personal circle, and in his international alliances. Although a Calvinist, he swallowed the Anglicanism of his wife, and many of his close advisors on English politics; he accepted the Lutheranism and indeed the Catholicism of many members of his front against France; and he even offered generous settlement to the Irish followers of the Roman communion who had been actively fighting against him. William, himself, came to belong to three rather different churches. He was Dutch Reformed by birth and upbringing, but he had had to become an Anglican to take on the English monarch's role as head of the churches of England and Ireland; and then, as king of Scotland, he had to lead a kirk which moved far away from its Anglican-style forms under the restoration monarchy. At the root of this tolerance was a belief that the core of Christianity was charity. So, William's rejection of Louis's religion was not founded in deep revulsion at its doctrines, but rather in conviction that its persecution of others was Antichristian. There was nothing so opposed to charity as using force in matters where Jesus himself had used nothing but prophecy and persuasion: true faith was an exercise in following Christian behaviour, not coercing others into one's version of it. William was therefore both a participant in the early modern European wars of religion, and a pioneer of escape routes from those conflicts.

All of these ambiguities have perhaps made William hard to categorise, and so difficult to place in the popular imagination. He seems to belong fully neither to the magnificence of renaissance politics, with its parallel heroism in defending national religions, nor to a later world of pragmatic and democratic politics within the framework of large and infrastructural states. He is therefore neither a Henry VIII (king of England, 1509 to 1547) or a William the Silent (leader of the Dutch revolt in the later sixteenth century) – whose gorgeous courts and martial prowess can linger in memory; nor is he a Victoria (queen of Britain and Ireland from 1834 to 1903) or a Wilhelmina (queen of the Netherlands, 1890 to 1962) – whose careful deployment of example and duty within limited monarchies have won respect and admiration. The same falling between stools may have also limited academic interest. The communities of scholars who deal with the early modern period and the high modern era are distinct, and they have too little overlap: in Britain this fissure may have been compounded by a falling off of interest after the excitements of the mid-seventeenth-century wars, and in the Netherlands by the perceived ending of the provinces' 'Golden Age' in the decades after 1672, which has made the later period less attractive.

Yet if the hybrid nature of William III's career may have made it difficult for him to gain recognition, it was, as this book has argued, the key to his success. He was a hinge figure between different ages – but he dealt brilliantly with the rapidly changing years in which he lived. He faced a blend of rapidly evolving cultures, societies, and polities; but he picked a superb, and appropriate, mix of backward- and forward-looking approaches to rule. As William did this, he had an impact on European affairs out of all proportion to his modest memorial in Westminster Abbey. But, perhaps, he would not have minded. His upbringing persuaded him he was called to great roles in the Orange-Nassau and Stuart families; to important places in Dutch, British, and Irish histories; and to a holy duty in the furtherance of God's work on earth. When he died, he left his countries and his religion with solutions to problems that had plagued them for decades. He could therefore reflect that he had met the high and demanding calls upon him.

Notes

1 Narcissus Luttrell, *A brief historical relation of affairs of state* (6 vols, London, 1857) V, 154.
2 Stephen B. Baxter, *William III* (London, 1966), p.396.
3 William's memory is fully integrated into the national Dutch celebration of the family which surrounds William I's tomb in Delft: for example, a stained-glass window is dedicated to him.
4 Gilbert Burnet, *Bishop Burnet's history of his own time: volume two* (London, 1734), pp.304–6; Manuel Schonhorn, *Defoe's politics: parliament, power, kingship, and Robinson Crusoe* (Cambridge,1991).

5 Thomas Babington Macaulay, *The history of England from the accession of James II* (5 vols, London, 1849–65).
6 Perhaps most clearly in Christopher Hill's reading of the seventeenth century – see, for example, Christopher Hill, *The century of revolution, 1603–1714* (Edinburgh, 1969).
7 See, for example, the essays in Jonathan Israel ed, *The Anglo-Dutch moment: essays on the Glorious Revolution and its world impact* (Cambridge,1991), or Dale Hoak and Mordechai Feingold eds, *The world of William and Mary; Anglo-Dutch perspectives on the revolution of 1688–9* (Stanford, 1996).
8 https://nl.wikipedia.org/wiki/De_grootste_Nederlander/genomineerden
9 *Journals of the House of Lords Vol 17, 1701–4*, p.68.

Suggestions for further reading

Primary sources

This biography made clear William was close to only a very few people – three figures who perhaps penetrated his inner circle have left records of their time with the stadhouder-king which are still prime sources for William. His wife, Queen Mary II, wrote annual reflections on her life; Gilbert Burnet, his chief propagandist, summarised his political career in a long manuscript published after his death; and Hans Willem Bentinck, William's closest friend until the rupture in the late 1690s, left an extensive correspondence with William, which was edited into a printed collection in the early twentieth century. See: R. Doebner ed, *Memoires of Mary, queen of England, 1689–1694* (London, 1886) – available on Google Books; Gilbert Burnet, *History of his own time* (London, 1724–34) – there are multiple later editions and abridgements; and N. Japikse ed, *Correspondentie van Willem III en van Hans Willem Bentinck* (Hague, 1932) – much of the correspondence is in French despite the Dutch editing. The key political moment in William's career, the Glorious Revolution, and his actions whilst king of the Stuart realms, generated thick commentary in the pamphlet press and in the emerging media of newspapers: all the surviving material can be consulted on the Jisc Historical Texts and the Burney Collection of British Newspapers websites. These sites sit behind paywalls, but can be consulted by becoming a reader at the British Library (any reasonable interest in the material will allow at least temporary access) or other libraries, including many university libraries across the world. The debates in the convention that appointed William king in Westminster can be followed in D.L. Jones, *A parliamentary history of the Glorious Revolution* (London, 1988); and the events of the winter of 1688–9 are reflected in the minutes of the provisional government, established in London after James II had fled the capital: Robert Beddard, *A kingdom without a king: the journal of the provisional government in the revolution of 1688* (Oxford, 1988). The *Calendar of State Papers Domestic* covering William's years also provide much useful information.

Biographies of William

The classic of large biography of William in English was Stephen B. Baxter, *William III* (London, 1966): it offers substantial, perhaps excessive, detail. More recently, a clear account of the events of the political life was provided by Wout Troost, *William III, the stadholder-king: a political biography* (Aldershot, 2005). Tony Claydon, *William III: profiles in power* (Harlow, 2002) attempted an analysis of William's identities and techniques rather than being a straight biography – but expands on some of the themes in this volume; while Tony Claydon and W.A. Speck, *William and Mary* (Oxford, 2007) – which reprinted the two *Oxford dictionary of national biography* articles on these figures – gave highlights of his life. More popular treatments can be found in John van der Kiste, *William and Mary: the heroes of the Glorious Revolution* (Aldershot, 2008) and Jonathan Keats, *William III and Mary II: partners in revolution* (London, 2015). One collection of essays offered some insightful reinterpretations of diverse aspects of William's career and world: Esther Mijers and David Onnekink eds, *Redefining William III: the impact of the king-stadholder in international context* (Aldershot, 2007).

William's career in the Netherlands

William's activities before 1688 form the bulk of the works by Troost and Baxter mentioned in the biographies section to this reading guide, while the relevant sections of Jonathan Israel, *The Dutch republic: its rise, greatness and fall* (Oxford, 1995) provide a clear narrative of Dutch politics from 1650 to 1702; and new perspectives on William's world are offered by David Onnekink and Gijs Rommelse, *The Dutch in the early modern world: a history of a global power* (Cambridge, 2019). William's relations with Bentinck, vital to understanding his role in the Netherlands, are described by David Onnekink, *The Anglo-Dutch favourite: the career of Hans Willem Bentinck, first earl of Portland 1649–1701* (Aldershot, 2007). Herbert H. Rowen, *The princes of Orange* (Cambridge, 1988) set William within the context of his family's role in the republic.

William's career in the British realms before 1688

As a nephew of the mid-Stuart kings, William weaves his way in and out of the standard biographies of those monarchs, providing insights into his approach to their realms: John Miller, *James II: a study in kingship* (London, 1989); Ronald Hutton, *Charles II: king of England, Scotland, and Ireland* (Oxford, 1989); John Miller, *Charles II* (London, 1991); David Wormersley, *James II: the last Catholic king* (London, 2015); and Clare Jackson, *Charles II: the star king* (London, 2016). The accounts of the Glorious Revolution listed in this guide to reading show William's strategy towards the Stuart realms in the years and months immediately before his invasion of England, while an older study concentrates on the European context of his actions down to 1688: John Carswell, *The descent on England: a study of the English revolution of 1688 and its European background* (London, 1969). The classic study of William's successful intervention in British politics in 1672 is K.H.D. Haley, *William III and the English opposition, 1672–4* (Oxford, 1953).

The Glorious Revolution

The old 'Whig' accounts of 1688–9, which set interpretations for decades, still have much to offer on the details of the revolution, and possible readings of it – see Thomas Babington Macaulay, *The history of England* (London, 1848–52) and G.M. Trevelyan, *The English revolution, 1688–9* (London, 1938) – but they perhaps over-celebrate William's arrival as a securing of English freedoms. The year 2006 saw a peculiar outburst of accessible, up-to-date, and scholarly accounts of the revolution: Edward Vallence, *The Glorious Revolution: England's fight for liberty* (London, 2006); Patrick Dillon, *The last revolution: 1688 and the creation of the modern world* (London, 2006); and Tim Harris, *Revolution: the great crisis of the English monarchy, 1685–1720* (London, 2006). Steven Pincus, *1688: the first modern revolution* (New Haven, CT, 2009) provided a thought-provoking interpretation, but it was controversial with some other scholars, and should be read in conjunction with reviews of the volume. The tricentenary of William's arrival in England sparked a number of collections of essays to mark the occasion: most still offer much insight, including Jonathan Israel ed, *The Anglo-Dutch moment: essays on the Glorious Revolution and its world impact* (Cambridge, 1991) and Robert Beddard ed, *The revolutions of 1688* (Oxford, 1991). A valuable and more recent collection is Tim Harris and Stephen Taylor eds, *The final crisis of the Stuart monarchy: the revolutions of 1688–91 in their British, Atlantic, and European contexts* (Woodbridge, 2013)

William as king of England

Perhaps the best all-round study of William's impact as king of England is Craig Rose, *England in the 1690s: revolution, religion and war* (Oxford, 1999). An older, but excellent, collection of essays surveys the way in which William's rule changed his new kingdom: Geoffrey Holmes ed, *Britain after the Glorious Revolution* (London, 1979). A powerful argument for the 1689 revolution breaking the pattern of English politics – echoed in the argument of this biography – is made by Jonathan Scott, *England's troubles: seventeenth-century English political instability in a European context* (Oxford, 2000); while the later chapters of the works by Dillon, Pincus, and Harris, mentioned in the section here on the Glorious Revolution, all offer readings of the 1690s and

William's effects on his new realm; and the case for the transformative infrastructural effects of William's war with Louis is made by John Brewer, *The sinews of power: war, money, and the English state* (London, 1989).

William in Scotland and Ireland

For William in Ireland, see the relevant chapters in Jane H. Ohlmeyer ed, *The Cambridge history of Ireland: Volume 2, 1550–1730* (Cambridge, 2018); as well as David Hayton, *Ruling Ireland, 1685–1730* (Dublin, 2004); and Toby Barnard, 'Ireland 1688–91', in the Harris and Taylor volume mentioned in the Glorious Revolution section of this guide. For the impact on Scotland, see Alasdair Raffe, *Scotland in revolution, 1685–1690* (Edinburgh 2018) and the relevant chapters of Tim Harris's *Revolution*, mentioned in the Glorious Revolution section of this guide – this volume also has a lot of useful stuff to say about Ireland. For a synthetic analysis of the problems of governing 'Three Kingdoms' at the end of the seventeenth century, see David Hayton, 'Constitutional experiments and political expediency' in Steven G. Ellis and Sarah Barber eds, *Conquest and union: fashioning a British state* (Harlow, 1995). Despite its title, Rose's *England in the 1690s*, cited in the 'king of England' section here, has good Scottish and Irish coverage.

William and public presentation

There is useful material on William's presentation of himself while stadhouder in some of the chapters in the Mijers and Onnekink volume listed under biographies in this guide; while William's propaganda as king of England is covered in Tony Claydon, *William III and the godly revolution* (Cambridge, 1996); Kevin Sharpe, *Rebranding rule: the restoration and revolution monarchy* (New Haven, 2013); and Julie Farguson, *Visualising Protestant monarchy: ceremony, art, and politics, after the Glorious Revolution (1689–1714)* (Woodbridge, 2021). Mary was also central to the public presentation of the post-revolutionary regime: her role is well summarised in Bill Speck's contribution the Claydon and Speck volume listed under biographies here. There are fascinating reflections on William's construction of his masculinity in Owen Brittan, 'The print depiction of William III's masculinity', *The Seventeenth Century*, 33:2 (2018), 219–39.

Index

Amsterdam 20, 21, 25, 60–1, 74, 104
Anglo-Dutch War, First 28–9
Anglo-Dutch War, Second 30, 32
Anne, queen of England, Ireland, and Scotland 151–2, 155, 161, 170, 176–7
anti-popery, English 49, 65, 127–8, 138, 140
army, standing 49, 136–140, 150, 162–3
Austria 24, 42, 51–2, 61, 76, 104, 113–14, 137, 155, 159–61
architectural patronage 15, 56–7, 119, 122–3, 148–9, 165–7
Atterbury, Francis 150–1
Aughrim, battle of 114

Bank of England 132
Beachy Head, battle of 117
Bentinck, Hans Willem 35–6, 54–5, 65, 74, 77, 96, 145–7, 163, 173–4
Boyne, battle of 1–3, 89, 105–07
Burnet, Gilbert 76, 77–8, 81–5, 95, 100–01, 121–2, 147, 174

Catholics, English 49, 67
Calvinism 16–7, 34, 41, 59, 78, 100, 179
Carlos II, king of Spain 158–60
Charles I, king of England, Ireland, and Scotland 10, 11, 16, 69, 96, 162
Charles II, king of England, Ireland and Scotland: and the army 139; and Anglo-Dutch wars 38, 42, 46, 50–1; career before Restoration 11; and Chelsea Hospital 119; and geopolitics 65; guardianship of William 31; and party 124–5; restoration of 29–30, 32; succession from 39, 49, 66; and William's marriage 63–4
'Child of state' scheme 30–2, 35–6

Church of England 68, 76–7, 83, 94, 100–03, 119–20, 149–51, 179
Churchill, John, first duke of Marlborough 155, 170
civil wars, in Britain and Ireland 11, 62, 124, 127–9, 139
Clarges, Thomas 128, 146
colonies 5–6, 130–1, 142
constitution of England 80–6, 96, 98
convention of 1689 in England 81–6
Cromwell, Oliver 29, 62, 110, 139

Darien scheme 142–3
Davenant, Charles 158
Defoe, Daniel 168–9, 174
De Hooghe, Romeyn 58
Denmark 105–6
De Ruyter, Michiel 30, 52
De Witt, Cornelius 27, 30
De Witt, Johan 27–32, 35–9, 41–6, 50
Declaration of Rights 85–6, 91, 94, 96–7, 179
Derry / Londonderry, 1689 siege of 92–3
dissenters in England 67–8, 77, 100, 102–03, 120, 149–50
Dordrecht 42, 44
Dijkvelt, Van Weede van 67
Dunkeld, battle of 91

East India Company 130–1, 142
Elizabeth I, queen of England and Ireland 3, 84, 94–5, 118, 120, 123, 137, 175
Evelyn, John 82
exclusion crisis 55–6, 74, 124, 128

Fagel, Gaspar 46, 54, 67, 76, 103–04
Finch, Daniel, earl of Nottingham 99, 122, 125–7

France 3, 4, 24, 35, 37–40, 60, 61, 74, 98; *see also* Louis XIV
Frederick Henry, prince of Orange 14, 16, 17, 57
Frederick William, elector of Brandenburg 31, 33, 38
Friesland 14, 19, 23, 40, 44
Fleurus, battle of 110

Gelderland 19, 23, 37, 40, 44, 53, 58–9
George, prince of Denmark 106, 151
Gibbons, Grinling 166
Ginkel, Godert de, earl of Athlone 114
Glencoe massacre 141–2, 179
Glorious Revolution in England 49, 73–86
Graham, John, of Claverhouse, viscount Dundee 91
Grand Alliance, First 104–5, 110–14, 136
Grand Alliance, Second 155, 161, 169
Groningen 14, 19, 23, 37, 40, 44, 51
Gunpowder Plot 78, 95

Harley, Robert 128, 158–60, 162–3, 168
Hampton Court 57, 122–23, 147–9, 165–7, 173
Heinsius, Anthonie 104, 112–13, 157
Hercules 166–7
Het Loo 57, 122, 159
Holland, province of 19, 20–3, 25, 31, 38, 40, 41, 44, 52–4, 59–61, 103
Huygens, Constantijn 74–5, 96–7

Ireland 1–3, 5–7, 11, 49, 81, 114–16, 143–4, 156–7; Catholics of 81, 114–16, 143–4, 157, 179; Jacobite rebellion in 89, 92–3, 105–07, 114–16; parliament of 116, 141, 143, 157, 178–9; resumption act 156, 162; woollens act 156–7
'Immortal Seven' 49, 54, 62–3, 67, 69, 70

Jacobitism 89–93, 114–16, 127–8, 137, 141–2, 144–7, 149–52, 161, 173
James VII and II, king of England, Ireland, and Scotland: and the army 139; and exclusion 66; in Ireland 89, 114; as king in the Stuart realms 49, 66–70, 160, 162, 167; and Louis XIV 90, 92; and party 98–9, 124–5; and revolution 73–4, 76–83; succession from 39, 68–9; and William 67
James Francis Edward Stuart 49, 68–9, 76–7, 79, 161

Kensington Palace 122, 148, 173
Keppel, Arnold Joost van 146–7
Killiecrankie, battle of 91
Kneller, Godfrey 164–5

La Hogue, battle of 117, 119
Landen, battle of 111–12
latitudinarianism 101, 103, 149
Lely, Peter 55–6
Limerick, sieges of 114–16
Limerick, treaty of 116, 143, 179
Locke, John 169, 177
Louis XIV, king of France: architectural patronage of 119, 165; and Carlos II's will 160–1; childhood 24–5; expansionism of 37–42, 50, 59–60, 75, 103, 110–11, 121; and James VII and II 81, 92, 161, 131, 144; and the *rampjaar* 37–42; religious policy 59, 74, 160, 179; William's attitude to 35, 40–1, 50, 59, 62, 64, 83, 101, 121, 131, 179

Maastricht 39, 52, 60
Macaulay, Thomas Babington 174–5, 177
Mary II, queen of England, Ireland, and Scotland: and Anne 151–2; coronation 73; and church of England 103, 120–1, 149, 172; death and funeral 148–9; as focus for Stuart loyalty 86, 93–4, 151; marriage 62, 64–7; propaganda centred on 84, 117–21, 123, 145, 148; as regent 105, 117; and relations with William 83–4, 148–9, 161, 172; and revolution 74, 84
Mary of Modena 49, 63, 68, 79
Mary Stuart, princess of Orange 10, 12–3, 19, 31, 33
masculinity 18–9, 36–7, 118; *see also* William III and masculinity
Maurice, prince of Orange 13, 17, 21
Molyneux, William 157
Münster 37–40, 42, 51, 52

Namur, siege of 110–12
Nantes, edict of 59, 74, 160
Nason, Pieter 17–8

Netherlands: constitution of 5, 19–20, 21–3, 29–30, 44, 51, 53, 58–9, 157, 169, 176, 178; nd geopolitics 24–5, 35, 37–9, 50–1, 75, 112, 141, 155, 157, 160–1; as model for English state 132–3, 175; political party in 21–3, 28–46, 112; origins of nation 13–4, 20, 24; religious culture in 34–5
Nijmegen, treaty of 60

Oldenbarnevelt, Johan van 21
Orange, city of 16, 59, 76, 137, 178
Orange-Nassau family 12–26, 35, 166, 176, 178
Orangist party 16, 23, 25, 25, 28–9, 30–2, 41, 42, 58, 157
Overijessel 19, 23, 37, 40, 44, 53

Parliament of England: and ceremony 123; constitutional position of 69, 73, 85, 94–9, 138, 162, 168–9, 178–9; and exclusion 65; and finance 94–9, 103, 128–30, 132, 178; and James II 67, 70; and religion 102; in the revolution 77, 80–1, 86, 94; tension with William III 127–8, 136, 146, 150, 156, 158–9, 163–4
partition treaties 161, 168
place bills 128, 130, 162–3
propaganda of William III 5, 8–9, 33–4, 38–9, 54–8, 63–4, 70, 75–8, 80–2, 93–5, 103, 119, 121–4, 129, 164–9, 178–9; propaganda in ceremony 25, 57, 78, 86, 91, 94–5, 105–6, 113, 123, 148, 151, 164, 166; propaganda, failures of 137–8, 140; propaganda in print 28, 43, 66–8, 75–7, 80–2, 110, 121, 164, 167–9; propaganda from pulpit 28, 43, 58, 110, 121–2; *see also* architectural patronage; public sphere; William III pictorial representation
Protestantism: in Dutch identity 12, 16, 34; survival in Europe 35, 49, 51, 59, 63, 74, 82, 119, 179; and William's identity and propaganda 43, 82, 94–5, 100, 121–2, 140, 164; and William's reputation 2–3, 6–7
public sphere: in the Netherlands 5, 8–9, 16, 27–9, 42–3, 45, 59; in the Stuart realms 5, 8–9, 69–70, 77, 81–2, 95, 138–9, 144–5, 158, 164, 167–9, 177
Purcell, Henry 148

rampjaar 5, 27, 39–46, 50, 75, 86
reformation of manners 120–2, 129, 149
Royal Africa Company 130–1
Russell, Admiral Edward 68, 158
Ryswick, treaty of 136, 158, 161

Savile, George, marquis of Halifax 68, 96, 98
Seymour, Sir Edward 78
Schomberg, Herman de 93, 103, 106–07
Scotland 5–6, 11, 90–2, 116–17, 141–3, 156; parliament of 92, 116–17, 141–2, 156, 178–9; religion in 90–1, 102, 120, 179; revolution in 90–1; union with England 92, 155–6
Scott, James, first duke of Monmouth 66
Seneffe, battle of 60
settlement, act of 161–3
slavery 131
smallpox 10, 31, 54
Solms, Amalia van 19, 31, 33, 38
Somers, John 127, 136, 139, 158, 169
Spain 14, 23, 24, 42, 51, 60, 61, 76, 104, 113, 142–3, 158–61
Spanish Netherlands 25, 37, 39, 51, 60, 104–5, 110, 136, 158, 161
Spanish Succession, War of the 155
Spenser, Robert, earl of Sunderland 126–7
stadoudership 14, 19–20, 28, 30, 32, 43, 44, 45, 53, 157, 178
states-general of the Netherlands 19, 20, 25, 27, 39, 41, 44–5, 50, 52–4, 58, 75, 103, 105, 157, 178
States-Republican party 22–3, 29

Talbot, Richard, earl of Tyrconnel 92
Temple, William 14–5
Tenison, John 148
Thirty Years War 24, 33, 51
Tillotson, John 101, 148
'toleration act 103, 120, 149
Tories 65–6, 76–7, 82, 85, 98–100, 102–03, 124–27, 138, 150–2, 158–60, 163, 167–9, 173, 174
treason bills 128, 130, 144
triennial bills 128, 130
Trigland, Cornelius 34–5
True Freedom 23, 25, 28–9, 35, 38, 42–3, 176

Utrecht, city of 40–1
Utrecht, province of 19, 23, 44, 52–3, 59

Villiers, Elizabeth 65, 147
Verrio, Antonio 147, 165–7

Waldeck, Georg Frederick 50
Wharton, Thomas 99–100, 125
Whigs 65–6, 76, 82, 85, 98–100, 103, 124–27, 136, 138, 150–1, 157–9, 163, 168–9, 173, 174
Willem Frederick, stadhouder of Friesland and Groningen 28–9
William I, prince of Orange 13, 16, 17, 18, 20, 57, 175
William II, prince of Orange 10, 18, 21, 22, 24, 25
William III, prince of Orange, king of England, Ireland and Scotland: abdication, threatened 136; assassination plot against 144; baptism 2; childhood 10–4, 19, 30–8; consolidation of power in the Netherlands 52–9; and the constitution of England 73, 76, 82–3, 85–6, 96–8, 127–30, 161–3, 178–9; and the constitution of the Netherlands 5, 44; coronation 73, 86, 94–5, 112; death and tomb 172–4; *Declaration of reasons* 76–7, 80–1, 84–5, 91; and de Witt's murder 45–6; and Gelderland sovereignty 58–61, 79, 178; health 36, 159–60, 164, 173; invasion of England 11, 16, 49, 73–9; and Ireland 1–2, 5–6, 92–3, 105–07, 114–16, 141, 143–4, 156–7, 162; and Louis XIV 45, 59, 6–2, 83, 95, 97–8, 104, 111, 132, 136, 158–9, 166–7, 177; marriage 64–5, 83–4, 93–4, 117–21, 148–9; and masculinity 19, 36–7, 41, 50, 64, 83–4, 93, 106, 112, 137, 146–7, 148–9, 159; and military leadership 40–1, 43, 50–2, 54, 75, 78, 82, 89, 93, 105–07, 110–12, 114, 177–8; and monarchy in England 4, 94–8, 122–3, 130, 178; and party in England 76–7, 98–100, 102–03, 124–7; pictorial representation of 11–2, 17–8, 33–4, 55–6, 58, 94, 114, 164–5; privacy of 8–9, 54, 64–5, 83, 96–7, 119, 123, 145–6, 149, 163, 166, 176; political style 43–4, 61, 69–70, 74, 75, 79–86, 91, 93, 94–100, 102–03, 105–06, 112, 116–17, 120–1, 124–132, 162–4, 173, 176–80; and the *rampjaar* 27–8, 32, 39–46, 50, 75, 86; religious attitudes 2–3, 6–7, 17, 34–5, 41, 44–5, 57–9, 67, 74, 78, 83, 91, 95, 100–03, 120–3, 144, 152, 179–80; reputation after death 1–9, 45–6, 172–80; and Scotland 5–6, 90–2, 105, 116–17, 141–3, 155–2; sexuality 37, 54, 65, 146–7, 166; and the Stuart kings 38–9, 60, 62–70, 76, 100; and the state in England 3–4, 103, 132–33, 137–140, 178; succession in the Netherlands 141, 157, 176; *see also* propaganda of William III
Wren, Christopher 122–3

xenophobia, English 145–6, 161, 163, 176–7

Zeeland 19, 23, 25, 38, 40, 41, 44, 53, 59
Zuylestein, Frederick Nassau of 37, 46

For Product Safety Concerns and Information please contact our
EU representative GPSR@taylorandfrancis.com Taylor & Francis
Verlag GmbH, Kaufingerstraße 24, 80331 München, Germany